RIGHTS, GROUPS, AND SELF-INVENTION

For Cara, Rachel, and Eli

Rights, Groups, and Self-Invention

Group-Differentiated Rights in Liberal Theory

ERIC J. MITNICK
Thomas Jefferson School of Law, USA

ASHGATE

Published by
Ashgate Publishing Limited
Gower House
Croft Road
Aldershot
Hampshire GU11 3HR
England

Ashgate Publishing Company
Suite 420
101 Cherry Street
Burlington, VT 05401-4405
USA

Ashgate website: http://www.ashgate.com

British Library Cataloguing in Publication Data
Mitnick, Eric J., 1966-
Rights, groups, and self-invention : group-differentiated
rights in liberal theory
1. Minorities - Legal status, laws, etc. 2.Law - Philosophy
I.Title
342'.087

Library of Congress Cataloging-in-Publication Data
Mitnick, Eric. J., 1966-
Rights, groups, and self-invention : group-differentiated rights in liberal theory / by Eric J. Mitnick.
p. cm.
Includes index.
ISBN 0-7546-4573-8
1. Social groups. 2. Civil rights. I. Title.

HM716.M58 2006
305--dc22

2006007630

ISBN-10: 0 7546 4573 8

Printed and bound by MPG Books Ltd, Bodmin, Cornwall

Contents

Preface

Law is a social practice. This is a book about one aspect of that social practice, the practice of affording legal rights to persons on the basis of their social or cultural group membership. Such rights, termed group-differentiated rights, are an increasingly common and controversial feature of modern liberal legal systems. This is the type of right petitioned for by members of religious groups, in order that they might engage in traditional rituals otherwise precluded by generally applicable laws. Group-differentiated claims might be raised, as well, by the members of ethnic or indigenous groups, asserting the need for public recognition of cultural differences, access to public institutions in native languages, or even collective rights to property or self-government. Members of social groups, differentiated according to race, gender, sexual orientation, or disability status, frequently are granted group-differentiated rights as part of an effort to remedy ongoing discrimination or past harms. Indeed, citizenship itself exists as a group-differentiated status, and so the rights pertaining exclusively to members of the political collective fall within this category as well.

Given the critical importance, and the frequently conflictual nature, of the values at stake in these sorts of rights-claims, it should come as no surprise that each of these claims, and all of these groups, has been the subject of numerous studies. The literature in political theory in particular in recent years has served as the setting for an extensive corpus of research concerning race, gender, religion, ethnicity, nationality, and other treatments of multiculturalism and the politics of difference. Yet, to date, there has been no comprehensive critical assessment of the group-differentiated form of right itself. This book is intended to fill this breach. Indeed, a focus on the form of right, rather than on the type of group in question, I shall argue, yields valuable insight into the rather striking constitutive effect group-differentiated rights often have on the construction of human identity.

The chapters below describe the group-differentiated form of right from the perspective of analytical and constitutive theory, delving into both the nature and sources of group-differentiated rights and the connection between this form of legal categorization and social identity. Then, in light of the influence the form of right is determined to have on human identity, the book considers as well the relationship between group-differentiated rights and fundamental principles of liberal theory—principles that privilege the individual capacity for self-invention. To this end, a liberal conception of membership is developed and applied contextually to three primary models of group-differentiated rights. For if we are indeed partially constituted by our rights, then we need to ask as well what this means for a liberal value system that claims to accord priority to individual constitutive autonomy.

In the course of seeking to understand the nature and effects of the group-differentiated form of right, this work has caused me frequently to encounter, and to attempt to cross, disciplinary boundaries. Group-differentiated rights unmistakably elicit deep questions of law and politics, issues that run to the heart of legal, political, and moral theory. But they also, in virtue of their correlation with social identity, raise questions that have received sustained examination primarily from within the fields of cultural sociology and cognitive and social psychology. In consequence, I owe a debt of gratitude to a number of people, both within my own field, and without, and it is a genuine pleasure to acknowledge these intellectual, institutional, and personal debts here.

This book is a revised version of my doctoral thesis, completed in the Department of Politics at Princeton University. I am grateful to my principal advisors, Robert George and Stephen Macedo, for their sustained commitment to this project. Both Robby and Steve daily set an example of intellectual depth and integrity that their graduate students can only aspire to emulate. Many others at Princeton, including especially Patrick Deneen, Amy Gutmann, George Kateb, Ken Kersch, and Keith Whittington, also served as sources of insight and criticism that have improved the arguments and ideas expressed in this book. I have been fortunate to be able to learn from such brilliant and dedicated scholars, and I thank them for their encouragement and attention to my work. My sincere thanks also to my fellow graduate students in the Political Theory Research Seminar at Princeton, all of whom listened to and commented upon early papers that eventually evolved into portions of the second, third, and fourth chapters in this book. The very earliest seeds of interest in the relationship between law and membership were planted in a seminar on Constitutional Membership in which I participated while still a student (many years ago) at the University of Michigan Law School, and so let me thank as well Alex Aleinikoff for that initial inspiration.

I have had the pleasure of presenting different portions of the material that has grown into this book at a number of academic conferences, colloquia and workshops. Unfortunately, I have neither the space nor the memory adequately to express my genuine appreciation to all of those who participated in these fora, and who commented upon earlier drafts of these chapters, but let me briefly address a few such experiences. An earlier version of the final chapter was the subject of discussion at the Law and Humanities Interdisciplinary Junior Faculty Workshop, held at Columbia Law School in June 2003. I am grateful to Robert Post and Anne Dailey for the illuminating criticism, advice, and encouragement they offered as discussants of that paper, and to Naomi Mezey, Austin Sarat, and Nomi Stolzenberg for their valuable commentary both at the workshop and thereafter. An earlier version of portions of the first and fifth chapters was presented at a conference on Ethno-Religious Cultures, Identities, and Political Philosophy, held at the University of Amsterdam in July 2002. My gratitude is due to the several participants in that conference who discussed my contribution, and especially to Veit Bader, Joseph Carens, and Roland Pierik, for comments that improved the contextual nature of my research in a number of ways. Most recently, I had the opportunity to present the entire introductory chapter at the University of San Diego Law School's Faculty Colloquium. I am grateful to my cross-town colleagues for generously lending their ears and minds to the betterment of this project.

Outside of formal presentations, a number of friends and colleagues have thoughtfully read and commented upon portions of the manuscript. Jack Nowlin, as a peer at Princeton, and later as a fellow law academic, has been unsparing in offering advice and commentary. Dennis Patterson is a giant in the field of law and philosophy, and I have been humbled by his support and encouragement and helped by his criticism. John Evans, of the Department of Sociology at the University of California San Diego, tolerated endless questions on cultural sociology and cognitive psychology and asked no more than a few pints of good quality ale in return. And no one deserves as generous a colleague as Steve Semeraro, who has read and commented upon virtually every corner of this manuscript.

For financial support, I am thankful to Princeton University and the Mellon Foundation for providing fellowship funds that made possible and helped advance the dissertation that would eventually become this book. I am grateful, as well, to my former Dean, Kenneth Vandevelde, for providing research support and for building such a fine academic home in the Thomas Jefferson School of Law. Ken's dedication to the project of legal education serves as an inspiration to all who come into contact with him. My thanks also to my faculty colleagues at Thomas Jefferson, with whom I have had innumerable informal conversations regarding the arguments contained in this book, and to Dorothy Hampton for her ever skillful research assistance.

Finally, and most profoundly, let me thank the group that is closest to my heart, and most constitutive of my identity. I am deeply grateful to my mother, Susan Mitnick, for her seemingly limitless support and kindness, and to my father, Richard Mitnick, whose love of knowledge and thirst for ideas continue to serve as an inspiration. I am grateful to my children, Rachel and Eli Mitnick, for the joy they bring me daily and for serving as constant reminders of what is most precious in life. And most of all I am grateful to my wife, Cara Ellen Mitnick, for her support, her spirit, and her love. She is with me in all things. I dedicate this book, with love, to her and to our children.

Some of the ideas expressed in this book appeared previously, often in very different form, in a number of journal articles, including: "Taking Rights Spherically: Formal and Collective Aspects of Legal Rights," *Wake Forest Law Review*, Vol. 34 (1999), p. 409; "Constitutive Rights," *Oxford Journal of Legal Studies*, Vol. 20 (2000), p. 185; "Liberalism and Membership," *University of*

Pennsylvania Journal of Constitutional Law, Vol. 4 (2001), p. 533; "Individual Vulnerability and Cultural Transformation," *Michigan Law Review*, Vol. 101 (2003), p. 1635; "Three Models of Group-Differentiated Rights," *Columbia Human Rights Law Review*, Vol. 35 (2004), p. 215; and "Differentiated Citizenship and Contextualized Morality," *Ethical Theory and Moral Practice*, Vol. 7 (2004), p. 163. I am grateful for permission to include in this book revised and extended versions of arguments that originally appeared in these journals.

Chapter 1

Introduction: Group-Differentiated Rights

Group-Differentiated Rights as a Distinct Form of Right

In a well-known essay, originally published nearly fifty years ago, H.L.A. Hart sought to describe virtually any right as falling within one of two broad categories.[1] Seeking to characterize "the circumstances in which rights are asserted with the typical expression 'I have a right to . . .,'" Hart wrote:

> It is I think the case that this form of words is used in two main types of situations: (A) when the claimant has some special justification for interference with another's freedom which other persons do not have ('I have a right to be paid what you promised for my services'); (B) when the claimant is concerned to resist or object to some interference by another person as having no justification ('I have a right to say what I think').[2]

The first type, Hart labeled "special rights." These are rights that arise in virtue of particular transactions among market participants (e.g., a promise to sell wheat for a certain price), or in virtue of some special relationship in which individuals stand (e.g., the special fiduciary relationship that exists between parent and child).[3] In contrast with special rights, Hart characterized the latter type as "general rights," or those rights (e.g., freedom of speech, due process of law) that arise not from particular transactions or relationships but from, in Hart's words, "the equal right of all men to be free."[4]

It is sometimes thought that Hart's distinction exhausts the universe of rights. Upon closer examination, however, there clearly are rights that fit neatly into neither category. This becomes plain once we consider Hart's categories from the vantage point of the duties they impose and the interests they protect.[5] For the

---

1 See H.L.A. Hart, "Are There Any Natural Rights?," in Jeremy Waldron, ed., *Theories of Rights* (Oxford: Oxford University Press, 1984), pp. 77–90. Hart's essay was originally published in *Philosophical Review* 64 (1955): 175–91.

2 Hart, "Are There Any Natural Rights?," pp. 83–4.

3 Ibid., pp. 84–7.

4 Ibid., p. 88.

5 That Hart conceptualized rights fundamentally as choices, rather than as benefits or in terms of the advancement of interests, has little bearing in this context. The critical point

critical distinction between Hart's two broad categories of rights lies in their differing scopes, both in terms of the anticipated beneficiaries of the rights and of those in whom the rights place corresponding obligations. Thus, special rights, which derive from particular interpersonal transactions and relationships, protect the interests of, and impose obligations upon, only those particular individuals involved in the specific transactions and relationships at issue. General rights, on the other hand, protect the interests of and impose obligations upon (virtually) everyone.

With this scheme in mind, then, we can see that there will be rights that, having nothing whatsoever to do with interpersonal transactions or relationships, cannot be considered "special," and that, while they may indeed impose obligations generally, yet protect only the interests of some *subset* of individuals in society, and so cannot be considered "general." A right that I intend to discuss at greater length in succeeding chapters, the right against discriminatory treatment on the basis of disability, is one example; the right is general in terms of the obligations it imposes, but protects the interests of just one segment of society, disabled persons.[6] Other prominent examples include rights arising from affirmative governmental action to combat racial discrimination, rights afforded same-sex couples to engage in civil unions, and rights granted to the members of particular religious or cultural groups to engage in traditional practices. Even the right to vote, which imposes duties of non-interference generally, but only benefits citizens, would seem to defy Hart's categories.

This is not to suggest that Hart was unaware of a specifically group-differentiated form of right. For his own part, it is important to recognize, Hart merely described the special and general categories of rights as the "two main types" of rights, leaving open the possibility that other categories might exist. In fact, more than a century before, Jeremy Bentham had noticed that certain rights would benefit only particular classes of persons,[7] and Hart, in his well-known treatment of Bentham's analysis of legal rights, made this plain: "not only individuals have rights; the public and also distinct classes included in it have, according to Bentham, rights in those cases where the persons intended to benefit are what he terms 'unassignable individuals.'"[8] The more interesting question,

---

here is not the essence of the constitution of rights but the extent of their applicability. On the choice theory of rights, see H.L.A. Hart, "Legal Rights," in *Essays on Bentham: Jurisprudence and Political Theory* (Oxford: Clarendon Press, 1982), pp. 162–93. On the interest theory, see, e.g., D.N. MacCormick, "Rights in Legislation," in P.M.S. Hacker and J. Raz, eds., *Law, Morality and Society: Essays in Honour of H.L.A. Hart* (Oxford: Clarendon Press, 1977), pp. 192–5; Joseph Raz, *The Morality of Freedom* (Oxford: Clarendon Press, 1986), p. 166.

6 See Americans with Disabilities Act, 42 U.S.C. §§12101–12213 (1994).

7 See Jeremy Bentham, *An Introduction to the Principles of Morals and Legislation*, J.H. Burns and H.L.A. Hart, eds. (Oxford: Clarendon Press, 1970), ch.XVI, para. 7, p. 189.

8 Hart, "Legal Rights," p. 168. Further analysis of Bentham's concept of

then, is not whether Hart was aware of this form of right, for surely he was, but why he chose to ignore it.[9]

The timing of Hart's writing makes this question particularly apt, for Hart's essay appeared in the wake of the Second World War. At first glance, one might suspect that at such a time of increased sensitivity to the plight of minority groups a liberal theorist such as Hart might well have noted especially the *need* for rights particularly protecting the interests of members of more vulnerable groups. In fact, however, Hart's strong focus at this time on general rights was shared by most liberal theorists interested in supporting members of at-risk minority groups. Consider, for example, the following depiction of the state of affairs in minority rights in the decade following World War II, a depiction that appeared in a work published the same year as Hart's essay: "The doctrine of human rights has been put forward as a substitute for the concept of minority rights, with the strong implication that minorities whose members enjoy individual equality of treatment cannot legitimately demand facilities for the maintenance of their ethnic particularism."[10] Indeed, not just within liberal rights theory, but more broadly among social scientists of the post World War II era, the sentiment began to take shape that American society was swiftly approaching ethnicity's end.[11]

The thought depicted here, and shared widely, was that by guaranteeing the fundamental rights of all individuals, the interests of members of minority groups necessarily would be protected as well. Had not history demonstrated, the thinking continued, the unique virtue of universal rights? After all, this formally egalitarian model of universal citizenship, grounded in enlightenment ideals, had been the approach used successfully to bring an end to the nightmarish wars of religion in sixteenth-century Europe. Those bloody clashes were resolved, in part, by affording universal rights of religious freedom, not by granting group-based rights to particular religious minorities.[12] Moreover, it had long been legally sanctioned group-differential treatment that had served to *subordinate* minority group members. From the institution of slavery, through categorical restrictions on citizenship rights in the United States, as well as the horrors of the Holocaust in

---

unassignability, and his consequent suggestion of class-held rights, appears in the next chapter.

[9] In his essay on Bentham's analysis of legal rights, Hart notes as well that "Bentham [himself] seems to have made very little use of his idea that in the sense explained the public or a class within it have legal rights." Ibid., p. 181, n. 79.

[10] Inis Claude, *National Minorities: An International Problem* (Cambridge, Mass.: Harvard University Press, 1955), p. 211.

[11] See, e.g., Robert Park, *Race and Culture* (Glencoe, Ill.: Free Press, 1950); William J. Wilson, *The Declining Significance of Race* (Chicago: University of Chicago Press, 1967); Joane Nagel, *American Indian Ethnic Renewal: Red Power and the Resurgence of Identity and Culture* (Oxford: Oxford University Press, 1996), p. 19.

[12] See Will Kymlicka, *Multicultural Citizenship: A Liberal Theory of Minority Rights* (Oxford: Clarendon Press, 1995), pp. 2–6.

Europe, group-based policy had engendered an appalling legacy. Hart, thus, hardly stood alone in his neglect at mid-century of a third, group-differentiated, form of right. The era in which Hart distinguished general from special rights was an era in which group-differentiated claims were viewed not as a solution but as a long-enduring problem.

Nearly a half-century after Hart invoked his famous typology, however, the universe of rights is a far less tidy place. Rights that vest on the basis of an individual's membership in a particular social or cultural group—rights that in Hart's terms could be described neither as special nor as fully general—are an increasingly common aspect of modern liberal legal systems throughout the world.[13] Such rights have been granted to members of a broad array of social groups to remedy inequities associated with, for example, the members' race, sexual orientation, gender, age, economic or disability status. Rights similarly have been afforded to the members of cultural groups constituted according to nationality, ethnicity or religion, to acknowledge and accommodate particular beliefs or practices, or in recognition of collective claims to self-government or property. Indeed, rights such as these, differentiated as they are according to group membership, might be afforded on the basis of virtually any shared human characteristic deemed socially relevant. Yet, since group-differentiated rights openly distinguish among classes of persons in the distribution of social benefits and burdens, this form of right remains a source of significant controversy.

The Contemporary Debate Over Group-Differentiated Rights

Like so many other ongoing discussions in modern liberal theory, recent debates over group-differentiated rights have their roots in John Rawls's conception of justice, and in particular in the well-known communitarian response to that conception.[14] The thrust of the communitarian critique, relevant for present purposes, contends that Rawls's theory is reliant upon an overly atomistic,

---

[13] For a recent assessment of the state of differentiated citizenship policies within western democracies, see Will Kymlicka and Wayne Norman, "Introduction," in Will Kymlicka and Wayne Norman, eds., *Citizenship in Diverse Societies* (Oxford: Oxford University Press, 2000), p.4.

[14] See John Rawls, *A Theory of Justice* (Cambridge, Mass.: Harvard University Press, 1971). Works illustrative of the communitarian critique of Rawlsian liberalism include Alasdair MacIntyre, *After Virtue: A Study in Moral Theory*, 2d ed. (Notre Dame, Ind.: University of Notre Dame Press, 1984); Michael J. Sandel, *Liberalism and the Limits of Justice*, 2d ed. (Cambridge: Cambridge University Press, 1998); Michael Walzer, *Spheres of Justice: A Defense of Pluralism and Equality* (New York: Basic Books, 1983); Charles Taylor, "Atomism," in *2 Philosophy and the Human Sciences: Philosophical Papers* (Cambridge: Cambridge University Press, 1985), pp. 187–211. For an overview, see Amy Gutmann, "Communitarian Critics of Liberalism," *Philosophy & Public Affairs* 14 (1985).

unrealistically universalized conception of the self as prior to its ends.[15] The Rawlsian conception of the person, communitarians charge, is both false, because individuals naturally exist encumbered by particular social attachments, and ultimately dangerous, because the radical valorization of individual right threatens the virtues of civic and communal life.[16] There was thus an obvious, though misleading, correlation at the outset of recent debates in liberal and multicultural theory between proponents of group-differentiated rights and communitarian critics of liberalism. For the early proponents of group-differentiated claims, like their communitarian counterparts, were similarly concerned with the affirmation of particular (i.e., cultural or communal group-differentiated) attachments.[17]

This initial correlation between communitarianism and multiculturalism was in part bred of confusion over the nature of group-differentiated claims. At first, both the proponents of group-differentiated rights and their detractors commonly assumed that claims for differential treatment were, in essence, assertions of communal privilege. On this basis, the multicultural debate was originally thought of as yet another front in the broader dispute between individualists and collectivists over the relative priority of the self and its ends. Liberal theorists thus routinely rejected group-differentiated claims for fear of sacrificing individual to collective interests. Even more, group-differentiated rights were (as it happens, correctly) perceived as claims to a formally unequal distribution of benefits and duties among persons in society on the basis of particular attachments. Liberal theorists thus initially also opposed claims for group-differentiated rights in defense of what they took to be liberal neutrality.[18] As a consequence, early proponents of group-differentiated rights faced a dual challenge: first, they needed to dispel the notion that group-differentiated policy is inherently detrimental to individual interests; and second, they needed to establish how it was that official group-differentiated policies and institutions, insofar as they distinguished among categories of persons in the distribution of benefits and duties, were not *prima facie* contrary to justice.[19]

---

15 Rawls, *A Theory of Justice*, p. 560.

16 See MacIntyre, "Atomism," pp. 204–5; Sandel, *Liberalism and the Limits of Justice*, pp. 152–4; Michael J. Sandel, *Democracy's Discontent: America in Search of a Public Philosophy* (Cambridge, Mass.: Harvard University Press, 1996), p. 14: "Unless we think of ourselves as encumbered selves, already claimed by certain projects and commitments, we cannot make sense of . . . indispensable aspects of our moral and political experience."

17 For an overview of the evolution of the debate over cultural rights, see Will Kymlicka, "The New Debate Over Minority Rights," in *Politics in the Vernacular: Nationalism, Multiculturalism and Citizenship* (Oxford: Oxford University Press, 2001), pp. 17–38.

18 For a recent articulation of the view that cultural rights contravene liberal principles, see Brian Barry, *Culture and Equality: An Egalitarian Critique of Multiculturalism* (Cambridge, Mass.: Harvard University Press, 2001).

19 See, e.g., Will Kymlicka, *Liberalism, Community, and Culture* (Oxford: Clarendon

Multicultural and rights theorists in particular thus set about the task of explaining that, although rights grounded in social and cultural differences might attach on the basis of group membership, most such rights (e.g., language rights, rights freely to practice one's religion) vest legally in *individuals* rather than in any collective entity.[20] There indeed may be group-differentiated rights that vest in, and can only be asserted by, a group *qua* group (e.g., a right to collective self-determination), but these group rights are exceedingly rare in modern liberal democracies.[21] Moreover, even those rights that logically can be pressed only by a collectivity nonetheless remain grounded, from a liberal perspective, in individual interests. Collective rights, on this view, remain legitimate only insofar as they benefit individuals, albeit on the basis of their membership in the particular group at issue.[22]

Further, the notion that modern liberal states, enduringly composed of a plurality of social and cultural groups, could be truly neutral with respect to group membership has been exposed, persuasively, as fiction.[23] Governments, of necessity, make decisions on a broad range of matters that affect members of social and cultural groups in disparate ways. Public schooling, for example, and the provision of other public services and institutions (e.g., court systems, health and welfare agencies) typically occur in some relatively limited number of languages, and so there inevitably will be members of particular groups placed at a disadvantage by such linguistic choices.[24] Similarly, decisions to close

---

Press, 1989); Charles Taylor, "The Politics of Recognition," in Amy Gutmann, ed., *Multiculturalism: Examining the Politics of Recognition* (Princeton, NJ: Princeton University Press, 1994).

[20] See, e.g., Michael Hartney, "Some Confusions Regarding Collective Rights," in Will Kymlicka, ed., *The Rights of Minority Cultures* (Oxford: Oxford University Press, 1995), pp. 202–27; Jan Narveson, "Collective Rights?," *Canadian Journal of Law and Jurisprudence* 4 (1991). For a discussion of the investitive conditions of rights in individuals, see D.N. MacCormick, "Rights in Legislation," pp. 204–5.

[21] See, e.g., Avishai Margalit and Joseph Raz, "National Self-Determination," *Journal of Philosophy* 87 (1990). For a helpful typology of cultural rights, see Jacob T. Levy, "Classifying Cultural Rights," in Ian Shapiro and Will Kymlicka, eds., *NOMOS XXXIX Ethnicity and Group Rights* (New York: New York University Press, 1997), pp. 22–66.

[22] On the relationship between collective rights and individual interests, see especially Raz, *The Morality of Freedom*, pp. 207–9.

[23] See, e.g., Joseph Carens, *Culture, Citizenship, and Community: A Contextual Exploration of Justice as Evenhandedness* (Oxford: Oxford University Press, 2000), p. 53, suggesting that "cultural neutrality is an illusion." See also Kymlicka, *Multicultural Citizenship*, p. 111, arguing that the idea of cultural neutrality is "patently false," and Kymlicka, *Politics in the Vernacular*, p. 32: "mainstream institutions are not neutral, but rather are implicitly or explicitly tilted towards the interests and identities of the majority group."

[24] Charles Taylor makes this point in "Nationalism and Modernity," in Jeff McMahan and Robert McKim, eds., *The Morality of Nationalism* (Oxford: Oxford University Press,

government offices on particular public holidays, including the structure of the "work week" itself, and decisions with respect to state symbols, rituals and uniforms, will disadvantage some persons on the basis of their group memberships while granting an advantage to others.[25] And it would likely surprise few to learn that most of these decisions have tended to privilege, implicitly or explicitly, the dominant or majority culture. Moreover, even efforts expressly to remedy group-based disadvantages by devolving decision-making authority to more local levels generate certain inequities, for the decisions regarding the drawing of geographical and jurisdictional boundaries themselves then become culturally sensitive. State sanctioned, minority group-differentiated policies thus commonly are defended by liberal theorists today as rational remedies for inevitable state partiality.

Hence, many of the more interesting contemporary debates over group-differentiated policy have tended to accept as an initial premise that official differential treatment is made necessary by state bias toward particular conceptions of the good, and so have focused instead on the appropriate extent of, and occasions for, such differential treatment. Missing from the literature, however, has been any comprehensive critical assessment of the group-differentiated form of right itself. First, what is the structure, and what are the sources, of the group-differentiated form of right? Despite Bentham's limited entrée into the field more than a century ago, relatively little analytical work has been done to describe more particularly the nature of group-differentiated rights.[26]

Second, *in light of their form*, in what sense might group-differentiated rights influence individual identity? Theorists of difference and identity, for the most part, have neglected close scrutiny of the types of rights involved in their analyses, emphasizing instead the character of the group to which differential treatment has or might be afforded. As a result, much of the literature that concerns group-differentiated rights concerns such rights and their constitutive effects only in an oblique way. Relatedly, such treatments largely have been confined narrowly to particular categories of groups, rather than seeking broadly to comprehend the normative implications of group-differentiated claims.[27] This balkanization in the

---

1997), p. 34: "a state-sponsored, -inculcated, and -defined language and culture, in which both economy and state function, is obviously an immense advantage to people if this language and culture are theirs."

[25] Kymlicka has suggested that in countries like Canada and the United States, state symbols, public holidays, the work-week and government uniforms tend to "reflect the needs of Christians." Kymlicka, *Multicultural Citizenship*, pp. 114–5. Carens similarly has suggested that public holidays and state symbols "are always culturally laden." Carens, *Culture, Citizenship, and Community*, p. 54.

[26] Raz is an important exception, see *The Morality of Freedom*.

[27] On rights that attach in virtue of an individual's membership in a particular racial, gender, disability or other social category, see, e.g., David M. Engel and Frank W. Munger, *Rights of Inclusion: Law and Identity in the Life Stories of Americans with Disabilities* (Chicago: University of Chicago Press, 2003); Ruth Rubio-Marin and Beverly Baines,

treatment of group-differentiated rights is hardly surprising, given the extraordinary breadth of interests this form of right might protect. And studies with a narrow focus on particular groups clearly are critical if we are to appreciate the underlying circumstances which give rise to group-differentiated claims. Indeed, a recurrent theme within the present treatment will be that the particular legitimacy of differentiated rights often remains contingent upon the social context within which the right is invoked. Yet, the analogous structure, and the comparable constitutive effects, displayed across the variety of group-differentiated rights, affords a basis for an integrated assessment of this critical form of right. Indeed, a focus on the form of right, rather than on the type of group at issue, I shall argue, yields valuable insight into the rather striking constitutive effect legal categorization often has on the construction of social groups and individual identities.

Third, given their form and their effect on human identity, to what extent are group-differentiated rights consistent with liberal values? One by-product of the segmentation that has characterized the literature on group-differentiated rights is the relative absence of integrated evaluations of differentiated policy according to core liberal principles. The usual starting point in such assessments has been with the question of formal equality, and often we have failed to move very far beyond either disparaging or defending departures from that standard. In particular, too little work has been done assessing group-differentiated rights from the perspective of liberal autonomy. In one segment of the literature, this has not been the case: the autonomy-based benefits of cultural rights have received significant attention from liberal multicultural theorists.[28] Yet, even here, we remain in need of an approach that protects cultural freedom while also safeguarding the autonomy of vulnerable individuals within cultural groups.[29] Moreover, the consequences for personal constitutive autonomy, as opposed to formal and substantive equality, of group-based claims differentiated not according to culture but according to racial,

---

Constituting Women (Cambridge: Cambridge University Press, 2004); David A.J. Richards, *Identity and the Case for Gay Rights: Race, Gender, Religion as Analogies* (Chicago: University of Chicago Press, 1999); K. Anthony Appiah and Amy Gutmann, *Color Conscious: The Political Morality of Race* (Princeton, NJ: Princeton University Press, 1996). On group-differentiated rights in the context of religious or cultural pluralism, see, e.g., Kymlicka, *Multicultural Citizenship*; Chandran Kukathas, "Are There Any Cultural Rights?," *Political Theory* 20 (1992); Bhikhu Parekh, *Rethinking Multiculturalism: Cultural Diversity and Political Theory* (Cambridge, Mass.: Harvard University Press, 2000); Joseph Raz, "Multiculturalism: A Liberal Perspective," in *Ethics in the Public Domain: Essays in The Morality of Law and Politics*, rev. ed. (Oxford: Clarendon Press, 1994), pp. 170–91; Barry, *Culture and Equality*.

[28] See especially Kymlicka, *Multicultural Citizenship*.

[29] See the analysis of Ayelet Shachar's work, *Multicultural Jurisdictions: Cultural Differences and Women's Rights* (Cambridge: Cambridge University Press, 2001), below in Chapter 7.

gender, disability and other social characteristics have been much less fully developed.

My core claim in this book will be that the group-differentiated form of right serves further to constitute aspects of human identities, and, further, that this constitutive aspect should be a cause for anxiety from a liberal perspective. Where liberal theorists have primarily viewed rights as instruments of self-invention, and rights-critics have seen rights as atomizing and self-destructive, the present treatment will demonstrate how group-differentiated rights function also as sources of social and self meaning. I shall argue that group-differentiated rights, through processes of inclusion and exclusion that are intrinsic to law and derivative of formal justice, sort and construct individuals as members of particular social groups. In this way, a legal system's invocation of the group-differentiated form of right affects the course of, indeed the human capacity for, individual self-invention. Hence, along with the more obvious, and more frequently remarked upon, sacrifice that group-differentiated rights exact in formal equality, and along with the substantial benefits and opportunities such differential policies often provide, group-differentiated rights present the prospect also of a significant moral loss in individual constitutive autonomy.

The Approach of this Book

This book assesses group-differentiated rights from a number of different perspectives. In order to describe the essential nature of this form of right, the book engages analytical theory. In order to understand the effects of group-differentiated rights on human identity, this book explores and applies a methodology grounded in constitutive theory. And in order to appreciate more fully the social consequences of group-differentiated rights from the perspective of liberal theory, the book adopts as well a normative, contextual approach. Moreover, as part of an effort to comprehend more fully the relationship found to exist between the group-differentiated form of right and aspects of persons' social identities, this book turns at points to related work on the nature of human identity and social cognition conducted within the disciplines of cultural sociology and social and cognitive psychology. Indeed, there remains a great deal that legal and political theorists working in the areas of rights and multiculturalism might learn from these other social scientific disciplines. As social psychologist Karmela Liebkind has suggested:

> The nature of the reality we are trying to understand is not dependent on the ad hoc divisions of academic disciplines ... if the domain of ethnic identity is ever to become illuminated by the joint efforts of different social and behavioral sciences, some amount of theoretical and empirical coordination and cooperation is imperative, thus cutting across the territorial chauvinism of the various disciplines participating in this venture.

> Social psychologists definitely need to know, not only what sociology and psychology, but also anthropology, philosophy, and political science have to say about ethnic identity.[30]

The reverse, obviously, is true as well, and, given the rate at which legal and political theorists have become interested in pursuing the nature and function of social identity, perhaps even more so. Hence, this volume's design proceeds from the conviction that no one perspective is capable of capturing the full character and significance of group-differentiated rights. The intent is to exploit a strategy of methodological and, to a certain extent, disciplinary, pluralism in order to arrive at a more comprehensive understanding of the group-differentiated form of right—an understanding, as it were, from the ground up.

The notion that social life, and with it individual identity, is partially a product of law is not new. Indeed, constitutive and institutional theories of law have been developed across a wide spectrum of schools of legal, political, and social thought.[31] Moreover, legal and political theorists, increasingly, are realizing the virtues of contextuality to conceptual analysis.[32] For just as theory may provide useful standards for the assessment of political practices, so may application of

---

[30] Karmela Liebkind, "Ethnic Identity—Challenging the Boundaries of Social Psychology," in Glynis M. Breakwell, ed., *Social Psychology of Identity and the Self Concept* (London: Surrey University Press, 1992), p. 179.

[31] The initial distinction between regulative and constitutive rules, and between brute and institutional facts, arose in the context of analytic linguistic philosophy. See John Searle, *Speech Acts: An Essay in the Philosophy of Language* (Cambridge: Cambridge University Press, 1969), pp. 33–53. Searle's conception of constitutive rules was, however, presaged in certain respects in an early essay by Rawls in which he described a "Practice Conception of Rules." See John Rawls, "Two Concepts of Rules," *Philosophical Review* 64 (1955). Variations on the institutional or constitutive theories of law have since arisen in the law and society movement, see, e.g., Austin Sarat and Thomas R. Kearns, eds., *Law in Everyday Life* (Ann Arbor, Mich.: University of Michigan Press, 1993); within the critical legal studies and critical race theory movements, see, e.g., Robert W. Gordon, "Critical Legal Histories," *Stanford Law Review* 36 (1984); Ian Haney Lopez, *White By Law: The Legal Construction of Race* (New York: New York University Press, 1996); within the discipline of political science, see, e.g., Rogers M. Smith, "Political Jurisprudence, The 'New Institutionalism,' and the Future of Public Law," *American Political Science Review* 82 (1988), and *Civic Ideals: Conflicting Visions of Citizenship in U.S. History* (New Haven, Conn.: Yale University Press, 1997); Michael W. McCann, *Rights at Work: Pay Equity Reform and the Politics of Legal Mobilization* (Chicago: University of Chicago Press, 1994); and within analytic jurisprudence, see, e.g., Neil MacCormick and Ota Weinberger, *An Institutional Theory of Law: New Approaches to Legal Positivism* (Dordrecht: Kluwer, 1986).

[32] See, e.g., Carens, *Culture, Citizenship, and Community*; Kymlicka, *Multicultural Citizenship*; Shachar, *Multicultural Jurisdictions*; Barbara Yngvesson, "Inventing Law in Local Settings: Rethinking Popular Legal Culture," *Yale Law Journal* 98 (1989).

theoretical constructs within particular contexts provide a critical corrective to theory. It will be my contention that adopting a constitutive and contextual approach will enable us better to appreciate the critical interactive relationship that often exists among rights, group membership and social identity. Such an approach will also prove instrumental in assessing previously neglected moral issues presented by group-differentiated rights. In the next section, then, I describe constitutive methodology and assess its merits as a contextual approach in the evaluation of differentiated citizenship policy. In the section thereafter, I discuss the relationship between a constitutive methodology and normative liberal theory.

Constitutive Theory and Contextualized Morality

Noting the predisposition within the discipline of political theory toward the conceptual and the abstract will hardly come as a revelation; moral theorizing and conceptual analysis are, after all, its hallmarks. Yet, recently, a significant contingent within the discipline has been particularly interested in engaging the situational, the historically contingent, the non-ideal, in their quest to respond to the fundamental problems of political life. While the deep and profound questions presented by life in political society continue to be stated in formal terms, the proposed solutions are increasingly articulated with reference to particular contexts. And nowhere is this new inclination toward contextualization more pronounced than in analyses of contemporary cultural conflict.

Michael Walzer, in perhaps the seminal expression of the modern contextualist political theory, both confessed and declared:

> My argument is radically particularist. I don't claim to have achieved any great distance from the social world in which I live. One way to begin the philosophical enterprise—perhaps the original way—is to walk out of the cave, leave the city, climb the mountain, fashion for oneself (what can never be fashioned for ordinary men and women) an objective and universal standpoint. Then one describes the terrain of everyday life from far away, so that it loses its particular contours and takes on a general shape. But I mean to stand in the cave, in the city, on the ground. Another way of doing philosophy is to interpret to one's fellow citizens the world of meanings that we share. Justice and equality can conceivably be worked out as philosophical artifacts, but a just or an egalitarian society cannot be. If such a society isn't already here—hidden, as it were, in our concepts and categories—we will never know it concretely or realize it in fact.[33]

Walzer's emphasis on the importance of context in moral theorizing has influenced numerous scholars.[34] Walzer's own theory, though, is contextual not only in a

---

[33] Walzer, *Spheres of Justice*, p. xiv.

[34] See, e.g., Carens, *Culture, Citizenship, and Community*, pp. 2–8; Shachar, *Multicultural Jurisdictions*, p. 8, n. 14; Veit Bader, "Citizenship and Exclusion: Radical Democracy, Community and Justice," *Political Theory* 23 (1995).

methodological but also in a deeper normative sense. For Walzer, attention to social context is not simply a useful means of discerning the justice or injustice of particular political institutions and social practices; rather, justice itself is contingent upon, indeed constituted by, social context. Central to Walzer's thought is the conviction that a society should be judged according to norms derived from the shared values of those who inhabit the particular society. "A given society is just," Walzer contends, "if its substantive life is lived in a certain way—that is, in a way faithful to the shared understandings of the members . . . Every substantive account of distributive justice is a local account."[35] The logical consequence of such a radically relativist conception of justice, though, is that Walzer must to a large extent countenance traditional local practices that would seem impossibly unenlightened to most anyone living within a modern liberal society.[36]

More recently, liberal theorists such as Will Kymlicka and Joseph Carens have demonstrated the virtues of a contextual methodology in political theorizing, while at the same time eschewing the more extreme elements of Walzer's normative relativism.[37] Carens, for instance, writes:

> In reading the ongoing and overlapping contemporary debates about liberalism and communitarianism, equality and difference, citizenship and multiculturalism, and public reason and pluralism, I have learned a great deal, but I have also felt that the discussions are usually conducted at such a high level of abstraction that it is often hard to tell whether disagreements are real or rhetorical and difficult to determine what concrete judgements can be inferred from alternative theoretical positions . . . To put the main point starkly, we do not really understand what general principles and theoretical formulations *mean* until we see them interpreted and applied in a variety of specific contexts.[38]

Not only can reference to context help elucidate abstract concepts, it can also help refine conceptual analysis by yielding aspects of theoretical questions, as well as potential solutions, that remain hidden at higher levels of generality. Moreover,

---

[35] Walzer, *Spheres of Justice*, pp. 314–15.

[36] In fact, however, Walzer's treatment in *Spheres of Justice* appears to revert to universalist liberal principles at critical points. This is particularly the case with his treatment of political asylum, which Walzer suggests should be liberally granted even where contrary to a political community's shared understandings, see ibid., pp. 48–51, and with respect to temporary guest workers, for whom Walzer would demand citizenship, see ibid., pp. 52–61. Indeed, in his more recent writings, Walzer appears to shift slightly his fundamental outlook to articulate a more universal, if minimalist, morality. See Michael Walzer, *Thick and Thin: Moral Argument at Home and Abroad* (Notre Dame, Ind.: University of Notre Dame Press, 1994).

[37] See Kymlicka, *Multicultural Citizenship*; Carens, *Culture, Citizenship, and Community*.

[38] Ibid., pp. 2–3.

examining conceptual problems in new, and particularly in less familiar, contexts may cause us to question, and again to refine, the very assumptions upon which our theoretical constructs are founded.

Of course, one consequence of recognizing this sort of contingency in theorizing about life in political society might well be the loss of satisfyingly tidy solutions to critical questions. A contextual approach will, indisputably, often yield complicated inferences and merely provisional results where we might naturally crave order and logical certainty. But order must at some point submit to social reality, logic to the corrective of fact. Indeed, the point is not to demean or encumber conceptual analysis but to help ensure its relevance and significance. After introducing the general attributes of constitutive theory just below, I will suggest why it is that a constitutive methodology naturally implicates a contextualized morality.

Constitutive theory, during roughly the last quarter of the twentieth century, and continuing into the twenty-first, has taken firm root in interdisciplinary legal scholarship.[39] As early as 1981, as part of his Storrs Lectures at Yale Law School, Clifford Geertz had already indicated the importance of adopting a constitutive perspective toward law. "[L]aw," Geertz said, "rather than a mere technical add-on to a morally (or immorally) finished society, is . . . an active part of it . . . Law, even so technocratized a variety as our own, is, in a word, constructive; in another, constitutive; in a third, formational."[40] From Geertz's perspective, the predominant, essentially descriptive, conception of culture as a relatively static inventory of norms and traditions was insufficiently complex, insufficiently interactive. Culture, Geertz and those who came after taught, should be conceptualized as a far more dynamic social phenomenon, continuously forming, and being formed by, human thought and social behavior. As Joane Nagel indicated in her study of the evolution of Native American culture, "That culture provides a blueprint for action is only one side of the culture-agency coin stamped by symbolic conceptions of culture; the other side of that coin depicts human action as forging culture itself."[41] Law, from the constitutive perspective, is viewed as an integral aspect of this broader culture-agency causal relationship, or as a critical participant in the ongoing dialectical constitution of social reality. Legal institutions, thus, can be seen to function in a transformative fashion,

---

[39] For recent illustrations of constitutive theory, see, e.g., Engel and Munger, *Rights of Inclusion*; Rogers M. Smith, *Stories of Peoplehood: The Politics and Morals of Political Membership* (Cambridge: Cambridge University Press, 2003); Efren Rivera Ramos, *The Legal Construction of Identity: The Judicial and Social Legacy of American Colonialism in Puerto Rico* (Washington, D.C.: American Psychological Association, 2001).

[40] Clifford Geertz, *Local Knowledge: Further Essays in Interpretive Anthropology* (New York: Basic Books, 1983), p. 218.

[41] Nagel, *American Indian Ethnic Renewal*, p. 44.

molding public and private values and even aspects of human identities.[42] Indeed, constitutive theory deems law a significant part of what makes us *who* and *what* we are.

The constitutive power of law lies in its seemingly ubiquitous structuring of the categories through which individuals perceive social life. As Austin Sarat and Jonathan Simon have written, "Most social relations are permeated with law. Long before we ever think about going to a courtroom, we encounter landlords and tenants, husbands and wives, barkeeps and hotel guests—roles that already embed a variety of juridical notions."[43] The law *defines* social roles such as these, *signifying* how we should be interpreted and how we should interpret others. Even more ominously, constitutive theory exposes "the subtle ways in which law operates to construct our understanding of the world and what we take to be the 'natural' order of things."[44] Hence, because we so readily internalize legally constructed categories, values and definitions, we are rarely specifically conscious of their influence on our perceptions.

In this sense, constitutive theory is related to the critical legal studies movement, though arguably more as sibling than as descendant.[45] The most fundamental commonality in the two traditions, owing to their common derivation from legal realism more generally, is their rejection of a purely internal approach to conceptualizing law. In the wake of realism's challenge to legal formalism, critical legal scholars argued that the allegedly authoritative principles said to underlie law are not only practically but also necessarily internally inconsistent, and that legal decisions are, therefore, inevitably exercises in political power.[46]

---

[42] For a discussion of the transformative potential of liberal political institutions, see Stephen Macedo, *Diversity and Distrust: Civic Education in a Multicultural Democracy* (Cambridge, Mass.: Harvard University Press, 2000), p. 217: "By recognizing and providing legal recourse for certain kinds of harms but not others, legal regimes represent us as certain kinds of persons with certain kinds of basic interests . . . We need to consider what the aims of a transformative constitutional order should be. What sorts of identities do we want to encourage citizens to adopt? How will the recognition of certain interests affect identity formation?"

[43] Austin Sarat and Jonathan Simon, "Beyond Legal Realism? Cultural Analysis, Cultural Studies, and the Situation of Legal Scholarship," *Yale Journal of Law and the Humanities* 13 (2001), p. 20.

[44] Paul Schiff Berman, "The Cultural Life of Capital Punishment: Surveying the Benefits of a Cultural Analysis of Law," *Columbia Law Review* 102 (2002), p. 1171.

[45] On the critical legal studies movement generally, see especially Mark Kelman, *A Guide to Critical Legal Studies* (Cambridge, Mass.: Harvard University Press, 1987). For a general treatment of constitutive theory, see Alan Hunt, *Explorations in Law and Society: Toward a Constitutive Theory of Law* (New York: Routledge, 1993).

[46] See, e.g., the essays contained in David Kairys, ed., *The Politics of Law: A Progressive Critique* (New York: Basic Books, 3d ed., 1998); Roberto Mangabeira Unger, *The Critical Legal Studies Movement* (Cambridge, Mass.: Harvard University Press, 1983).

Yet where critical legal studies grew out of realism's rejection of legal objectivity, constitutive theory developed from the felt need of sociolegal scholars further to conceptualize law's role within social life. And while critical legal studies was nearly everywhere criticized for its incessant tendency toward abstraction, constitutive theory is nearly always introduced within a particular social context.

The reasons for this are not far to seek. The emphasis that constitutive theory places on the construction of meaning, as opposed merely to function or ideology, entails that constitutive theory is ineluctably contextual. We can see this, first, by examining further the particular conception of causation assumed by constitutive theorists. In deciphering the complex relationship that exists between law and social life, adopting a constitutive perspective involves adopting a less strictly linear attitude toward causality than would a traditional social scientific or instrumental view.[47] Where a primarily instrumental model of law and social change would seek to establish particular legal rules as the specific cause of some aspect of social life, a constitutive model conceives of that effect in far less sequential and unidirectional terms. Constitutive theory recognizes that while law is itself a social practice, initiated by and dependent upon human agents, all social practices take place against a backdrop of preexisting legally constituted forms.[48]

The constitutive process is, then, conceptualized as interactive and ongoing, with prior effects subsequently functioning as causes.[49] Legal meaning, on the constitutive view, is constructed according to a reciprocal or dialectical process, or according to what Naomi Mezey has called "the dance of mutual constructedness."[50] According to this view, law plays a critical role in shaping individuals and communities, and individuals and communities in turn shape the law. Further, the constitutive perspective recognizes, in ways that linear models cannot, that legal meanings and legally constituted relationships may permeate social and individual consciousness and become in that sense unseen and seemingly natural constituents of persons' lives. What this means, however, is that

---

47 See Michael McCann, "Causal versus Constitutive Explanations (or, On the Difficulty of Being so Positive)," *Law and Social Inquiry* 21 (1996).

48 For discussions of constitutive methodology, see Gordon, "Critical Legal Histories"; Hunt, *Toward a Constitutive Theory of Law*; Austin Sarat and Thomas R. Kearns, "Beyond the Great Divide: Forms of Legal Scholarship and Everyday Life," in Sarat and Kearns, *Law in Everyday Life*, pp. 21–61; McCann, "Causal versus Constitutive Explanations"; Paul Kahn, *The Cultural Study of Law: Reconstructing Legal Scholarship* (Chicago: University of Chicago Press, 1999); Austin D. Sarat, "Redirecting Legal Scholarship in Law Schools," *Yale Journal of Law and the Humanities* 12 (2000), pp. 129–150.

49 Martha Minow suggests that in this sense constitutive methodology is derivative of post-Cartesian scientific inquiry associated with persons such as Einstein, Bohr and Heisenberg. See Martha Minow, *Making All the Difference: Inclusion, Exclusion, and American Law* (Ithaca, NY: Cornell University Press, 1990), p. 180.

50 Naomi Mezey, "Out of the Ordinary: Law, Power, Culture, and the Commonplace," *Law and Social Inquiry* 26 (2001), p. 152.

in order fully to appreciate the constitutive nature and effects of law, one must explore the particular social and cultural contexts that construct, and are constructed by, law.

Moreover, constitutive theory conceptualizes law not only as a social or cultural practice, but also as an essentially local practice, "as a mode of giving particular sense to particular things in particular places."[51] The meanings signified by law may ultimately apply across a large number of persons, or they may apply only within a small jurisdiction, but they remain always grounded, always historical, always situational. This explains why many of the studies conducted according to a constitutive methodology have involved research strategies that emphasize aspects of social life drawn from the everyday.[52] It also helps to explain why the fit between a contextual methodology and constitutive theory is so natural. To adopt a constitutive perspective is to take account of social context.

Relating Constitutive and Liberal Theory

Liberalism, in very broad terms, is primarily a normative theory of government and social policy privileging some combination of individual freedom, equality, and the rule of law (among, perhaps, other values). Constitutive theory is primarily a descriptive theory (though ideology is rarely far from the surface) regarding the interactive, transformative relationship said to exist between legal institutions and other aspects of social life. Very little has been said to date about the relationship between constitutive and liberal theory. In part, this might be due to the boundaries of the respective disciplines within which these theories typically are articulated and employed.

Indeed, in coming to terms with the subject of group-differentiated rights, I have often felt as if I were making significant progress only to bump up against a wall. Most of the time, at least, these walls were not the physical walls of a library (though this is always a risk for clumsy academics), but the virtual walls of an academic discipline. Constitutive methodology, as noted in the previous section, is grounded in a particular perspective toward law and legal institutions prevalent especially within sociolegal and law and culture research. Liberalism, on the other hand, although of far greater influence within legal studies generally, remains essentially a theory of politics and general philosophy. Yet, in its rendering of the

---

[51] Geertz, *Local Knowledge*, p. 232.

[52] These "everyday" studies include approaches that emphasize particular narratives, see, e.g., Patricia Ewick and Susan S. Silbey, *The Common Place of Law: Stories from Everyday Life* (Chicago: University of Chicago Press, 1998); as well as more traditional case studies, see, e.g., Barbara Yngvesson, *Virtuous Citizens, Disruptive Subjects: Order and Complaint in a New England Court* (New York: Routledge, 1993) and Sally Engel Merry, *Getting Justice and Getting Even: Legal Consciousness Among Working-Class Americans* (Chicago: University of Chicago Press, 1990).

relationship between rights and human identity, constitutive theory rather directly implicates fundamental liberal values. That is, constitutive theory, in the context of describing rights, reveals an important sense in which law may influence self-invention. For this reason, the disciplinary wall, so to speak, needs to come down.

Admittedly, this is not so radical a proposition. The constitutive perspective is, at least in part, derivative of significant earlier traditions in political philosophy conceptualizing the relationship between society and the formation of the individual. Moreover, substantial parallels between constitutive theory and contemporary critiques of liberalism already exist. To continue the (perhaps already too tired) metaphor, it might be said that the roots of constitutive theory stretch back beneath the disciplinary wall that otherwise separates sociolegal and political theory. For instance, the underlying insight of constitutive theory as it is applied in sociolegal research—the idea that law is not only constituted by, but also perpetually constitutes, aspects of social life, including elements of our individual identities—may be rooted in the earlier Hegelian tradition conceptualizing, in varying degrees, the natural and social worlds as the preponderant sources of individual desires. According to Hegel, it is our communal membership that supplies the basis for our moral existence; we are who and what we are only in virtue of that common membership, only in virtue of our public life and our relations and participation with others as part of a cultural whole. As Hegel put the thought, "Everything that man is he owes to the state; only in it can he find his essence."[53]

More recently, the background idea of the social as the source of the individual self has played an important role in the communitarian response to Rawlsian liberalism. In brief, in articulating his theory of justice, Rawls famously posits a conception of persons as self-inventors. We may all be subject to particularity; we are all born into particular families, communities and cultures, for instance. But according to Rawlsian liberal theory, as human beings we are also possessed of an essential capacity rationally to select and revise our attachments and conceptions of value. We choose our own paths; we are the authors of our own identities. In Rawls's words, "the self is prior to the ends which are affirmed by it; even a dominant end must be chosen from among numerous possibilities."[54] The communitarian response to Rawls's conception of a self-inventing citizenry coheres in certain ways with the social constructionism underlying constitutive theory. This is so both in terms of the alternative substantive conception of the self communitarian theorists commonly propose, and in terms of the fundamental

---

[53] Georg Willhelm Friedrich Hegel, *Lectures on the Philosophy of History* (1835), trans. J. Sibree (New York: Dover, 1956), p. 111; see also Hegel, *Philosophy of Right* (1821), trans. T.M. Knox (Oxford: Oxford University Press, 1990), and for commentary on this aspect of Hegel's thought, Charles Taylor, *Hegel* (Cambridge: Cambridge University Press, 1975), pp. 378–88.

[54] Rawls, *A Theory of Justice*, p. 560.

sources of that self. Michael Sandel, for instance, has prominently criticized Rawls's basic conception of freely choosing selves as neglecting the deep sense in which persons exist already strongly encumbered by their own particularity.[55] And Charles Taylor has challenged the asocial individualism of the Rawlsian conception of the person, conceptualizing the self instead as self-defining only within the context of some broader linguistic community.[56] There are, hence, both in the Sandelian conception of constitutive attachments, and in Taylor's account of the constitutive role of language in the formation of the self, correlates within contemporary political theory to the underlying perspective of constitutive theory within sociolegal research.

Even beyond the communitarian critics, we find modern canonical echoes of the fundamental influence of the social on human conceptions of our own and others' identities. In *The Human Condition*, for instance, Hannah Arendt, emphasizing the requirement, limits, and consequences of human speech and action, at one point writes of our enduring existence as individuals within a "web of human relationships": "The moment we want to say *who* somebody is, our very vocabulary leads us astray into saying *what* he is; we get entangled in a description of qualities he necessarily shares with others like him . . . with the result that his specific uniqueness escapes us."[57] Neither has the influence of our essential social matrix been lost even among core liberal theorists. Isaiah Berlin, for instance, in his famous essay on positive and negative liberty (published, interestingly, precisely the same year as Arendt's *Human Condition*) similarly noted "that some, perhaps all, of my ideas about myself, in particular my sense of my own moral and social identity, are intelligible only in terms of the social network in which I am . . . an element."[58] Indeed, while much has been made (and rightly so) of Rawls's later shift in his theorizing about justice toward the accommodation of particularity among different groups of persons,[59] there is even in his earlier work an acknowledgment of the weight of social influence in the interpretation of individual identity: "No doubt even the concepts that we use to describe our plans and situation, and even to give voice to our personal wants and purposes, often presuppose a social setting as well as a system of belief and thought that are the

---

55 See Sandel, *Liberalism and the Limits of Justice*.

56 "Later, I may innovate. I may develop an original way of understanding myself and human life, at least one which is in sharp disagreement with my family and background. But the innovation can only take place from the base in our common language." Taylor, *Sources of the Self*, pp. 35–6. Taylor further describes the powerful effect of social understandings on individual identity in "Politics of Recognition."

57 Hannah Arendt, *The Human Condition* (Chicago: University of Chicago Press, 1958), p. 181.

58 Isaiah Berlin, "Two Concepts of Liberty," in *Four Essays on Liberty* (Oxford: Oxford University Press, 1969), p. 155.

59 See John Rawls, *Political Liberalism* (New York: Columbia University Press, 1993).

outcome of the collective efforts of a long tradition."[60] The difference, of course, is that where communitarian (and some multicultural) theorists tend to privilege social attachments, Rawlsian and other liberal (and liberal-multicultural) theorists instead conceptualize the capacity to revise one's allegiances and beliefs as an integral aspect of human dignity.

There is, thus, within the received tradition in political theory, and even within liberalism itself, nothing so extravagant or radical in locating the source of aspects of individual identity in the social world. Yet, the constitutive perspective adopted within sociolegal research may yield an additional dimension to our appreciation of the relationship between the social and the individual human self. This is so because constitutive theory seeks to describe not merely the character or depth of our cultural and communal memberships, but rather the influence of our distinctly *political* (including legal) institutions on the construction of human identity.[61] Where communitarian theory emphasizes self-discovery within a pre-existing web of group memberships, and liberal theory prioritizes self-invention by means of individual rational thought, constitutive theory offers a view of human beings as, partially, politically and legally constructed. In this light, the present study applies constitutive theory to group-differentiated rights in order both to understand the role of such rights in the construction of social identity and to assess the senses in which such rights may frustrate, and facilitate, liberal self-invention.

An Overview of the Book

The ensuing chapters in this volume engage analytical, social cognitive, constitutive and liberal theory to explore the critical relationships that exist among rights, social groups and the ideals of membership and self-invention. The final chapter then depicts three distinct models of group-differentiated rights, and evaluates each model in light of core principles of liberal and constitutive theory introduced in the earlier chapters.

More specifically, Chapter 2 places this work in the context of contemporary debates in legal and political theory concerning the nature of rights and the relationship between rights and individualism. The primary concern here is to demonstrate that, although rights are intimately (and appropriately) related in liberal thought to individual well-being, fundamental precepts of liberal theory provide room for, indeed mandate, as well a view of rights in collective form. After preliminarily defining rights in light of prevailing interest and choice theories, and distinguishing among rights in terms both of their sources (i.e., law;

---

60 Rawls, *A Theory of Justice*, p. 522.

61 For an essay describing the importance of studying "political identities," see Rogers M. Smith, "Identities, Interests and the Future of Political Science," *Perspectives on Politics* 2 (2004), pp. 302–4.

morality) and the nature of their bearers (i.e., individuals; groups), this chapter proceeds to describe previous treatments of collective aspects of legal rights, including especially treatments apparent in or derived from the work of John Stuart Mill, T.H. Green, Jeremy Bentham, Wesley Hohfeld and Joseph Raz.

Chapter 3 then suggests a further basis for concluding that legal rights are necessarily collective. While from a liberal perspective rights remain ever grounded in the interests of individuals, rights both in legislation and adjudication also serve, in virtue of fundamental precepts of law and formal justice, to relate persons one to another, and in the process inherently to categorize rights-bearers. In light of the necessary categorization of rights-bearers, the chapter then explores related work undertaken within sociology and cognitive psychology with three primary goals in mind: first, to understand how and why, given our cognitive makeup and limitations, we tend naturally to categorize aspects of the social world, including human beings; second, to grasp the basic nature of social categories and their relationship to social prejudice and stigma; and third, to appreciate, in view of the indeterminacy apparent in social and legal categorization, the degree of influence legal actors and institutions may possess over the constitution of social identities. This chapter concludes with an assessment of social labeling theory and a consideration of the role of law in the dissemination of social labels. Law is, thus, described as one among many vital agents of socialization, spreading and further constructing social and self conceptions of categories of human beings.

The fourth chapter describes more particularly the nature and significance of the categories of rights-bearers engendered by legal rights. Often these classes persist as nothing more than aggregates of individual rights-bearers. When the investitive criteria of rights correspond to socially salient characteristics, however, the categories engendered by legal rights serve also to constitute individuals as members of critical social and cultural groups. This understanding of the impact of legal rights on group membership stands in strong contrast to the prevailing view of rights purely as the instruments of self-invention. Indeed, the primary aim of this chapter is to seek a reconceptualization of the relationship between rights and human identity. To that end, the chapter examines the nature of identity as it has been described in social theory, as well as the role of social salience in the creation of collective identities. The chapter then explores the constitutive influence of legal rights, in particular, by drawing further upon Hart's distinction between special and general rights and describing the inclusionary and exclusionary conditions under which these forms of right might constitute social groups and self-meaning. Through the processes of adjudicative and legislative classification, a legal system may be seen to distribute membership among the persons subject to it in critical ways. The image drawn of persons sorted, and identities constructed, by law, the chapter suggests, would seem a cause for anxiety among those who value self-invention.

Given the constitutive relationship found to exist between legal rights and social groups, Chapter 5 assays our current conceptual understanding of membership in order to derive a standard against which to assess group-differentiated rights. In contrast with Michael Walzer's relativist and Michael Sandel's communitarian conceptions, this chapter constructs and adopts a liberal conception of membership. Within the context of official differential treatment of categories of persons, liberal principles have received particularly sustained examination within contemporary debates in multicultural theory. The search for a liberal conception of membership thus naturally begins here. Indeed, it seems fair to say that recent debates over multicultural policies have now become debates not only *within* but also fundamentally *about* liberal theory, or about the nature and principal commitments of liberalism and the liberal state. In that vein, recent liberal-multicultural theory has been marked by two major stances, which are in this chapter labeled the autonomy and toleration perspectives on liberalism. Adherents of both perspectives generally countenance reasonable differentiated policies designed to protect cultural groups from external social forces. Where the perspectives differ, however, is with respect to cultural group claims internally to restrict individual members' liberty.[62] Where in such cases theorists of the autonomy perspective would privilege individual over collective freedom, theorists who perceive toleration as the core of liberalism would more readily sacrifice individual liberty to cultural tradition. Although this chapter suggests reasons to view toleration and diversity as instrumental to the project of autonomy, once the toleration perspective is exploited to justify cultural repression it becomes difficult to conceptualize in liberal terms.

The liberal conception of membership invoked in Chapter 5 therefore privileges rational self-invention, or what is here termed individual constitutive autonomy. The idea of constitutive autonomy is intended to create an explicit link between constitutive and liberal theory. The invocation of autonomy is meant to reflect the view, manifest particularly in the thought of Mill, and more recently in that of Rawls and Raz, that individuals must remain free, consistent with an equal freedom for all, to act in accordance with their own rationally and independently derived sense of what is good and valuable in life.[63] In this context, the modifier

---

[62] This description is based on Kymlicka's distinction between external protections and internal restrictions, see Kymlicka, *Multicultural Citizenship*, pp. 35–44.

[63] John Stuart Mill, *On Liberty* (1859), Gertrude Himmelfarb, ed., (New York: Penguin, 1974); John Rawls, "Kantian Constructivism in Moral Theory," *Journal of Philosophy* 77 (1980), reprinted in *John Rawls: Collected Papers*, Samuel Freeman, ed., (Cambridge, Mass.: Harvard University Press, 1999), pp. 303–58; Raz, *The Morality of Freedom*, pp. 369–78. Thus, in this project, I am primarily concerned with personal autonomy, or the virtue inherent in rationally deciding for oneself one's own beliefs and direction in life. I do not here engage the contemporary debate concerning the relationship between personal and Kantian moral autonomy. In short, Kantian moral autonomy, like liberal theories of personal autonomy, is a theory fundamentally about human self-direction. But unlike most such theories of personal autonomy, Kantian moral autonomy raises further the question of one's moral relationship with others. Persons act autonomously, in the

"constitutive" comprehends the sense in which an autonomous person is a maximally self-defined person, a person free to the greatest possible extent to constitute one's self and determine one's life path. Although, of course, it remains impossible ever entirely to remove oneself from social forces, all things equal, the liberal self is more likely to flourish within a society that seeks to constrain social forces constructive of the self and instead promotes conditions conducive to individual constitutive autonomy. Yet, at the same time as the liberal conception privileges constitutive autonomy, it simultaneously strives to reflect a range of human values, even values to some extent in conflict with autonomy. Drawing upon Isaiah Berlin's suggestion of a conflict among ultimate values, this chapter also suggests that liberal membership will at times curtail individual autonomy in order to advance other critical values, such as equality, fairness, or public order. The chapter concludes with an assessment of the relationship between liberal and political membership in the context of immigration and border policy. Consistent with the principles of liberal membership, the analysis commends a presumption in favor of inclusion but notes also the existence of specifically *liberal* grounds upon which borders may be closed and persons excluded.

Chapter 6 seeks to defend liberal membership against an important objection, an objection, indeed, that would challenge even the characterization of the conception constructed *as* liberal. Brian Barry has sought to critique multicultural theory and policy by reintroducing a purportedly egalitarian view of liberal justice.[64] Invoking dogmatically a precept of formal equality, Barry condemns the view that any degree of state accommodation of minority cultural practice may be required as a matter of justice. This chapter contends that, although certain aspects of Barry's response to liberalism's more extreme multicultural critics are credible, indeed even edifying, the universalist's adoration of formal equality above all else fails to capture the complex moral calculus inherent in group-differentiated policy. After outlining the major strands of Barry's universalistic conception of justice, and assessing the cogency of his justification of social and economic rights in light of his critique of cultural rights, the final portion of this chapter suggests why, in contrast to Barry's proceduralist approach, we do better by asking whether differentiated citizenship policies threaten to impede individual constitutive autonomy.

Kantian moral sense, when they are free to guide their actions in accordance not only with their own ends but also constrained by universalized attention to the interests of others. For discussions of the relationship between personal and Kantian moral autonomy, see, e.g., Gerald Gaus, "The Place of Autonomy within Liberalism," and Jeremy Waldron, "Moral Autonomy and Personal Autonomy," both of which appear in John Christman and Joel Anderson, eds., *Autonomy and the Challenges to Liberalism: New Essays* (Cambridge: Cambridge University Press, 2005), pp. 272–306, 307–29.

[64] See Barry, *Culture and Equality*.

Chapter 7 then describes three distinct models of the process by which social groups and identities may be constituted by rights, and evaluates each model according to the principles which inform the liberal conception of membership previously constructed. The first model treated is the ascriptive form of group-differentiated right. The analysis begins with the assumption, explored in Chapter 3, that any right granted will of necessity be granted to a class of persons. It then suggests that where the dissimilarity between the classes of persons included in and excluded from a right is founded upon an ascribed characteristic (e.g., a moral or intellectual trait associated with the rights-claimant's race or gender), both the inclusion and exclusion result in the further construction of social groups characterized according to the particular capacity or incapacity at issue. Membership in such an ascriptive group will thus influence social and self-perceptions of any individual member's identity. The examples explored in this section include exclusions from constitutional (e.g., slavery and alienage) and political (e.g., citizenship and voting rights) membership, as well as exclusions in private law. In each such instance, persons will have been sorted, and aspects of human identity defined, by law on the basis of ascriptive characteristics. Hence, the ascriptive exclusionary model of group-differentiated right severely constrains constitutive autonomy. Indeed, the denial of personal liberties and opportunities to categories of individuals on the basis of ascriptive characteristics resembles ancient and feudal forms of differentiated citizenship.

Group-differentiated rights of affirmation are considered in the second portion of the chapter. Such rights are afforded solely to a particular subset of persons as part of an effort to remedy a previous exclusion, or to remedy the exclusionary effect of social practices other than law itself. Although formally similar, in that the right is afforded exclusively to a particular class of persons, this type of legal exclusion is of a substantively different nature than the ascriptive exclusionary process described above. The exclusion of a dominant class from a right granted to subordinated persons may function affirmatively to include a category of persons in need of special protection. At the same time, however, in light of their common form, affirmative rights serve also further to constitute individuals as members of social groups, and so also present the prospect of a loss in constitutive autonomy. This is so, because the bearers of such rights similarly are sorted and further defined by law as members of particular social groups. Group-differentiated rights of affirmation are, therefore, like ascriptive rights, inherently constitutive, but at times they also may be crucial to the realization of liberal justice. Examples explored in this section include rights to affirmative action, rights afforded same-sex couples to engage in civil unions, and rights that attach on the basis of disability. Through a contextual analysis, this section demonstrates both the ways in which such rights might curtail individual constitutive autonomy, and ways in which such rights might further that same, as well as other, liberal values.

In contrast both to rights that ascriptively constitute individuals as members of social groups, and rights that seek affirmatively to include persons on the basis of their group membership, the third model focuses on rights that permit individual members of groups, or the groups themselves in a collective capacity, the freedom to exclude themselves from some aspect of social life. Typically rights such as these are claimed by members of ethnic, national or other types of cultural groups seeking recognition or accommodation of group practices or identities. Again through a contextual analysis, this section demonstrates that, unlike ascriptive or affirmative rights, such culturally-differentiated rights often directly foster constitutive autonomy by enabling cultural group members to construct their own particular social identities in contrast to broader social groups. Yet the analysis also considers ways in which cultural rights might facilitate the intra-group repression of more vulnerable individuals and sub-groupings within cultural groups, and suggests that where this is the case the moral costs apparent in the ascriptive differentiated model are merely revived at a different level.

A final introductory note. While this book aims to achieve a more integrated and comprehensive assessment of group-differentiated rights than has appeared in the literature to date, it certainly is no part of this project to claim that there is nothing further to say on this subject. It is my hope, of course, that the constitutive understanding of rights offered here will make a valuable contribution to the burgeoning literature on rights and liberal multiculturalism. I hope, as well, that the interdisciplinary nature of the project serves as an illustration of the virtue of remaining open to alternative perspectives and methodologies. One cost of breadth of treatment and method, however, is a want of concentration in any one subject area or approach. Indeed, the present study is intended in part to establish the importance of context in assessing group-differentiated rights, and yet the surface can only be scratched within these pages. Further, the present study assesses group-differentiated rights from a distinctly liberal perspective, and so it assumes the truth of a particular view of the world and social order. Such an assessment should prove useful, insofar as numerous theorists who have engaged the topic of social and cultural group claims share many aspects of this worldview. But I remain cognizant of the fact that the liberal perspective has been rejected, if it has even been considered, throughout much of the world today.

In both of these senses, then, this work is intended more as a beginning than an as an end. It is an invitation for further inquiry, directed both to those who would approach the subject of rights and identity from a broad theoretical perspective and to those who would focus more intently on particular types of rights or social groups, both to those theorists who share a fundamentally liberal conception of justice and to those with substantially different perspectives.

Chapter 2

Collective Aspects of Legal Rights

Rights and Individualism

Critics of liberalism commonly lament liberalism's fascination with rights. The usual plaint is that rights are too fiercely individualistic constructs, and that the liberal dependency upon rights ultimately portends disaster for social relations.[1] In this sense, the recent critique echoes the earlier sentiments of Marx, who warned that "liberty as a right of man is not founded upon the relations between man and man, but rather upon the separation of man from man. It is the right of such separation. The right of the circumscribed individual, withdrawn into himself."[2] Today, similarly, we find rights critics denouncing the liberal "priorit[ization] of the individual and his rights over society,"[3] and decrying the liberal "image of citizens as free and independent selves."[4] By taking rights as primary, these rights critics contend, liberals atomize humanity and so neglect civic virtue, sacrifice community, and fundamentally misrepresent humanity's social status.

It is, of course, true that much of the intimacy between rights and individualism originates at the core of liberal thought. Liberals conceive of rights as critical elements in the constitution of individual freedom.[5] And insofar as freedom is a necessary condition for, and an instrument of, human self-realization, according

---

[1] On criticism of liberalism's prioritization of rights, see, e.g., Michael J. Sandel, *Liberalism and the Limits of Justice*, 2d ed. (Cambridge: Cambridge University Press, 1998); Alasdair MacIntyre, *After Virtue: A Study in Moral Theory*, 2d ed. (Notre Dame, Ind.: University of Notre Dame Press, 1984); Charles Taylor, "Atomism," in *2 Philosophy and the Human Sciences: Philosophical Papers* (Cambridge: Cambridge University Press, 1985), pp. 187–211.

[2] Karl Marx, "On the Jewish Question" (1843), in *The Marx-Engels Reader*, 2d ed., Robert C. Tucker, ed. (New York: W.W. Norton, 1978), p. 42.

[3] Taylor, "Atomism," p. 187.

[4] Michael J. Sandel, *Democracy's Discontent: America in Search of a Public Philosophy* (Cambridge, Mass.: Harvard University Press, 1996), p. 350.

[5] For a classic statement of this view, see John Locke, *The Second Treatise of Government* (1690), in *Two Treatises of Government*, Peter Laslett, ed. (Cambridge: Cambridge University Press, 1960). For a more contemporary statement, see George Kateb, *The Inner Ocean: Individualism and Democratic Culture* (Ithaca, NY: Cornell University Press, 1992).

rights to individuals expresses respect for basic human dignity.[6] In this light, we find contemporary liberal thinkers, led by Rawls, asserting as fundamental the priority of the right over the good,[7] and Dworkin, portraying rights as political trumps such that the interest of the individual may override broad considerations of general utility or community will, even where that utility or will has been democratically determined.[8] Others have gone even further, claiming that individualism is intrinsically linked to the concept of rights, or that individuality is essential to the very logic of possessing a right.[9]

I have few qualms with this depiction, common to liberals and their critics alike, of rights characterized primarily in individualized form. Rights pertain predominantly to individuals because they are rooted ultimately in the interests of individuals, and because normally they may be pressed by any individual who fits the relevant criteria.[10] Rights permit us the liberty necessary to behave and believe in ways we, as individuals, choose. Rights afford persons the freedoms necessary to *be* individuals, to revise our ends, our attachments, and thus our selves.

At the same time, however, rights are not the purely individualistic constructs they are commonly depicted to be. Far from exhibiting the sort of "hyper-individualism" generally assumed by rights critics and proponents, rights inherently portray critical and collective aspects. What most rights critics, and indeed most proponents of rights-based liberalism, appear to have missed in their debates is that rights, under law, attach not because (or not merely because) a subject is an individual separate and apart from all others, but specifically because the subject is an individual *similar* in some crucial respect(s) to some number of others. This is the difference that *law* makes. It is an elementary consequence of formal justice. Indeed, as I shall argue below, rights possess certain formal and collective properties inapposite to the claims of rights critics and proponents alike.

---

6 See Immanuel Kant, *Groundwork of the Metaphysic of Morals* (1785), trans. H.J. Paton (New York: Harper & Row, 1964); John Stuart Mill, *On Liberty* (1859), Gertrude Himmelfarb, ed. (New York: Penguin, 1974); Kateb, *Inner Ocean*, pp. 1–10.

7 John Rawls, *A Theory of Justice* (Cambridge, Mass.: Harvard University Press, 1971), p. 31.

8 Ronald Dworkin, *Taking Rights Seriously* (Cambridge, Mass.: Harvard University Press, 1977), p. xi: "Individual rights are political trumps held by individuals."

9 See Jeremy Waldron, "Can communal goods be human rights?," in *Liberal Rights: Collected Papers 1981–1991* (Cambridge: Cambridge University Press, 1993), pp. 339–69; D.N. MacCormick, "Rights in Legislation," in P.M.S. Hacker and J. Raz, eds, *Law, Morality and Society: Essays in Honour of H.L.A. Hart* (Oxford: Clarendon Press, 1977), pp. 192–5. Even Raz, who more than most liberal theorists is interested in attending to collective aspects of rights, asserts that rights only exist "if they serve the interests of individuals." Joseph Raz, *The Morality of Freedom* (Oxford: Clarendon Press, 1986), p. 208.

10 The interest theory of rights is discussed in greater detail in the next section.

The Language of Rights and Groups

Let us take as our initial presumption Joseph Raz's well-known definition of a right: "'X has a right' if and only if X can have rights, and, other things being equal, an aspect of X's well-being (his interest) is a sufficient reason for holding some other person(s) to be under a duty."[11] The first portion of this definition is intended broadly to incorporate an extensive range of views on the capacity of different types of entities to hold rights. Clearly we often envision not merely natural persons but also artificial entities (e.g., corporations) as bearing rights.[12] But can a fetus bear a right? A person who is comatose? Members of future generations? An animal? Raz's definition is potentially consistent not only with natural and artificial persons as rights-bearers, but it also largely remains agnostic on a host of other sensitive and substantive moral issues.[13]

The second portion of Raz's definition, however, is possessed of significantly more substantive content. It suggests that rights are correlative to duties, and that rights fundamentally protect interests. Both of these essential characteristics of rights are derivative ultimately of Bentham's theory of rights.[14] We will take up Bentham and the relational nature of rights later in this chapter, but it is important to note here that Hart and others have long disputed the notion that rights are, at heart, benefits, or the embodiments of interests. Hart's alternative to the benefit or interest theory of rights conceptualizes rights as, in essence, choices or exercises of individual will.[15] What is critical, from the point of view of the choice or will theory of rights, is the rights-bearer's control over the duty imposed upon another. According to this view, in any case where a person X has the power to release another from a duty, X may be said to possess a right.

The choice theory has been the subject of extensive criticism, and in fact Hart himself partially repudiated the idea as an all encompassing theory of rights.[16] For

---

[11] Raz, *The Morality of Freedom*, p. 166.

[12] Indeed, Raz further specifies a standard governing this capacity: "An individual is capable of having rights if and only if either his well-being is of ultimate value or he is an 'artificial person' (e.g. a corporation)." Ibid.

[13] See ibid., pp. 176–80.

[14] For an account, and critique, of Bentham's benefit theory of rights, see H.L.A. Hart, "Legal Rights," in *Essays on Bentham: Jurisprudence and Political Theory* (Oxford: Clarendon Press, 1982), pp. 162–93.

[15] See ibid. and H.L.A. Hart, "Are There Any Natural Rights?," in Jeremy Waldron, ed., *Theories of Rights* (Oxford: Oxford University Press, 1984), pp. 77–90. On the interest and will theories more generally, see also Jeremy Waldron, "Introduction," in *Theories of Rights*, pp. 9–11; Peter Jones, *Rights* (New York: St. Martin's Press, 1994), ch. 2; Matthew H. Kramer, N.E. Simmonds and Hillel Steiner, *A Debate Over Rights: Philosophical Enquiries* (Oxford: Oxford University Press, 1998).

[16] See Hart, "Legal Rights," pp. 192–3, repudiating the choice theory of rights with respect to non-"ordinary" legal rights, such as moral and constitutional rights; see also

one thing, the choice theory appears unduly to limit the types of entities capable of bearing rights. For example, it seems reasonable to ascribe rights to very young children even though they may not yet be capable rationally of exercising their wills in ways envisioned by the choice theory. Something very similar might be said of persons with a severe mental disability; surely such persons, despite a certain incapacity for choice, should be deemed capable of bearing at least certain, if not most, rights. Further, the criminal law presents seemingly insurmountable obstacles to a choice theory of rights. For example, it seems reasonable to presume that we all have the right not to be killed without also presuming that we all have the power to release our assassins from the duty to avoid murder.[17]

Even once we presume to describe rights, following Raz and others, in terms of the protection of interests, however, there remains significant complexity within contemporary rights language. Indeed, there has been, in modern times, a virtual explosion in our rights vocabulary. Some have come to view this as a great problem, while others tend to see in any such expansion a cause for modest celebration.[18] There is at least some truth in both positions, for while not every moral claim can or should be stated in terms of a right, it is also the case that beneath the seemingly limitless linguistic outbreak lies a more fundamental and welcome turn toward concern for individual human well being.

We thus frequently hear reference today to moral rights, natural rights, human rights, constitutional rights, fundamental rights, legal rights, political rights, civil rights, individual rights, group rights, and so on. According to the context, and according to our particular theory of rights, we may not see meaningful differences among these terms, or we might see each as vitally distinct.[19] Certainly human and natural rights are often spoken of at once, and these are as often linked with the concept of moral rights, though they are as certainly not identical.[20] Constitutional,

---

H.L.A. Hart, "Introduction," in *Essays in Jurisprudence and Philosophy* (Oxford: Clarendon Press, 1983), p. 17; Waldron, *Liberal Rights*, p. 463, n. 19.

[17] See Waldron, "Introduction," in *Theories of Rights*, p. 9.

[18] For an example of the former position, see Mary Ann Glendon, *Rights Talk: The Impoverishment of Political Discourse* (New York: Free Press, 1991), pp. x–xi, and for an example of the latter, see Richard Dagger, *Civic Virtues: Rights, Citizenship, and Republican Liberalism* (Oxford: Oxford University Press, 1997), p. 4.

[19] For example, Austin and, perhaps most famously, Bentham dismissed the idea of non-legal rights. See Jeremy Bentham, *Anarchical Fallacies* (1824), in *The Works of Jeremy Bentham*, ed. John Bowring (Edinburgh, 1843), Vol. II, p. 501; John Austin, *Lectures on Jurisprudence*, Vol. II, Lecture XII, pp. 1–2 (London: John Murray, 1863); Hart, "Legal Rights," p. 163. On the other hand, Ronald Dworkin presents perhaps the best known argument for law's fundamental dependence upon morality. See Ronald Dworkin, *Law's Empire* (Cambridge, Mass: Harvard University Press, 1986) and Dworkin, *Taking Rights Seriously*, pp. 81–130.

[20] Human or natural rights may best be conceptualized as that subset of moral rights that are of a truly general scope. Human or natural rights become requisite in light of some

political and civil rights are normally considered species of legal rights, but the connection between these legal rights and the previous and more abstract categories of rights is, of course, a matter of substantial controversy.[21] It is certainly not my intention here to parse all the various contrasts and kinship in contemporary rights-talk. It is even less my intention, in suggesting the importance of exploring group-differentiated rights, simply to multiply further our already burdened rights vocabulary. There are, however, two distinctions worth making. The first concerns the positive, as opposed to moral, basis for legal rights, for clearly much of the perplexity in rights-talk falls along this division. The second concerns the distinction between individual and group rights, and the place of group-differentiated rights across that axis.

Clearly when we say that someone has a "right" to something, or that it would be "right" to do something, we may be saying any of several things at once. We may mean that it is right, in a normative sense, for an individual, call her Jane, to lay claim to object X or to do act Y; that is, we might think that Jane should have X or do Y as a matter of ethics or in virtue of some moral principle. We might also think that not only should Jane be able to lay claim to object X or to do act Y, but that, where X is withheld from Jane or where Jane is in some way impeded from doing Y, the legal system should mediate the conflict in Jane's favor; that is, Jane should have a legally enforceable right. We might even, as Ronald Dworkin has suggested, think that Jane, from her perspective, should proceed with Y despite our feeling that the law will rightly seek to impose punishment upon her.[22] More commonly, however, we expect legally enforceable rights to correspond to normatively right outcomes. Where this is not the case, we might applaud Jane's challenge for X or Y as a morally justifiable effort to change what we consider unjust law.[23]

In this sense, then, we may say that the classification "legal rights" best describes those positive rights that arise by virtue of legislation (including constitution) and adjudication, and that are thus intended to be secured by the coercive power of the state.[24] The more abstract categories of rights we may refer

---

moral principle, but there are also moral principles which prescribe rights of more limited applicability. See John Finnis, *Natural Law and Natural Rights* (Oxford: Clarendon Press, 1980), pp. 198–9.

[21] Constitutional and other civil and political rights represent perhaps the most comprehensible nexus between morally right outcomes and positive legal rights. See, e.g., Dworkin, *Taking Rights Seriously*. For a helpful discussion of the relationship between positive and constitutional law, see Frederick Schauer, "Constitutional Positivism," *Connecticut Law Review* 25 (1993).

[22] See Dworkin, *Taking Rights Seriously*, pp. 188–92.

[23] See especially Martin Luther King, "Letter from Birmingham City Jail" (1963), in *A Testament of Hope: The Essential Writings and Speeches of Martin Luther King, Jr.*, James M. Washington, ed. (New York: Harper Collins, 1986), pp. 289–302.

[24] As Neil MacCormick has written, "The first point to be made about legal rights must

to as "moral rights," or those rights that, whether they be affirmed by the state or not, are requisite given some normative principle of direction.[25] When, within a given legal system, a decision is made that a right should attach on the basis of some particular group membership, the result will be a group-differentiated legal right. Of course, depending upon the particular context, there may be a legitimate moral claim to differential treatment as well, and where this is the case we may in addition point to the existence of a group-differentiated moral right.

Further, when the investitive criteria indicated by a right do happen to coincide with membership in a particular social or cultural group, it has become common, particularly among theorists of difference and multiculturalism, to speak of such rights broadly as "group rights."[26] Jeremy Waldron has disclaimed the wisdom even of expressing such claims in the language of rights.[27] We need not go this far, but if we are at all concerned with the general coherence and precision of rights language we would do well to heed the spirit of Waldron's message and tread cautiously in pronouncing the existence of group rights, and in clarifying the scope of group-differentiated rights. I shall reserve the term "group rights" for those rights which, although they may remain grounded in the interests of individuals, can only logically be pressed by groups *qua* groups.[28] All other rights are individual rights, or simply rights.

Hence, group-differentiated rights, or rights that vest on the basis of some particular group membership, may be either group rights or individual rights. Consider, for instance, a tribal right to collective ownership of property, or the right of a nation to collective self-determination.[29] Rights such as these are group rights because they can only logically be asserted by groups. But since these rights

---

seem, when made, to be of breath-taking banality. The point is that legal rights are conferred by legal rules, or (if you will) by laws." MacCormick, "Rights in Legislation," p. 189; see also H.L.A. Hart, *The Concept of Law* (1961), 2d ed. (Oxford: Clarendon Press, 1994), ch. 5. For the contrary view, that a conceptual separation between legal and moral rights is not possible, see Dworkin, *Taking Rights Seriously*, pp. 14–46, and *Law's Empire*.

[25] The division between morally right outcomes and rights as possessory interests is, according to Finnis, a relatively recent phenomenon. Confusion was more limited in pre-modern times with the use of the classical term *jus*, or "the right," which in Roman law, and for Aquinas, meant roughly "that which is just in a given situation." *Jus*, and rights, principally became something individuals were capable of possessing in the much later thought of Francisco Suarez, Hugo Grotius, and ultimately Hobbes, Locke and Pufendorf. Finnis, *Natural Law and Natural Rights*, pp. 206–10.

[26] See, e.g., the essays collected in Will Kymlicka, ed., *The Rights of Minority Cultures* (Oxford: Oxford University Press, 1995).

[27] Waldron, "Can communal goods be human rights?," pp. 360–67.

[28] Peter Jones adopts essentially the same definition of "group rights." See Jones, *Rights*, pp. 182–7.

[29] On collective rights to self-government, see Avishai Margalit and Joseph Raz, "National Self-Determination," *Journal of Philosophy* 87 (1990).

attach on the basis of group membership, they also constitute group-differentiated rights. All group rights, then, are also group-differentiated rights. On the other hand, a right to free religious practices, instantiated in the form of an exemption from an otherwise generally applicable safety standard such that, say, Sikhs might wear turbans rather than helmets while driving motorcycles, is properly conceptualized as an individual rather than a group right.[30] For though the right reflects the importance of a group-based belief, it may nonetheless be exercised by individual members of the group at issue. At the same time, the individual exemption right remains a group-differentiated right (call it an "individual group-differentiated right," if you like) since the religious practitioner possesses the right only in virtue of their particular group membership.

Collective Aspects of Rights

To the extent that we are prepared to admit the existence of group rights, then one fundamental sense in which rights may be conceptualized in collective terms has already been established. In this section I shall be interested in bringing more directly to light previous treatments of collective aspects of rights, particularly including collective aspects of rights that may be derived from certain classical works in liberal theory.[31] Often, these theorists did not in their discussions of rights pointedly describe rights in collective terms, yet implicit within their writings are valuable insights into the collective nature of rights. I will also consider here Joseph Raz's contemporary analytical conceptualization of rights in other than purely individualistic terms. In the ensuing chapter, I shall suggest that law itself provides an additional basis upon which to conclude that rights are inherently collective.

Utilitarian and Perfectionist Justifications for Rights: J.S. Mill and T.H. Green

In differing ways, nineteenth-century thinkers John Stuart Mill and T.H. Green brought together ideals which contemporary rights critics and proponents often

---

[30] See Brian Barry's discussion in *Culture and Equality: An Egalitarian Critique of Multiculturalism* (Cambridge, Mass.: Harvard University Press, 2001), pp. 112–13.

[31] It is, of course, possible to discern collective aspects of rights in works other than those treated here. For instance, Hegel's reconstruction of the relationship of the individual to state and society, in effect turning consent based theory on its head, results in a vision of the social as the source of rights. See Hegel, *Philosophy of Right* (1821), trans. T.M. Knox (Oxford: Oxford University Press, 1990). Natural law theorists, too, have conceptualized rights as partially constitutive of the common good rather than as mere restraints thereon. See Finnis, *Natural Law and Natural Rights*, pp. 210–18; Robert P. George, *In Defense of Natural Law* (Oxford: Oxford University Press, 1999). My emphasis here, though, is on collective aspects of rights within liberal theory.

view as essentially in opposition. In contrast to the predominantly individualist suppositions reflected in current debates, both Mill and Green sought to justify liberal rights in virtue of the social benefits they thought rights would provide. Both considered individual freedom, and thus an expansive array of rights, to be essential to human dignity and the development of human capacities. Yet their accounts of rights also reflected highly divergent conceptions of the relationship between individuals and society, of freedom and the good, and of the role of the state in advancing the most beneficial state of affairs. Where Mill's justification of rights was grounded in his utilitarianism, Green's sprung from his perfectionist view of the state.

Mill envisioned expansive liberal rights as instrumentally conducive to the social good in at least three essential ways. First, and most narrowly, Mill defended freedom of expression as instrumental to the discovery of truth:

> But the peculiar evil of silencing the expression of an opinion is that it is robbing the human race, posterity as well as the existing generation—those who dissent from the opinion, still more than those who hold it. If the opinion is right, they are deprived of the opportunity of exchanging error for truth; if wrong, they lose, what is almost as great a benefit, the clearer perception and livelier impression of truth produced by its collision with error.[32]

In this sense, insofar as truth itself should be deemed a social good, the liberal right to freedom of expression, upon which the search for truth is said to depend, should be conceived of even as a "necessity to the mental well-being of mankind."[33] Second, and more generally, Mill perceived great social utility in enabling "individuality [to] assert itself," in affording freedom to individuals to engage in "different experiments of living," for insofar as "mankind are imperfect" an expansive array of liberal rights would constitute "the chief ingredient [both] of individual and social progress."[34] Mill's thought here was that the liberal granting of individual rights would facilitate an evolutionary process whereby alternative modes of individual and social life might compete with one another, leading ultimately toward greater individual and social fulfillment. And finally, through individual freedom, Mill suggested:

> human life also becomes rich, diversified, and animating . . . strengthening the tie which binds every individual to the race, by making the race infinitely better worth belonging to. In proportion to the development of his individuality, each person becomes more valuable to himself, and is, therefore, capable of being more valuable to others. There is

---

[32] Mill, *On Liberty*, p. 76.

[33] Ibid., p. 115.

[34] Ibid., p. 120.

> a greater fullness about his own existence, and when there is more life in the units there is more in the mass which is composed of them.[35]

Mill thus evoked, in the broadest possible sense, the prospect of a noble community of individuals, a vision of a liberal society composed of persons committed to their own self development, and, *in that sense*, contributing to the virtue of all.

Green too saw in the exercise of rights a vital means by which individuals might develop their capacities and in the process serve communal life. "There ought to be rights," he wrote:

> because the moral personality—the capacity on the part of an individual for making a common good his own—ought to be developed; and it is developed through rights; i.e. through the recognition by members of society of powers in each other contributory to a common good and the regulation of those powers by that recognition.[36]

The difference, of course, is that where Mill would have avoided interfering with liberty even where such interference might be in the interest of the individual, Green saw in rights the opportunity for human development in a particular direction. "At first sight," Green lectured, "you might say that you are not free, for your individuality is repressed. But this is to lose sight of what is the highest in man."[37] Freedom, from Green's perspective, is not merely the liberty to behave as one likes, but "the liberation of the powers of all men equally for contributions to a common good."[38] Freedom is a claim to participate in, and contribute more fully to, social life, and the end of government is to facilitate the individual's moral development by extending the prospects for the exercise of this vital freedom. In emphasizing government's role in individual moral development, Green's point was not that the state, through law, can make men moral, for he viewed moral character and responsibility as primarily internal spiritual matters not susceptible to external coercion.[39] But Green did maintain, strongly, that through legislation and

---

[35] Ibid., p. 127.

[36] T.H. Green, "Lectures on the Principles of Political Obligation" (1879), in *Lectures on the Principles of Political Obligation and Other Writings* (Cambridge: Cambridge University Press, 1986), p. 26.

[37] T.H. Green, *Miscellaneous Writings, Speeches and Letters*, Peter Nicholson ed. (Bristol: Thoemmes Press, 2003), p. 181.

[38] *Collected Works of T.H. Green*, Peter Nicholson ed. (Bristol: Thoemmes Press, 1997), Vol. 3, p. 372.

[39] See Green, *Miscellaneous Writings*, p. 218, noting the "difference between that liberty of the subject which is compatible with the real freedom of others, and that which merely means freedom to make oneself a social nuisance; between the possibility of making men moral by Act of Parliament and that of removing positive social obstacles to their morality . . ."; ibid., p. 452: "That the Law cannot make men good, that its business is to set

education government could engender social conditions that would enable moral self-development.[40] Indeed, it was this vision of the role of government that led Green in his *Lectures on Moral and Political Philosophy* to characterize "the state [as] an education machine."[41]

Green's conception of freedom is therefore positive where Mill's is essentially negative, and Green's conception of the relationship between rights and the common good is intrinsic where Mill's is primarily instrumental. Yet for both Green and Mill, in contrast to most contemporary rights critics and proponents, the fundamental legitimacy of rights turns on the social benefits such rights produce.[42]

Collective Aspects of Rights in Analytical Theory: Wesley Hohfeld and Jeremy Bentham

In the past several decades, we have been witness to an unparalleled degree of, and appreciation for, analytical rigor in the specification of legal concepts. Our conceptions of such ideas as rights and obligations, rules and law itself have been made far more precise as a result. Two of the more important strands of thought that have developed in the context of this broad analytical project bear importantly on our understanding of a social dimension in legal rights. The first, associated most closely with the typology of rights developed by Wesley Hohfeld, consists of an effort to enhance conceptual precision of the notion of rights by describing rights as forms of jural relations. The second, initiated in large part by Jeremy

---

them free to make themselves good, I quite agree."

[40] Indeed, Green frequently attempted to turn his theoretical convictions into political realities, as in his participation in the temperance movement. For instance, one report of a speech given by Green paraphrases him as having said: "In pursuance of this same war against slavery he was now amongst them preaching against the dominion of strong drink, and in some ways he thought they would agree with him that this bondage of strong drink was harder to deal with than negro slavery, because this was a bondage whose victims were scarcely aware of it. They were told very often that those who wished to put restraints on the liquor traffic were not the friends of freedom, but its enemies . . . He should like to consider the word 'freedom.' If it was doing exactly what a person pleased, if he desired to go into a publichouse, and get drunk, and if he thought it was interfering with his liberty for any one to restrain him, then all he could say was, if that was the sort of freedom they desired they must go back to the naked savage in order to find it. By freedom he meant every man to make the best of himself, to turn to the best account all the talents and capabilities God had given him. Only in that sense was freedom worth having." Green, *Miscellaneous Writings*, p. 255.

[41] Ibid., p. 110.

[42] For contemporary analyses of the role of the state in engendering a liberal public culture, and the promotion of liberal community through expansive liberal rights and social policy, see Stephen Macedo, *Liberal Virtues: Citizenship, Virtue, and Community in Liberal Constitutionalism* (Oxford: Clarendon Press, 1990); Raz, *The Morality of Freedom*.

Bentham, seeks to locate that which is essentially the same in any form of right. Indeed, in important respects, both Hohfeld and Bentham anticipated the substance of many of the aspects of the contemporary analytical debates which bear most crucially on our understanding of the relationship between rights and social relations.

Hohfeld famously aspired to encompass within a four-part typology any and all relationships that might give rise to a legal right.[43] John Finnis has usefully summarized Hohfeld's analysis in the following form:

> (1) A has a *claim-right* that B should do X, if and only if B has a *duty* to A to do X.
> (2) B has a *liberty* (relative to A) to do X, if and only if A has *no-claim-right* (a 'no-right') that B should not do X.
> (2') B has a *liberty* (relative to A) not to do X, if and only if A has *no-claim-right* ('a no-right') that B should do X.
> (3) A has a *power* (relative to B) to do X, if and only if B has a *liability* to have his legal position changed by A's doing X.
> (4) B has an *immunity* (relative to A's doing X), if and only if A has no power (i.e. a *disability*) to change B's legal position by doing X.[44]

Hohfeld's own conclusion was that "the term 'rights' tends to be used indiscriminately" and that only the first type of right, a claim-right, should be characterized as a "right in the strictest sense."[45] Given the intransigence of rights-language, though, this particular recommendation never gained much of a footing. Moreover, a given right plainly might fall within more than one Hohfeldian category. For example, the right to freedom of expression might be characterized as a *liberty*: insofar as A has no claim-right that B should or should not speak, B will have a liberty freely to express herself or not. But the same liberty right might also be characterized as a *claim-right*: insofar as B has a duty to avoid interfering with A's speech, A has a right to speak freely or not.[46] It is hard, then, to justify calling the second a right but not the first, for they are, in essence, one thing.

---

[43] See Wesley Newcomb Hohfeld, "Some Fundamental Legal Conceptions as Applied in Judicial Reasoning," in *Fundamental Legal Conceptions as Applied in Judicial Reasoning*, Walter Wheeler Cook, ed. (New Haven: Yale University Press, 1919), pp. 23–64.

[44] Finnis, *Natural Law and Natural Rights*, p. 199; see also Joel Feinberg, *Social Philosophy* (Englewood Cliffs, NJ: Prentice-Hall, 1973), ch. 4.

[45] Hohfeld, "Some Fundamental Legal Conceptions," p. 36.

[46] See Jones, *Rights*, pp. 13–14; Finnis, *Natural Law and Natural Rights*, pp. 200–201: "But a liberty thus protected by a claim-right is not a distinct type of Hohfeldian right; it is a conjunction, never logically necessary but always beneficial to the liberty-holder, of two distinct Hohfeldian relationships . . . Most 'legal rights' . . . are in fact combinations, often very complex, of Hohfeldian rights . . ."

Hohfeld's principle claim that all legal rights are ultimately entirely reducible to atomic relationships has been the subject of much critical attention. Jeremy Waldron, for instance, has pointed to ways in which ambiguities in the idea of a duty, a concept left largely untreated by Hohfeld, pose difficulties for Hohfeld's theory.[47] Finnis, too, has suggested that though Hohfeld's scheme of translating without remainder any legal right into component relationships might be theoretically possible, in practice it fails to reflect the various ways in which legal rules might from the outset envisage temporal shifts among various parties contingently involved in rights claims.[48] Still, the influence of Hohfeld's larger strategy has been extensive, for his categories do seem to capture, to a great if not an unqualified extent, the essential structures of those legal constructs we term rights. Indeed, Hohfeld's most enduring legacy, from the perspective of social theory, may be his fundamental recharacterization of rights in *relational* terms.[49] Early theorists and proponents of rights, from Suarez, Grotius, Hobbes, and Pufendorf, through Locke, Jefferson, and Paine, conceptualized rights primarily as faculties, aptitudes or powers.[50] Rights, in essence, were things that persons could in some sense *have*; individuals were deemed to be "endowed" with, or "possessed" of, rights.[51] Hohfeld, though, provided good reason for us to conceptualize rights instead *as* relationships. For every claim, liberty, power or immunity, there is a corresponding duty, no-right, liability or disability. And each of these positions represents persons, connected now, *by legal rights*, one to another.

Although Hohfeld's typology of rights has taken grasp of analytical rights-consciousness, it is important to remember that roughly one century earlier Bentham too had noticed this relational aspect of rights. As Hart noted, "Bentham

---

47 See Waldron, "Introduction," in *Theories of Rights*, p. 8.

48 Finnis explains: "To take the simplest example: if A has the right to 10 pounds under a contract, he may at one time have a Hohfeldian claim-right to be paid 10 pounds by B, and at a later time (B's debt having been assumed by C) another Hohfeldian claim-right, to be paid 10 pounds by C; and the procedural rights (Hohfeldian claim-rights, powers, etc.) that A enjoys to enforce his right may be shifting, either in step or out of step with the shift between the earlier claim-right to be paid 10 pounds and the later. Yet this series of differing sets of Hohfeldian rights is intelligibly unified; for the shifting applications of the various relevant legal rules all relate to one topic, the 'right to 10 pounds under the contract', a non-Hohfeldian right of which the benefit, the burden, and the procedural props and incidents can all be shifted more or less independently of each other without affecting the 'right itself' which is the constant focus of the law's concern." Finnis, *Natural Law and Natural Rights*, pp. 201–2; see also MacCormick, "Rights in Legislation," pp. 205–7.

49 Richard Dagger makes this point in *Civic Virtues*, p. 22.

50 See Finnis, *Natural Law and Natural Rights*, pp. 206–10; Dagger, *Civic Virtues*, p. 19.

51 This is the sense of rights manifest, for example, in the Declaration of Independence.

certainly anticipated much of Hohfeld's work and he has moreover much to say about important aspects of the subject on which Hohfeld did not touch."[52] Indeed, while analysis of the social aspects of Bentham's work have tended naturally toward his utilitarianism, two aspects of Bentham's analytical thought afford a largely unexplored (perhaps because unintended) basis for examining the nature of rights from a social perspective, namely: (i) the correlativity he described between persons as rights-bearers and persons as bearers of duties (i.e., the correlativity that served also as a basis for Hohfeld's later work); and (ii) his theory that rights may be held not merely by individual persons but also by classes of unassignable persons, or by the public generally.

Bentham asserted that legal concepts were not susceptible to meaningful elucidation in isolation; the meaning of legal words, including the term "right," he claimed, may be gleaned only in connection with proximate terms and ideas.[53] For Bentham, then, as for those theorists who have followed in his wake, the critical factor for understanding the concept of legal rights, and the factor primarily determinative of the type of legal right at issue, was the nature of the relationship between the right and the notion of duty or obligation.[54] Bentham claimed that where the law fails to impose a duty upon persons with respect to some action, either because it affirmatively leaves the decision to the discretion of individuals, or because it simply does not address the issue, such persons are at liberty, that is they have a liberty-right, to engage in or to refrain from engaging in the action.[55] And whenever the law does impose a duty with respect to some action, Bentham suggested, it also thereby creates a legal right, that is, a claim-right, in the person(s) who stand to benefit from the performance of the obligation.

Thus, though perhaps best known for his emphatic denunciation of the enlightenment notion that rights with other than a legal basis might exist—that is, of the "nonsense" of moral or natural rights—given his expansive conception of what it means to have a legal right, Bentham's rights-skepticism clearly did not carry over into the realm of positive law. Indeed there are moments in Bentham's writings when he seemed virtually to conflate the points at which laws and rights might be said to exist: "On what occasion soever the law does anything in favour of any person, it thereby confers on that person a right. But there is no law whatsoever that does not operate in favour of some person or other: consequently

---

[52] Hart, "Legal Rights," p. 162.

[53] See generally H.L.A. Hart, "Definition and Theory in Jurisprudence," in *Essays in Jurisprudence and Philosophy* (Oxford: Clarendon Press, 1983), pp. 21–47, and, with special regard to rights, Hart, "Legal Rights," pp. 163–4.

[54] The concepts of obligation and duty are interchangeable for Bentham. See Jeremy Bentham, *Of Laws in General* (1782), H.L.A. Hart, ed. (London: Athlone Press, 1970), p. 294; Hart, "Legal Rights," p. 165, n. 20.

[55] Ibid., p. 166.

there is no law whatsoever that does not confer on some person or other a right."[56] In fact, with the exception of "self-regarding" duties, or duties imposed solely for the benefit of the person so obligated, and "barren" duties, or duties which can be said to benefit no one, for Bentham *every* failure to perform a legal obligation results in the breach of some legal right.[57]

Still, Bentham's analysis seems reasonable, at least when considered from the perspective of the individual person to whom a legal duty is owed. The idea, for instance, that breach by one party of a duty resulting from a legally enforceable contractual provision will violate a legal right held by another party conforms generally to our understanding of what it means to hold a legal right. The notion becomes a bit more awkward, however, and so more controversial, when considered in the context of duties imposed by the criminal law. This is partly why Hart and other critics of benefit theories expressed reservations with Bentham's theory. Deriving legal rights in victims not to be the subject of crimes from the criminal duties themselves adds little of substance to the extant notion of legal duty.[58] But even Hart eventually conceded that, once we base such rights on "needs" rather than benefits, we can indeed conceive of criminal duties as securing general legal rights to life and personal security.[59]

So far, so good. But what of duties imposed by the law which have clear social utility, and so are not "barren" duties, but which benefit *no person in particular*, as is the case, for example, with the duty to pay one's income taxes? When this sort of duty is breached, whose right is violated? We might want to say that somewhere down the line some yet to be named person will lose an important governmental service on account of the diminishment in public funds, but that seems a rather indirect and highly contingent chain of events upon which to found an individual right. And so it seemed to Bentham.[60] And yet the duty exists and therefore on Bentham's reckoning so must a right.

Hence, acknowledging the need for some meaningful degree of proximity between the obligation and the entity (i.e., the rights-bearer) harmed by its offense, Bentham sought to expand the category of rights-bearer beyond particular individuals to include those sorts of entities which stand nearer on the causal chain of events to the offense in question. Thus, while no particular individual might be directly harmed as a result of a violation of one's legal duty to pay one's taxes, surely society as a whole would be injured thereby and so society as a whole, according to Bentham, holds a legal right not to be so injured. And while no particular individual might be harmed by, say, a lunatic parading naked through the street, surely the neighborhood affected would suffer as a result, and so it too is

---

56 Bentham, *Of Laws in General*, p. 220.

57 Hart, "Legal Rights," pp. 169, 174.

58 Ibid., pp. 181–2.

59 Ibid., p. 192.

60 See Bentham, *Of Laws in General*, p. 62; Hart, "Legal Rights," p. 177.

deemed capable of holding a right not to be subjected to such treatment. More specifically, Bentham developed an intricate catalogue of the sorts of "offences," or violations of legal duties, in which one might take part, distinguishing among such violations according to the relative generality of the entity intended to benefit from the performance of the obligation. Thus "private" offenses, such as thievery or the failure to perform a legally enforceable contractual duty, were said by Bentham directly to violate individual rights, or rights held by "assignable" individuals.[61] On the other hand, "semi-public" and "public" offenses threaten a more "distant mischief" to "unassignable" persons, and so are held, in the case of the latter, by the entire community or populace, and in the case of the former, by some class within that community.[62]

Insofar, then, as bearers of rights may consist not merely of individual persons but also collective entities, Bentham's analysis would seem to support a unique connection between rights and social relations. A useful metaphor with which to explore this connection, and one which Bentham himself employed, is mentally to draw a circle around the intended beneficiaries of the legally imposed duty. Thus, a private offense to an assignable person would result in a circle of one, but public offenses would result in a whole series of concentric and cross-cutting circles, the dimensions of which would be dependent on a long series of contingencies some of which are external to the law but others of which derive from the effects of the legal obligation itself:

> When it appears, in general, that there are persons to whom the act in question may be detrimental, but such persons cannot be individually assigned, the circle within which it appears that they may be found, is either of less extent than that which comprizes the whole community, or not. If of less, the persons comprized within this lesser circle may be considered for this purpose as composing a body of themselves; comprized within, but distinguishable from, the greater body of the whole community. The circumstance that constitutes the union between the members of this lesser body, may be either their residence within a particular place, or, in short, any other less explicit principle of union, which may serve to distinguish them from the remaining members of the community.[63]

The result of all of this circle drawing is an image of society united and divided in diverse but collective ways. Still, we must be careful not to attach to Bentham views which clearly he did not hold. While it seems beyond doubt that Bentham conceptualized bearers of rights in collective form, he did not seek to ascribe to any of these collective entities an ontological status independent of its individual

---

61 Jeremy Bentham, *An Introduction to the Principles of Morals and Legislation* (1780), J.H. Burns and H.L.A. Hart, eds (Oxford: Clarendon Press, 1970), ch. XVI, para. 6, pp. 188–9.

62 Hart, "Legal Rights," p. 175; see also Jones, *Rights*, pp. 27–8.

63 Bentham, *Principles of Morals and Legislation*, ch. XVI, para. 7, p. 189.

members.[64] Rather, Bentham explicitly constrained the notion of offenses detrimental to the public with the condition that such offenses be detrimental to one or more of its individual members.[65] And the critical point for Bentham here was not the collective or individual nature of the rights-bearing agent but rather the notion that we will at times be unable to discern a direct harm to any particular individual. In such a case, the individual beneficiaries of the legal duty will be "unassignable," that is "[in]sufficiently distinguish[able] from all the others."[66]

Now, this is, for Bentham, hardly a watertight formulation. The most obvious ambiguity is temporal: at just what point in time are we to determine the assignability of the beneficiaries of legal obligations? Given that Bentham has in mind *intended* beneficiaries, probably the most logical interpretation would suggest that we examine the issue of assignability at the time the legal obligation is imposed. But this interpretation would all but eliminate the category since laws are rarely drafted with specifically identifiable persons in mind. At least under certain circumstances, we might instead think that assignability should be determined not at the time a law is drafted but at the time an individual performs some action under which he assumes a legal duty, as for example when a party enters into a contract. This interpretation would seem feasible in the context of voluntarily assumed obligations, but it makes little sense of Bentham's claim that criminal laws engender individual rights for assignable persons, since obligations not to engage in crime are not assumed in any manifest way and since the identity of the rights-bearing victim remains unknowable until such laws are actually violated.[67]

Indeed, noting this difficulty in Bentham's analysis, Hart sought to resurrect Bentham's conception of assignability by reversing the temporal order; that is, by discerning assignability at the time of violation rather than imposition of an obligation. Under Hart's reformulation, a violation of a legal obligation will be considered a private offense, giving rise to an individual right, in any case where it is possible *to demonstrate harm* to an assignable individual.[68] And so my failure to pay taxes, or my decision to sell confidential information to an enemy state, should be considered instead a public offense against unassignable persons, and so a public- or class-held right, because it cannot be shown that I have violated a legal duty with reference to any individual victim.

---

[64] See ibid., para. 3, p. 188, describing the state as an "imaginary compound body" composed of individual members.

[65] Ibid., para. 4, p. 188.

[66] Hart cites as Bentham's most explicit description of this idea that persons "may be assignable 'by name or at least by description in such manner as to be sufficiently distinguished from all others.'" Hart, "Legal Rights," p. 178, citing Bentham, *Principles of Morals and Legislation*, chap. XVI, para. 4, p. 188, n. c.

[67] See Hart, "Legal Rights," p. 178.

[68] Ibid., p. 179.

Hart is thus able to resurrect Bentham's conception of assignability, but we should notice too what has been lost. By making the distinction between public and private offenses dependent on the extent to which the benefit (i.e., not being harmed) is necessarily directed toward assignable persons, Hart has stressed the generality not of the rights-bearer but of the *benefit* itself. Under Hart's reformulation, an offense can be said to violate the rights of the public or a class only where "general compliance with the law creating an offence is intended to constitute an indirect benefit for any one or more individuals who are or may be included in the community or in a class within it but who are not otherwise identified."[69] The rights-bearer thus retains its public or class character but now is clearly viewed even less as a significant entity and more as a mere repository for a public benefit. It is the benefit now, rather than the beneficiary, that is in some meaningful sense collective. In the next chapter, I shall attempt to reinvigorate the idea of a generality implicit among rights-bearers themselves. First, though, we should consider the predominant contemporary treatment of collective aspects of rights, a treatment which, like Bentham's, focuses on the public nature of the benefits rights secure.

Raz on Rights to Collective Goods

With so much recent attention paid to the relationship between rights and individualism, it is surprising that so few contemporary theorists interested in understanding that relationship have thought to look to the structure of rights themselves. Joseph Raz is one who has. In *The Morality of Freedom*, in the course of depicting his larger perfectionist doctrine of autonomy, Raz proposes a public and collective understanding of liberal rights. The strict association of liberal rights with individualism, common among anti-perfectionist liberals and communitarian critics of liberalism, he argues, is false. Liberal rights, according to Raz, pertain not merely to the procurement of private and individuated goods, but rather "depend on and serve collective goods."[70]

Raz's argument depends on some technical language, especially concerning the nature of rights and the sorts of public goods around which he believes liberal rights revolve. Recall that, for Raz, rights are not simply correlative to duties; rather, rights *ground* duties. Further, a person may be said to have a right only if that person's interest in a particular good is sufficient to hold some other person(s) to be under a duty.[71] The correspondence of rights to duties, in Raz's formulation,

[69] Ibid.

[70] Raz, *The Morality of Freedom*, p. 255.

[71] Recall that Raz defines the concept of a right according to the following formula: "Definition: 'X has a right' if and only if X can have rights, and, other things being equal, an aspect of X's well-being (his interest) is a sufficient reason for holding some other person(s) to be under a duty." Ibid., p. 166.

thus results in a delicate balance between the value anchoring any proposed right and the extent of the various burdens required to secure its advantages. The greater the potential burden to be imposed upon those persons to whom it falls to consummate the right, the more extensive must be the good achieved by the right's affirmation. "If conflicting considerations show that the basis of the would-be right is not enough to justify subjecting anyone to any duty, then the right does not exist."[72] In this sense, Raz builds a consideration of the common good directly into his rights formula. For the very notion that individual interests may be valued against, and indeed may be outbalanced by, collective burdens, presupposes a fundamental concern for the well-being of the members of society taken generally.[73] Indeed, this presupposition coheres with Raz's larger point that individual freedom serves and depends ultimately upon publicly oriented goods, and so the state has a positive role in the generation of freedom and in the generation of the conditions of freedom.[74]

The benefit secured by a right will be a "public good," in Razian terminology, only when no one other than any particular beneficiary may control that beneficiary's enjoyment of the good.[75] So, for example, a water supply system that runs uninterrupted to everyone's house is a public good. But then public goods come in two varieties; they may be either "contingent" or "inherent." The example of a public water supply system depicts a merely *contingent* public good because the system may be altered (now or at some point in the future) to enable voluntary control over one's enjoyment; that is, my water supply may be capable of being turned off by someone other than me. A public good is, on the other hand, *inherent* to the extent that it is truly general or (virtually) nonexcludable. Thus, for example, the tolerant nature of a given society is an inherent public good; its benefits are wholly diffuse. It is precisely this sort of inherent public good that Raz has in mind when he refers to the "collective goods" secured by liberal rights.[76]

From the general course of his argument, then, we may distill four somewhat overlapping elements in the Razian justification to conceive of liberal rights in collective terms.[77] First, Raz contends that liberal rights tend to promote "general beneficial features of society," or distinctive and general forms of public culture.[78] Rights infused with liberal values would, Raz claims, nourish the formation of a

---

[72] Ibid., p. 183.

[73] Ibid., pp. 187–8.

[74] See ibid., especially Part V.

[75] Ibid., pp. 198–9.

[76] On the distinction between "inherent" and "contingent" public goods, and the identity of "inherent" and "collective" goods, see ibid.

[77] As discussed above, Raz also treats separately the concept of group or collective rights, potentially a fifth rationale for conceptualizing rights in collective terms. Ibid., pp. 180, 207–9.

[78] Ibid., p. 199.

generally liberal or tolerant, or perhaps even an educated or artistic society. Of course the diffuse advantages of living in such a society would fall on citizens in varying degrees and respects; clearly individuals would continue to assert their particularity through diverse responses to such general environments. "But the degree to which they benefit depends on their character, interests, and dispositions, and cannot be directly controlled by others."[79] And so, in that sense, individual distinctiveness may coexist with the irreducibly collective goods secured by liberal rights.

Raz's definition of rights supplies his second rationale for conceptualizing liberal rights as collective constructs. As indicated above, Raz follows the general outlines of an interest or benefit theory of rights, suggesting that rights are founded upon individual interests. Raz goes further, however, by claiming also that rights serve as the ground for duties.[80] In an initial sense, then, Raz acknowledges, on a structural level, the relational character of rights along some of the same veins explored by Bentham and Hohfeld; that is, rights are relational insofar as they delineate persons' interests that other persons will be obligated to, in some sense, satisfy. For instance, in the context of an argument that there may exist self-regarding duties, Raz notes the impossibility of their opposite, or self-regarding rights: "Nothing, however, can legitimize the notion of rights against oneself. The very idea is self-contradictory, for rights are essentially interpersonal. Their existence entails consequences to others."[81] Rights entail obligations, and so wherever there exists an entity (i.e., an individual or a group) determined to possess a right, there must also be a second entity related to the rights-bearer in virtue of that second entity's duty.

Yet, in claiming also that rights *ground* duties—in claiming that, for a right to exist, the interests served by the right must be of sufficient importance to *justify* holding others to a duty—Raz conceptualizes the idea of a right in a way that both reveals the prospect of a further collective quality in the right and becomes critically contentious.[82] This becomes apparent once the frame for our analysis shifts from special to general (or, frequently in Raz's terms, liberal) rights. For, as we have seen, general rights impose duties upon all persons, and hence the weight of the duty carried by general rights will be substantial indeed. According to Raz, then, while liberal rights, like all rights, remain based on the interests of individuals, it is only interests *taken collectively* that may account sufficiently for liberal rights. For no individual's interest, in itself, on Raz's view, can justify the imposition of the sorts of far-reaching obligations contemplated by liberal rights.[83]

---

79 Ibid.

80 Ibid., pp. 183–6.

81 Joseph Raz, "Liberating Duties," in *Ethics in the Public Domain: Essays in the Morality of Law and Politics*, rev. ed. (Oxford: Clarendon Press, 1994), p. 33.

82 Raz, *The Morality of Freedom*, p. 249.

83 Ibid., pp. 250–55.

Given that the fulfillment of liberal rights, and the attainment of the collective goods they are meant to secure, requires massive society-wide collective action, then any particular individual's interest in a public good is unlikely to be of sufficient weight to establish a duty on the part of society generally.[84]

This, as noted above, seems the most contentious segment of Raz's justification. For one thing, to accede to Raz's conceptualization of rights we must assume that the various individualist and collectivist considerations implicated in the rights calculus represent, in some sense, commensurable values, and yet a moral reckoning such as this may lie beyond our grasp.[85] Further, even if we do accept the possibility or practical necessity of engaging in Razian interest/burden balancing, we may nevertheless conclude that Raz has radically underweighted the interests individuals possess in the procurement of public goods. And further still, the focus on burdens in this context ultimately may be illusory, for one can easily imagine a substantial deflation of the burden placed on society insofar as every member (or nearly every member) has an interest in maintaining the particular public culture fostered by the liberal right in question.[86] Finally, to the extent that rights are, in Raz's own terms, "dynamic" constructs, such that the precise duties they ground are never (or are rarely) entirely foreseeable, we may question whether the perpetual variation in the burdens imposed would either yield intolerably inconstant rights or render the Razian rights-calculus itself practically infeasible.[87]

Raz's third rationale for conceptualizing rights in other than purely individualistic terms is more convincing. Raz demonstrates how liberal rights tend, rather directly, to promote or depend upon certain types of public goods. For example, religious toleration both serves communal peace and secures the continued existence of particular religious communities.[88] Freedom of contract

[84] Raz argues that such a "duty is not grounded in my interest alone. It is based on my interest and the interests of everyone else . . . It is difficult to imagine a successful argument imposing a duty to provide a collective good on the ground that it will serve the interests of one individual." Ibid., pp. 202–3; see also ibid., p. 208: "one may indeed doubt the possibility of a justification for a fundamental individual right to a collective good."

[85] See, e.g., John Finnis, "Natural Law and Legal Reasoning," in Robert P. George, ed., *Natural Law Theory: Contemporary Essays* (Oxford: Clarendon Press, 1992), pp. 134, 145–51.

[86] See Waldron, "Can communal goods be human rights?," p. 349, citing Denise Reaume, "Individuals, Groups and Rights to Public Goods" (1985) (unpublished manuscript presented to the Centre for Criminology and the Social and Philosophical Study of Law, University of Edinburgh).

[87] See Raz, *The Morality of Freedom*, pp. 185–6: rights "are not merely the grounds of existing duties. With changing circumstances they can generate new duties."

[88] Raz writes: "Thus while religious freedom was usually conceived of in terms of the interests of individuals, that interest and the ability to serve it rested in practice on the secure existence of a public good: the existence of religious communities within which people pursued the freedom that the right guaranteed them." Ibid., p. 251.

presupposes the collective good of a free market.[89] The freedoms of speech and of the press help to preserve the collective good of an open society and protect or enable political processes.[90] And rights against discrimination foster tolerance and enable persons to take pride in shared aspects of their particular identities.[91] Thus, although rights to fair treatment and religious, economic or expressive freedom might accrue in individuals, each such right has as well a significant collective aspect closely associated with the content of the particular right.

Finally, Raz's analysis at least implicitly suggests an institutionally-based rationale for the conception of liberal rights in collective terms. "Why," he asks, "should one use constitutional rights as a means of dividing political power between the different organs of government?"[92] Raz's principal answer echoes his earlier themes: by removing the settlement of disputes over individual rights from the normal fray of majoritarian politics, we accord enhanced stability to the collective good of a society's particular political culture.[93] Yet underlying this point may be a distinct and even more fundamental rationale. Raz's institutional claim is based on the assumption that the constitutional protection of liberal rights encourages the division of political power, presumably by enhancing judicial influence over that of other agencies.[94] And so, insofar as the devolution of political power, in the Madisonian sense, forestalls oppression, such division might *itself* be considered a collective good.[95]

So Raz provides a wealth of reasons, some more controversial than others, and some more implicit than others, to conceive of rights in other than purely individualistic terms. Liberal rights are founded upon mutual interests. They engender a public culture, and they serve and depend upon diverse, including

---

[89] "The free market is a normative social institution consisting not only in individual rights, but also in a network of practices and conventions relating to the conduct of negotiations, the communication of information, the avoidance of actions in restraint of trade, etc. The existence of that institution is a collective good." Ibid., p. 253.

[90] The "primary role [of freedom of speech] has been to provide a collective good, to protect the democratic character of the society." Ibid., p. 254.

[91] "Discrimination on grounds of religion, nationality or race affects its victims in a more fundamental way. It distorts their ability to feel pride in membership in groups identification with which is an important element in their life." Ibid., p. 254; see also Joseph Raz, "Multiculturalism: A Liberal Perspective," in *Ethics in the Public Domain: Essays in The Morality of Law and Politics*, rev. ed. (Oxford: Clarendon Press, 1994), p. 178.

[92] Raz, *The Morality of Freedom*, p. 259.

[93] Ibid., pp. 258–60.

[94] Raz means this conclusion to apply not just to political systems operating under written constitutions, but to any system where "there is a legal tradition which views the defence of civil rights as a special charge of the judiciary," including the British parliamentary system. Ibid., pp. 257–8.

[95] For a classic statement of this position, see "Federalist No. 51 (James Madison)," in Clinton Rossiter, ed., *The Federalist Papers* (New York: Mentor, 1961), pp. 320–5.

institutionally oriented, collective goods. The common link, the critical factor which Raz returns to time and again, is the character of the good secured: it is general, or non-excludable. It is, says Raz, only interests taken collectively that may justify the provision of goods to so many persons; public culture approaches the very definition of an inherent public or non-excludable good; and particular rights serve and depend upon a variety of goods necessarily made generally available.

Above we noticed how Bentham conceptualized certain rights to unassignable persons in a collective sense, but, in order to make sense of the notion of assignability, stress needed to be placed on the generality of the benefit rather than the rights-bearer. In articulating the various bases upon which rights should be conceptualized in collective terms, Raz too focuses on the generality of the goods secured by rights. In part for this reason, Raz's account excludes consideration of most legal rights, focusing instead solely on liberal rights. There is, however, a far more fundamental generality inherent in rights, a sense of generality that cuts across all legal rights and that relates not merely to the benefits secured but also to the rights-bearers themselves. To see why, let us consider a different sort of right to a different sort of good, say a contractual right to an excludable good.

Imagine that you have an interest in holding me to a duty. Imagine that you and I sign a contract for the sale of some valuable piece of artwork. As we negotiate the terms of sale, we stand beneath a Picasso, we repeatedly allude to the Picasso above our heads, and you wisely make a point of noting the artist's name and certain aspects of the particular painting in the margins of our agreement. When the appointed time comes to transfer the Picasso, I deliver to you a perfectly nice painting, but it is not the Picasso we discussed. As a result, you bring a cause of action against me in a court of law for allegedly breaching our contract. Based on its review of relevant precedent, imagine the court determines that while our negotiating location and oral references to the Picasso might be irrelevant, your margin notes legally became part of our agreement. The court thus finds that you have a legal right to receive the Picasso, and I reluctantly turn the painting over to you.

Now assume that some years pass and you agree to sell the painting to a museum. A contract is signed and once again one of the parties notes the particulars of the transaction in the margin. But when it comes time to deliver the painting, you simply cannot let the painting go. It holds you as it held me, and so you attempt to substitute another piece. If the museum decides to pursue the matter in court, assuming the jurisdiction is the same, the rule of law announced in the previous case will control. The rule will be held generally applicable. Indeed that is how it attains the status of a rule. To put this in Raz's terms, once an interest has been deemed sufficient to anchor a duty, the resultant right must be acknowledged generally, in all rights-claimants possessing sufficiently similar interests.

The generality of rights thus persists beyond any question of the public or private character of the goods secured; it inheres in the structure of the right itself.[96] Of course, this sort of generality pertains as well to the liberal rights Raz chooses to analyze. But the effect of the generality of liberal rights, which exclude no one, forms such a natural background that its significance is all too easy to miss. For as rights become more general, the less perceptible become the implications of their generality; some degree of exclusion is useful simply to throw the collective effect more dramatically into relief.[97] Does this further species of generality suggest an additional collective basis for rights? I think that it does. To see why, though, we shall need to consider justice itself.

---

[96] Jeremy Waldron makes a similar sounding but ultimately very different argument on behalf of the "generality of moral rights." Waldron's point is that a given right to engage in a specific action is almost always a particular instance of some broader claim to perform actions of a certain general type. So, for instance, the right to join a particular political party is typically defended not of its own accord but as part of the right to free political association. See Jeremy Waldron, "A right to do wrong," in *Liberal Rights*, pp. 77–8.

[97] Or, as Iris Marion Young has said, "the similar can be noticed only through difference." Iris Marion Young, *Justice and the Politics of Difference* (Princeton, NJ: Princeton University Press, 1990), p. 98.

Chapter 3

Law and Social Categories

Formal Justice and Legal Generality

Rawls tells us that the concept of justice concerns the proper distribution of benefits and duties across persons in society.[1] The concept of justice provides us with a formula, the formula of formal justice, the purpose of which is to arrive at an appropriate balance among competing claims: like cases are to be treated alike, and different cases are to be treated differently. In this sense, formal justice provides a principle of direction for social institutions.[2] At its core are principles of impartiality, and thus of fairness and equality. As Rawls says, formal justice exists where "institutions are impartially and consistently administered by judges and other officials . . . [L]aws and institutions should apply equally (that is, in the same way) to those belonging to the classes defined by them."[3] The way that formal justice is expressed in law is through law's generality. Indeed, "this sort of equality is implied in the very notion of a law or institution, once it is thought of as a scheme of general rules."[4]

Law's generality operates in two contexts.[5] The first condition of legal generality consists in the requirement that legislation be drafted impersonally, or

---

1 John Rawls, *A Theory of Justice* (Cambridge, Mass.: Harvard University Press, 1971), pp. 5–10.

2 Ibid., pp. 54–60, 235–9.

3 Ibid., p. 58.

4 Ibid. See also Henry Sidgwick, *The Methods of Ethics*, 7th ed. (1907) (Indianapolis, Ind.: Hackett Publishing, 1981), p. 267.

5 The doctrine of the generality of law has a substantial lineage. See, e.g., Thomas Aquinas, *Summa Theologiae* I–II, q. 96, a. 1, Fathers of the English Dominican Province, trans. (1915), wherein Aquinas asks: "Whether Human Law Should Be Framed for the Community Rather Than for the Individual", and answers, in part: "law would be of no use if it did not extend further than to one single act. Because the decrees of prudent men are made for the purpose of directing individual actions; whereas law is a general precept . . ."; Baron de Montesquieu, *The Spirit of Laws*, Bk. XII, ch. XIX, Thomas Nugent trans. (1873), wherein Montesquieu notes the existence of "bills of attainder" or special "laws by which a single person is deprived of [liberty] in order to preserve it for the whole community." Though he admits of "cases in which a veil should be drawn for a while over liberty, as it was customary to cover the statues of gods," he too acknowledges that "the force of a law consists in its being made for the whole community."

according to a universalizable format.[6] Rousseau describes this requirement of generality in the *Social Contract*:

> When I say that the object of the laws is always general, I have in mind that the law considers subjects as a body and actions in the abstract, never a man as an individual or a particular action. Thus the law can perfectly well enact a statute to the effect that there will be privileges, but it cannot bestow them by name on anyone. The law can create several classes of citizens, and even stipulate the qualifications that determine membership in these classes, but it cannot name specific persons to be admitted to them . . . In a word, any function that relates to an individual does not belong to the legislative power.[7]

Indeed, today legislation that pertains to specific individuals will often be of questionable constitutionality, in particular where the effect is to punish the subject of the legislation.[8] In its second, and perhaps more fundamental, sense, legal generality is concerned with instituting the rule of law.[9] In the simple but significant terms used by Lon Fuller in his explication of an "internal morality of law," the requirement that the law be general means that "there must be rules," as opposed to merely particularistic decision-making.[10] In this sense, then, the law's generality has vast social implications. For the extent to which a society seeks to satisfy this condition of legal generality will dramatically influence the nature of that society's governmental institutions.[11]

It is not far to see, then, how generality serves political justice. In its first aspect, generality ensures that no individual may be legislatively singled out for

---

6 See Lon L. Fuller, *The Morality of Law*, 2d ed. (New Haven, Conn.: Yale University Press, 1969), p. 47: "the desideratum of generality is sometimes interpreted to mean that the law must act impersonally, that its rules must apply to general classes and should contain no proper names;" see also Rawls, describing the formal constraints of his principle of right: "First of all, principles should be general. That is, it must be possible to formulate them without the use of what would be intuitively recognized as proper names, or rigged definite descriptions." Rawls, *A Theory of Justice*, p. 131.

7 Jean-Jacques Rousseau, *On The Social Contract* (1762), trans. Donald A. Cress (Indianapolis, Ind.: Hackett Publishing, 1983) Bk.II, ch. 6, pp. 36–8.

8 See U.S. Const. art. I, sec. 9, cl. 3, forbidding "bills of attainder;" *Platt v. Spendthrift Farm Inc.*, 514 U.S. 211, 239 n. 9 (1995); Fuller, *The Morality of Law*, p. 47: "Constitutional provisions invalidating 'private laws' and 'special legislation' express this principle."

9 "Formal justice in the case of legal institutions is simply an aspect of the rule of law which supports and secures legitimate expectations." Rawls, *A Theory of Justice*, p. 59. "Formal justice . . . becomes the rule of law when applied to the legal system." Ibid., p. 235.

10 "The first desideratum of a system for subjecting human conduct to the governance of rules is an obvious one: there must be rules. This may be stated as the requirement of generality." Fuller, *The Morality of Law*, p. 46.

11 See Rawls, *A Theory of Justice*, pp. 54–60.

pain or benefit, and so endeavors to treat persons impartially and as equals. In its second aspect, the law's generality strives to place the burden of decision on the rule rather than on the arbiter, and so promotes fairness and individual freedom by constraining official discretion and oppression.[12] "The precept forces [government officials] to justify the distinctions they make between persons by reference to the relevant legal rules and principles."[13] Indeed, in this respect generality strives not just on a horizontal plane, as between individual subjects, but for vertical neutrality as well; it endeavors to treat *all* citizens, including government officials, fairly and as equals.[14] In addition, the effort to create stable rules serves the end of certainty. Commercial economies may therefore develop with some sense of surety, and citizens may plan their lives with an enhanced measure of predictability.[15] And

---

12 For varied articulations of this view, see, e.g., Friedrich A. Hayek, *The Constitution of Liberty* (Chicago: University of Chicago Press, 1960), p. 153: "The conception of freedom under the law . . . rests on the contention that when we obey laws, in the sense of general abstract rules laid down irrespective of their application to us, we are not subject to another man's will and are therefore free;" John Locke, *The Second Treatise of Government* (1690), in *Two Treatises of Government*, Peter Laslett, ed. (Cambridge: Cambridge University Press, 1960), para. 57, p. 306: "the end of Law . . . is to preserve and enlarge Freedom;" Rawls, *A Theory of Justice*, p. 235; John Finnis, *Natural Law and Natural Rights* (Oxford: Clarendon Press, 1980), p. 273: "The fundamental point of [the Rule of Law] is to secure to the subjects of authority the dignity of self-direction and freedom from certain forms of manipulation. The Rule of Law is thus among the requirements of justice or fairness."

13 Rawls, *A Theory of Justice*, p. 237; see also ibid.: "In any particular case, if the rules are at all complicated and call for interpretation, it may be easy to justify an arbitrary decision. But as the number of cases increases, plausible justifications for biased judgments become more difficult to construct:" Gerald F. Gaus, *Justificatory Liberalism: An Essay on Epistemology and Political Theory* (Oxford: Oxford University Press, 1996), p. 199: "Citizens are to be treated equally unless relevant grounds can be demonstrated for unequal treatment. This requires that the state advance public reasons for its treatment of citizens."

14 On this point, see Hayek, *The Constitution of Liberty*, p. 155: "The chief safeguard [of liberty] is that the rules must apply to those who lay them down and those who apply them—that is, to the government as well as the governed—and that nobody has the power to grant exceptions." In this way, the notion of the law's generality neatly captures the nearly proverbial sentiment that legitimate government will consist "of laws and not of men." See, e.g., President's Remarks Following His Swearing in as the 38th President of the United States, 10 *Weekly Comp. Pres. Doc.* 1023, 1024 (Aug. 9, 1974) (Gerald Ford): "My fellow Americans, our long national nightmare is over. Our Constitution works; our great Republic is a government of laws and not of men. Here the people rule;" *Marbury v. Madison*, 5 U.S. (1 Cranch) 137, 163 (1803): "The government of the United States has been emphatically termed a government of laws and not of men."

15 As Justice Rehnquist once commented: "Hundreds of years ago in England, before Parliament came to be thought of as a body having general lawmaking power, controversies were determined on an individualized basis without the benefit of any general law. Most students of government consider the shift from this sort of determination, made on an ad hoc

certainty, too, may be conducive to freedom; for when "the boundaries of our liberty are uncertain . . . liberty is restricted by a reasonable fear of its exercise."[16]

Now, of course, a truly general system of law has never existed. In its first aspect, this is, at least in part, because sheer logical generality, the condition in which legislation would in the abstract relate to circumstances of an indeterminate variety, is in itself an insufficient gauge of legal generality.[17] In reality, an imaginative but disingenuous legislature might simply evade the criterion of logical generality—as indeed many have[18]—by describing a particular subject of legislation in apparently generic terms.[19] Further, in virtue of the simple reality that any piece of legislation (short, perhaps, of a universal declaration of human rights) will be adopted within a given legal system, there necessarily will be jurisdictional barriers to true generality.[20] More importantly, however, a *truly* general system of law—understood in the second sense of legal generality described above—would need to be devoid of human beings, for no rule of law can

---

basis by the King's representative, to a relatively uniform body of rules enacted by a body exercising legislative authority, to have been a significant step forward in the achievement of a civilized political society." *Cleveland Board of Education v. LaFleur*, 414 U.S. 632, 657–8 (1974) (Rehnquist, J., dissenting). Then Justice Rehnquist's dissent criticized the Court's refusal to let stand an irrebuttable presumption standard in an equal protection case, a decision that resulted in individual determinations rather than generalized rulemaking. See ibid., p. 660 (Rehnquist, J., dissenting). For a more general discussion of the "movement from Status to Contract," see Hayek, *The Constitution of Liberty*, p. 154, and citations therein.

16 Rawls, *A Theory of Justice*, p. 239.

17 On logical aspects of the generality of law, see especially Edwin W. Patterson, *Jurisprudence: Men and Ideas of the Law* (Brooklyn, NY: Foundation Press, 1953), pp. 107–16.

18 A prominent example of charges of this sort were leveled at legislation passed by the New York State Legislature enabling Kiryas Joel, a village of orthodox Satmar Hasidic Jews, to form its own school district. Though the legislation was drafted using seemingly generic language, Kiryas Joel is allegedly the only municipality intended to fall within its purview. See Raymond Hernandez, "Albany Vote Defies Courts Again To Back a Hasidic School District," *New York Times*, August 5, 1997, at A5.

19 The avoidance of proper names in such a case would be considered, under proper scrutiny, a voidable subterfuge. Remarking on just such a case, Justice Cardozo suggested: "An act is not general when the class established by its provisions is at once so narrow and arbitrary that duplication of its content is to be ranked as an unexpected freak of chance, a turn of the wheel of fortune defying probabilities . . ." *In re Elm Street in City of New York*, 153 N.E. 24, 26 (N.Y. 1927).

20 Along these lines, the Supreme Court has noted: "Indeed, the greater part of all legislation is special, either in the extent to which it operates, or the objects sought to be attained by it." *Home Insurance Co. v. New York*, 134 U.S. 594, 606 (1890).

entirely prescind interpretation, and no regime can be so fully ensconced in rules as to wholly eradicate official discretion.[21]

Nor would we wish to live in such a society.[22] Although there is indeed a strong sense in which the generality of law serves political justice, it will not, of course, ensure a substantively good or right outcome. Think in this regard of an artist, obsessed with the more formal aspects of her craft, with composition, line, and color. The artist's focus on form surely influences the content of her work, but it fails ultimately to dictate its meaning or interpretation. So, too, may procedural conformity in the law influence greatly, but not finally enjoin, law's substance. As Neil MacCormick has written, "Fuller's principles . . . can in principle be as well observed by those whose laws wreak great substantive injustice as by those whose laws are in substance as just as can possibly be."[23] Thus, for example, even a most rigid system of racial segregation might perfectly cohere with the formal dictates of the rule of law, but would yet be unjust. Perhaps first among many, Aristotle noticed that when "decency" conflicts with "what is legally just," there arises a need for "rectification of law in so far as the universality of law makes it deficient. This is . . . the reason why not everything is guided by law. For on some matters legislation is impossible, and so a decree is needed."[24] Neither did Fuller envision the generality of law as a universal prescript for government action. Indeed, he recognized that there may be "situations in which an application of this morality may be inappropriate and damaging."[25]

---

[21] There is, of course, a certain amount of what Hart famously called "open texture" in any legal rule, including legal rights. H.L.A. Hart, *The Concept of Law* (1961), 2d ed. (Oxford: Clarendon Press, 1994), pp. 127–8; see also Rawls, *A Theory of Justice*, p. 237: "we must suppose that the criteria of similarity are given by the legal rules themselves and the principles used to interpret them." For further discussion of Hart's conception of "open texture," see *infra*, this chapter.

[22] See, e.g., Jerome N. Frank, *Law and the Modern Mind* (New York: Brentano's, 1930), p. 120: "The constant development of unprecedented problems requires a legal system capable of fluidity and pliancy. Our society would be straight-jacketed were not the courts . . . constantly overhauling the law and adapting it to the realities of ever-changing social, industrial, and political conditions . . . Much of the uncertainty of law is not an unfortunate accident: it is of immense social value."

[23] Neil MacCormick, "Natural Law and the Separation of Law and Morals," in Robert P. George, ed., *Natural Law Theory: Contemporary Essays* (Oxford: Clarendon Press, 1992), p. 105; see also Rawls, *A Theory of Justice*, pp. 59–60: "Treating similar cases similarly is not a sufficient guarantee of substantive justice . . . Nevertheless, formal justice, or justice as regularity, excludes significant kinds of injustice."

[24] Aristotle, *Nicomachean Ethics*, trans. Terence Irwin, Bk. v., ch. 11, 1137b (Indianapolis, Ind.: Hackett Publishing, 1985), pp. 144–5.

[25] Fuller, *The Morality of Law*, p. 168. In particular, Fuller concluded that when our administrative agencies attempt "to accomplish through adjudicative forms what are essentially tasks of economic allocation," the result is likely to be "inefficiency, hypocrisy, moral confusion, and frustration." Ibid., pp. 171, 173; see also Lon L. Fuller, "The Forms

Situations such as these arise specifically because the generality of law is an instinctively determinate instrument pressed against a sometime indeterminate task; insofar as law seeks to direct future events, events which by their nature are, at least to some extent, unpredictable, perfect generality is an impossible ideal.[26] But then the essence of the law's generality must lie in its aspiration, not in its perfection.[27] And so while we cannot expect all things from the law's generality, "we can say," together with Rawls, "that, other things equal, one legal order is more justly administered than another if it more perfectly fulfills the precepts of the rule of law."[28] Both precepts of legal generality—that the law remain impersonal and that there be rules of law—are essential to the existence of a legal system. The distinction offered here may thus best be described as one between a requirement acutely aware of the particular subject or object of law and a broader condition engaged with the institutional design of government. Where the first condition of law's generality is concerned foremost with ensuring the procedural fairness of any given piece of legislation, the second aspires to ensure official impartiality through an essentially adjudicative form. It is this sense of legislative fairness, and this aspiration toward adjudicative impartiality, with which I want to work here.

---

and Limits of Adjudication," *Harvard Law Review* 92 (1978), discussing tasks that may be appropriately assigned to adjudicative agencies and how adjudication should be organized. Rousseau draws a similar distinction in the *Social Contract*. According to Rousseau, law or legislation must come from all and apply to all for the state to remain legitimate, but there remains a critical need for an institution capable of particular acts: "Since the citizens are all equal under the social contract . . . no one has the right to demand that someone else do what he does not do for himself. Now it is precisely this right, indispensable for making the body politic live and move, that the sovereign gives the prince in instituting the government." Rousseau, *On The Social Contract*, Bk. III, ch. 16, p. 76. As Rawls suggested, just "[h]ow far we are justified in [deferring generality], especially at the expense of expectations founded in good faith on current institutions, is one of the tangled questions of political justice." Rawls, *A Theory of Justice*, p. 59.

[26] Gaus well expresses this idea in *Justificatory Liberalism*, p. 200: "settled rules that dictate the proper resolution of all future disputes, taking into account all the relevant details of every case that may arise, seem beyond the ability of even a legal Hercules . . . this problem can only be mitigated, never completely solved . . ."

[27] Fuller famously characterized the "internal morality of law" as a "morality of aspiration." Fuller, *The Morality of Law*, p. 170. Rawls and Hayek similarly have expressed the aspirational quality of law's generality. See Rawls, *A Theory of Justice*, p. 236: "This is not, of course, to say that existing laws necessarily satisfy these precepts in all cases. Rather, these maxims follow from an ideal notion which laws are expected to approximate, at least for the most part;" Hayek, *The Constitution of Liberty*, p. 208: "complete certainty of the law is an ideal which we must try to approach but which we can never perfectly attain."

[28] Rawls, *A Theory of Justice*, p. 236. Indeed, in an imperfect world we must "aim for the least injustice that conditions allow." Ibid., p. 243.

Legal Rights and Categorization

We have said that, insofar as law is to serve as a legitimate means of social control, it must be expressed in general terms. Indeed, the law must be general specifically because the eventualities of social life are relentlessly unique and variable. Law, to be just, must provide individuals with a basis for anticipating the consequences of their actions in advance of the occasions on which decisions are made to engage in or refrain from such actions.[29] When this condition is combined with the great diversity of human activity, the effect is a disposition in the law toward categorization.

The requirement that the law be general means, therefore, that the law must classify the facts of social life. Included among the diverse "facts" of social life are characteristics associated with individual human beings. To govern human conduct, persons must often be classified alongside the range of circumstances in which individuals might find themselves. Formal justice makes differences and similarities among human beings central to the function of law. The law takes account of such disparities, and sorts individuals according to the particular characteristics deemed relevant to the regulation of social life.

Legal categorization occurs in two primary ways, corresponding to the two primary forms of generality through which legal rules are forged; that is, by legislation and adjudication. First, legislative, including constitutional, rights are acknowledged in individuals upon satisfaction of certain investitive criteria. The categorization of persons occurs, then, because the investitive conditions of legislation—the conditions under which legislation becomes pertinent to a given individual—are drafted according to a universalizable format. In his essay, *Rights in Legislation*, Neil MacCormick elucidates the rationale for fulfilling the requirement of investitive generality:

> To ascribe to all members of a class C a right to treatment T is to presuppose that T is, in all normal circumstances, a good for every member of C, and that T is a good of such importance that it would be wrong to deny it to or withhold it from any member of C. That as for moral rights; as for legal rights, I should say this: when a right to T is conferred by law on all members of C, the law is envisaged as advancing the interests of each and every member of C, and the law has the effect of making it legally wrongful to withhold T from any member of C.[30]

---

[29] Of course, given the limitations of human language, and the impossibility of anticipating and comprehensively attending to every eventuality, this effort must remain an aspiration. See especially Hart, *The Concept of Law*, p. 128.

[30] D.N. MacCormick, "Rights in Legislation," in P.M.S. Hacker and J. Raz, eds, *Law, Morality and Society: Essays in Honour of H.L.A. Hart* (Oxford: Clarendon Press, 1977), p. 204.

The core of this rationale is familiar to us. As a matter of formal justice, it would be unfair to afford disparate treatment to comparable cases. But notice, too, what is novel in MacCormick's explanation: an individual right has been attributed "to all members of a class C." This notion, that the right being ascribed is not being ascribed to individuals merely as such, but to individuals as members, would seem necessarily to suppose the existence of a collective quality in the right. The very idea of membership, after all, presupposes the existence of both constituent beings and some larger category to which all have been, in some sense, attached.

Now we should hasten to note that MacCormick himself seemed not very much impressed with his own revelation. Not only is this a terribly thin conception of membership, but MacCormick took great pains to restrain the notion that there were classes of rights-bearers from overwhelming the essentially individualistic character of legal rights. Rights, he wrote:

> concern the enjoyment of goods by individuals separately, not simply as members of a collectivity enjoying a diffuse common benefit in which all participate in indistinguishable and unassignable shares. But since necessarily the qualifications and conditions which must be satisfied for the application of such a rule of law in favour of any given individual have to be expressible and expressed in generic terms, it is therefore correct to say that such rules of law must be concerned with classes of individuals, but the benefit secured is secured to each and every individual severally upon satisfaction of the 'institutive' or 'investitive' conditions.[31]

MacCormick, thus, is even more hostile than was Hart to Bentham's ascription of rights to unassignable goods to classes or the public as a whole.[32] Nonetheless, MacCormick has suggested an additional basis upon which to conceptualize individual rights in collective terms. The individualization of the benefit secured need not alter the essential relationship of similarity drawn among individuals who fall within the relevant class. For the generality we are focused upon here accrues not at the level of the good secured, but at the level of the rights-bearers themselves. MacCormick thus has demonstrated that legal rights may secure benefits for individuals, and yet sort rights-bearers as potential members of collectivities. He has suggested a sense in which the investitive conditions of legislation serve inherently to relate individuals one to another.

We can further discern this relational property by imagining the position of a hypothetical rights-claimant. To be accorded the status of rights-bearer, one must demonstrate congruity between one's own circumstances and those generically described in the relevant legislation. The rights-claimant must show that she matches the investitive criteria, that she is like the persons contemplated by the legislative right, that she "fits in." If the rights-claimant is successful, then she becomes not merely a rights-bearer, but also a member of a class of similarly

---

31 Ibid., p. 205.

32 See *supra*, Chapter 2.

situated rights-bearers. Given the prescription of legal generality, one simply cannot hold a legislative right without simultaneously becoming a formally equal member of some more general set.

By way of example, consider the following prominent piece of legislation. In 1990, noting "discrimination against individuals with disabilities" as a "serious and pervasive social problem," and one of which the law had largely failed to take notice, Congress resolved to provide a more certain avenue of "legal recourse to redress such discrimination."[33] Congress passed The Americans with Disabilities Act (the "ADA"), seeking thereby to prohibit discrimination in the workplace, and in the provision of public services and accommodations, on the basis of disability.[34]

What persons then bear this right? To fall within the protections of the ADA, one must be "disabled" within the meaning of the Act, which means that one must have a "physical or mental impairment that substantially limits one or more of the major life activities of such individual."[35] This definition constitutes the ADA's central investitive criterion and so describes the characteristics required for classification within the set engendered by the legislative right. Hence, an inmate with a degenerative spine disorder that caused him to suffer pain when using certain prison facilities was determined to fall within the purview of the ADA.[36] So, too, did an epileptic employee prone to seizures that rendered him unconscious; a police officer suffering from depression; a student with a learning disorder; a store manager with hearing loss; and an employee with cerebral palsy.[37] Each of these individuals became a rights-bearer because each was deemed relevantly similar to the prospective class of rights-bearers envisioned by Congress when it enacted the ADA. Each fell within the set engendered by the legislative right.

Of course, no such set materializes spontaneously upon the enactment of a legislative right; the class of rights-bearers exists only prospectively. Moreover, legislative rights are not self-interpreting; hence, the precise borders of any such set are left, at least in part, for adjudicative specification. There is a certain amount of what Hart called "open texture" in nearly any legal rule, and, thus, in nearly any legal right.[38] Hard cases will inevitably arise, and with them the need for careful

---

[33] 42 U.S.C. §12101(a)(2), (a)(4) (1994).

[34] 42 U.S.C. §12182.

[35] 42 U.S.C. §12102(2)(A).

[36] *Saunders v. Horn*, 959 F. Supp. 689, 697 (E.D. Pa. 1996).

[37] *EEOC v. Kinney Shoe Corp.*, 917 F. Supp. 419, 425 (W.D. Va. 1996) (epilepsy); *Krocka v. Reigler*, 958 F. Supp. 1333, 1340 (N.D. Ill. 1997) (depression); *Price v. National Bd. of Med. Examiners*, 966 F. Supp. 419, 427 (S.D. W.Va. 1997) (learning disorder); *Wilson v. Gayfers Montgomery Fair Co.*, 953 F. Supp. 1415, 1421 (M.D. Ala. 1996) (hearing loss); *Fouraker v. Publix Super Markets, Inc.*, 959 F. Supp. 1504, 1507 (M.D. Fla. 1997) (cerebral palsy).

[38] "Whichever device, precedent or legislation, is chosen for the communication of

adjudication, both to construe any new claim of right in light of the statutory language itself and to fit fresh judicial interpretations appropriately within previous constructions. But adjudicative generality, thus necessarily operative even in the presence of explicit legislative standards, serves to relate individuals in an even more apparent sense. For the common law system of reference to precedent is based upon the principle of formal justice that like cases must be treated alike. Courts will thus determine any new claim of legislative right both with reference to explicit legislative criteria and by reasoning analogically from prior cases. The result, once again, will be a class of persons related by law one to another by virtue of some common characteristic(s).

Indeed, even in the absence of legislation, adjudicative generality works to similar effect, though the investitive conditions tend necessarily to develop in the opposite direction.[39] That is to say, where legislative rights begin as abstract rules of law subsequently deemed applicable to particular claimants, a right fashioned exclusively in adjudication begins with a particular claimant pressing a particular claim and then only gradually broadens into a rule of law. Nevertheless, given the dictates of formal justice, any such rule generates a prospective class of rights-bearers which is in other respects identical to that engendered by rights founded in legislation. For once a court grants a right to a particular claimant, any subsequent claimant with a sufficiently similar claim must be afforded, as a matter of justice

---

standards of behaviour, these, however smoothly they work over the great mass of ordinary cases, will, at some point where their applicability is in question, prove indeterminate: they will have what has been termed an open texture." Hart, *The Concept of Law*, pp. 127–8; see also ibid., p. 126: "In all fields of experience, not only that of rules, there is a limit inherent in the nature of language, to the guidance which general language can provide." Yet Hart recognized too that the *degree* of open texture in any given rule may vary according principally to the human capacity to anticipate. Ibid., p. 130. Hence, certain fields might be more responsive to control by rule, with relatively less open texture, than others. Such fields, Hart claimed, "are characterized by the fact that certain distinguishable actions, events, or states of affairs are of such practical importance to us, as things either to avert or bring about, that very few concomitant circumstances incline us to regard them differently." Ibid., p. 133. In other words, the relative intensity of our beliefs may at times place us in a better position to make a rule of law. Might rights, or at least some of them, be one of these areas of relatively firm conviction? Hart's Postscript suggests a basis for concluding that he thought so: "legal rights and duties are the point at which the law with its coercive resources respectively protects individual freedom and restricts it or confers on individuals or denies to them the power to avail themselves of the law's coercive machinery . . . rights and duties demand attention as focal points in the operation of the law which are of supreme importance to human beings . . ." Ibid., p. 269.

[39] Hart writes: "Two principal devices, at first sight very different from each other, have been used for the communication of such general standards of conduct in advance of successive occasions on which they are to be applied. One of them makes a maximal and the other a minimal use of general classifying words. The first is typified by what we call legislation and the second by precedent." Ibid., p. 124.

and fairness, consistent treatment and, hence, admittance to the set of rights-bearers constituted by the legal right at issue.

Notice, then, that where in the previous chapter Hart's revision of Bentham, and Raz's analysis of liberal rights, conceptualized rights as collective in virtue of the nature of the goods rights secure, law's generality suggests a collective aspect of rights inherent among the bearers of rights themselves. Similarly, where Hohfeld's typology and modern interest theories of rights posit relationships existing across the rights equation, formal justice provides a basis to conceptualize rights as relational with reference to just one side of that divide. Rights, that is, serve to relate persons whose interests the rights are designed to protect, or the rights-bearers themselves. Given their inherent generality, rights in legislation and adjudication necessarily engender sets of formally equal rights-bearers.

In the next chapter we shall begin more precisely to examine the nature of these sets. Here, though, let us notice too what occurs when a rights-claimant is denied her claim. For, in formal terms, any legal right engenders at least two classes of persons. The first class is composed of individuals deemed relevantly similar to the investitive criteria described in the particular legal rule at issue, and to each other; these individuals are thus *included* in the set of rights-bearers. The second class is composed of individuals who fail to match the investitive criteria, and who are thus deemed in some important respect dissimilar to those entitled to press the right; these individuals are thus *excluded* from the set of rights-bearers. Now, it may appear that those individuals who are included within or excluded from any particular set of rights-bearers will in fact be quite scattered, and will thus form a class only in the most formal of senses. But this depends entirely on the right in question. For exclusion from or inclusion within the class of persons deemed rights-bearers will at times powerfully affect an individual's social identity, and even one's self-perception. And when this is the case, rights will be seen to constitute persons as members of critical social groups.

Law and Social Cognition

Hence, legal rights, in light of formal justice, categorize persons. And formal justice, in various ways, serves the goals of fairness, freedom, and efficiency. These are values absolutely central to any meaningfully liberal legal system, but is this *why* we categorize? To begin to think further about this question, let me introduce a brief story from my own life. One Sunday afternoon, on a visit to Central Park in New York City, I walked with my then twenty-month old son along a path near a reservoir. At one point, my son dropped a piece of a large pretzel I had purchased for him on the ground, and almost immediately a small group of pigeons gathered, attempting to tear the piece of pretzel apart. My son pointed at the pigeons, turned to me, and proudly said, "duckie." I laughed, and then corrected my son. "*Pigeon*," I said, "those are pigeons." For the rest of the day, whenever we saw a group of pigeons walking about, my son would point at the group and say, "pin." At that moment, for him at least, the category of virtually all winged creatures that were in the habit of walking around parks taking food from humans had just been expanded from one to two types. There were "duckies," and there were "pin."

My son's early experience of birds is, of course, a perfectly ordinary example of the sort of human childhood development that occurs everywhere, everyday. And that is precisely the point. We naturally think in terms of categories, not only children as they are developing, but all human beings as we experience the social world. Simply look out the window and try to avoid the process of categorization. I suspect you will find it nearly impossible. We inherently categorize nearly everything we perceive, from cars to trees to buildings to people. In his seminal work on *The Nature of Prejudice*, Gordon Allport had cause to consider this process: "A million events befall us every day. We cannot handle so many events. If we think of them at all, we type them. Open-mindedness is considered to be a virtue. But, strictly speaking, it cannot occur. A new experience *must* be redacted into old categories. We cannot handle each event freshly in its own right."[40]

Today, many of the same insights that animated Allport's study are stimulating research advancements within the branches of sociology and social and cognitive psychology concerned with social cognition.[41] As described by social psychologist Judith Howard:

> Social cognition is a theory of how we store and process information. Social cognition has close roots to psychology and a reliance on experimental laboratory methodologies. Several central assumptions underlie social cognitive theories of identity: that human cognitive capacities are limited; that, therefore, we process information as cognitive misers, streamlining information to manage the demands of everyday interaction; that, following from this need for cognitive efficiency, we categorize information about people, objects, and situations before we engage memory or inferential processes.[42]

As Allport suggested several decades ago, and as cognitive psychologists continue to demonstrate experimentally today, social stimuli would overwhelm the human brain were it not for our inherent tendency to categorize our perceptions of the world and draw inferences from the classes that result. Our cognitive categories are thought to be maintained mentally as abstract structures, or "schemas."[43] Such cognitive schemas are composed of generalized characteristics,

---

[40] Gordon W. Allport, *The Nature of Prejudice* (Reading, Mass.: Addison-Wesley, 1979, 1954), p. 20.

[41] Gordon B. Moskowitz, *Social Cognition: Understanding Self and Others* (New York: The Guilford Press, 2005), p. vii.

[42] Judith A. Howard, "Social Psychology of Identities," *Annual Review of Sociology* 26 (2000), p. 368.

[43] On cognitive schemas, see Moskowitz, *Social Cognition*, pp. 155–63.

such as traits or behaviors, descriptive of the constituents of any given cognitive category. As human beings encounter the social world, our perceptions are filtered through these mechanisms of social cognition, these cognitive categories and schemas, that we have all come reflexively to develop. In this way, then, our cognitive categories and associated schemas dramatically influence the ways in which we interpret, process, and use social and self information, and they do so largely on a subconscious level.

As an example, consider the social category of doctors. We all have a somewhat different schema, or a series of overlapping schemas, associated with our cognitive category of doctors. Upon encountering relevant doctor-related stimuli in the world, our doctor schema enables our minds to summon a series of traits and behaviors we associate with members of this social cognitive category. The same holds true for innumerable other cognitive categories. We all subconsciously maintain schemas for our cognitive categories of academics, taxicab drivers, Catholics, women, and so on. Schemas such as these serve, in conjunction with the cognitive processes of categorization for which they provide an organizational structure, as instinctive mental shortcuts, enabling human beings to navigate our otherwise overwhelmingly complex social and inner worlds.

One byproduct of our reflexive mental recourse to cognitive categorization is that different persons with different backgrounds, and so different cognitive schemas, may perceive the same events in radically different ways. For example, in an early experiment conducted by the social psychologists Albert Hastorf and Hadley Cantril, undergraduates studying psychology at Princeton University and Dartmouth College were shown identical films of a notoriously nasty and violent football game between the two schools.[44] In the game, Dick Kazmaier, the star player for Princeton, an All-American quarterback playing in his last game for his college, suffered a critical injury. During the following quarter, the Princeton team seemed to retaliate when they tackled the Dartmouth quarterback aggressively in his own backfield, breaking his leg. Hastorf and Cantril instructed the students who watched the film to keep track of the number of so-called "dirty" plays committed by each team. The Dartmouth participants found roughly an identical number of infractions committed by each squad, but the Princeton participants, viewing the identical sequences, perceived more than twice as many violations committed by the Dartmouth side.

Now, it may have been that the Princeton participants overestimated the number of infractions committed by Dartmouth players, or perhaps the Dartmouth participants underestimated their own team's aggressiveness, or, more probably, both. The important point, though, is that a membership bias clearly existed, demonstrating the operation of a certain degree of group-dependent perception.

---

[44] Albert Hastorf and Hadley Cantril, "They Saw a Game: A Case Study," *Journal of Abnormal and Social Psychology* 49 (1954), pp. 129–34; see also Moskowitz, *Social Cognition*, pp. 40, 157.

The two categories of students, in light of their membership in different groups, came to the experiment with different social cognitive schemas, leading them to interpret identical events in radically divergent ways. As shown by this and numerous other experiments, our perceptions of the social world are framed by and filtered through the cognitive categories and schemas, or the mental baggage, so to speak, that we carry with us. As Gordon Moskowitz has suggested, "What we see and what we think we have seen are determined in large part by schemas."[45] Indeed, in the next chapter we will begin to examine more closely the consequences for social blaming and group prejudice of cognitive categories and schemas associated with social group membership, or what Allport more plainly but just as profoundly referred to above simply as "closed-mindedness."

Some theorists of social cognition have speculated, as does Judith Howard above, that our reflexive mental processes that serve to construct cognitive categories and associated schemas are a reflection of adaptive cognitive efficiency. Yet other cognitive psychologists, through experimentation, seemingly have demonstrated that we operate mentally according to the same processes of categorization even in circumstances where stimuli are limited and the resources for drawing fine distinctions abound.[46] This is the basis for the notion, presently foundational within social cognition theory, that human beings are "cognitive misers." Hence, it could be that by functioning mentally in virtue of generalization and inference, we are simply economically seeking to conserve our cognitive faculties, a trait which in turn reflects an evolutionary adaptation maximizing the prospects for human survival in a hostile world. On the other hand, social cognitive experimentation seems to demonstrate, alternatively, "that people are simply lazy...Responding with minimal effort when it is possible to act in a mindful, deliberate, and systematic fashion would seem to be better characterized as acting in a fashion that is stingy and miserly in the use of their cognitive abilities."[47]

Whether it is in virtue of efficiency or apathy, social cognition theory shows that it simply is the case that our mental capacities, including especially our working memory, are subject to critical limitations in social perception. When this limited capacity is combined with what Walter Lippmann referred to as "the great blooming, buzzing confusion of the outer world,"[48] the result, as we have seen, is an inherent tendency toward generalization, and with it, categorization. Notice, then, the strong parallel between social cognition theory and the functioning of formal justice. Formal justice mandates the classification of persons according to legally relevant characteristics. Social cognition theory provides evidence that the

---

[45] Ibid., p. 155.

[46] See ibid., pp. 174–8.

[47] Ibid., p. 177.

[48] Walter Lippmann, *Public Opinion* (New York: Harcourt Brace, 1922), p. 55, quoted in Moskowitz, *Social Cognition*, p. 173.

classification of persons is in fact an innate aspect of brain functioning. The legal-institutional parsing of relevant similarities and differences among persons does indeed serve the goals of fairness and predictability identified above, but the cause of this process may, at least in part, lie deep within our own cognitive makeup. Indeed, it might be fair to say that we "do" formal justice—that we treat similarly situated people similarly, and differently situated people differently—not, at the most fundamental level, because it is fair or just or conducive to freedom or predictability, but because that is simply how our brains function. I suppose it might even be possible that we consider the process of formal justice fair because we innately perceive the social world through the lens of social categories. But that, for now at least, must remain merely a supposition.

The Nature of Social Categories

Social cognition theory is important not merely because it aids our understanding of why we categorize persons, but also because it reveals significantly how we categorize, or the mechanisms and tendencies underlying the processes of social classification and identification. Before we can begin to consider their construction, however, we shall first need to gain a clearer understanding of the nature of social categories.

As defined by Moskowitz, "A category is a grouping of similar objects/people in memory—a grouping based on the important or essential features that define the class of things constituting the category."[49] There are two aspects to this definition that are worthy of some attention here. The first, which to some extent we've been assuming all along, is that cognitive categories relate not merely to objects but also to people. When we glance out our window, we see not only different types of motor vehicles, buildings, and trees; we are also apt to see different "types" of people. The existence of these different types of people is, of course, largely the result of the shared social classifications that we have, over time, collectively come to construct. As with objects, when we encounter a new person, we encounter an entity with certain physical properties, an entity of a certain form, even a certain color. And as with object perception, upon encountering a person, we need mentally to process the nature of the entity that stands before us, to try to understand its function in our lives and discern in what ways we are to react to it. Of course, person perception also differs significantly from object perception, in large part because persons *behave* in ways intended to affect us.[50] A person might approach us seeming somewhat melancholy, which might cause us to categorize them as depressed, and from which we might infer that their approach signals an

---

[49] Ibid., p. 111.

[50] On the similarities and differences between object and person perception, see ibid., pp. 16–20.

appeal for comfort, concern, or cheer. Or a person might come across as wildly uninhibited and flirtatious, which might cause us to categorize them as promiscuous, and from which we might infer that their approach signals an amorous interest. A typical object, of course, can be neither depressed nor interested in romance.

Person perception also differs significantly from object perception in terms of the consequences of any serious misperception. If we are mistaken, either in our classification of a particular person, or in ascribing a characteristic to an entire category of people, the result may be undeserved social stigma or harmful stereotypes. Indeed, the possibility of such mis- or irrational categorization brings to the fore the second important aspect of our definition of a category; that is, that a category is a "grouping based on the *important* or *essential* features that define the class of things constituting the category."[51]

In his study of prejudice, Allport, following the so-called "classical view" of social classification, approached the idea that categories are defined through their essential features by distinguishing rational from irrational categories.[52] Consider, for example, the category of automobiles. According to Allport, we might quite rationally say that all automobiles exhibit (or at least at some point did exhibit) the potential for ground transport upon a wheel base. Some automobiles will also contain powerful engines while others will be less aggressive; some will be quite large while others are relatively small, and so on. To say, however, that all automobiles are large or powerful or, for that matter, green, would be irrational, since these aspects are not essential to the category.[53] And so with categories of people. We know that there are Jews and Christians and Muslims; we know that there are lawyers and dentists and acrobats; we know that there are goths and punks and preppies. Each person category, regardless of its derivation, will have, according to Allport, some essential or defining characteristics, though it will often be difficult to discern precisely which these essential characteristics might be. Take, for example, the category of Muslims, the defining characteristic of which likely relates to one's association with a particular religious tradition.[54] Beyond this religious affiliation, there is probably no other essential characteristic that accurately describes the category. Yet there may exist any number of ascriptively derived characteristics irrationally associated with the category; for example, that Muslims tend to be dangerous, or even terroristic. Such an ascription in the categorization of persons obviously can result in treacherous social stigma or stereotypes in a sense unparalleled in the irrational categorization of non-social objects.

---

[51] Ibid., p. 111 (emphasis added).

[52] See ibid., p. 114; Allport, *The Nature of Prejudice*, pp. 22–3.

[53] Ibid., p. 171.

[54] Allport makes this point with respect to the person category of Jews. See ibid., pp. 171–2.

Allport's perspective on the nature and origins of stigma and stereotype has remained highly influential within social and cognitive psychology. Yet his more rigorous view of the nature of categories as embodying certain essential characteristics, without which the category simply would not exist, has given way to a more subtle conception of constitutive or defining categorical characteristics. Indeed, the distinction between Allport's classical view of the nature of social categories and its more modern counterpart tracks, in a certain fashion, the distinction between legal formalism and legal realism.[55]

To be a member of a social category, under Allport's classical conception, an individual would need to possess or display each and every characteristic deemed essential to the category. Moreover, as each such defining characteristic would be deemed essential, each would also be considered equally critical to membership.[56] More recent developments in cognitive and experimental psychology, however, have demonstrated that both of these assumptions are problematic. First, note that one consequence of the classical perspective should be that every member of a particular social category should be essentially identical to, or interchangeable with, every other member of the category according to the characteristic deemed essential. Yet it simply is not the case that every member of a socially recognizable category will be uniformly descriptive of the category. As Moskowitz suggests, "not all African Americans are equally representative of the category 'African Americans.' Tiger Woods is classified by most people as a member of the category ... but he is not perhaps as representative of the group as other famous members of the category one could imagine, such as Jesse Jackson."[57]

Second, more recent experimentation in social cognition seems to have belied the notion that categories can be described in terms of necessary or essential traits. For instance, in one well-known set of experiments, the cognitive psychologist Eleanor Rosch put a series of statements to research participants in the form, "X is a Y," where X stood for some species that varied in the extent to which the species was an obvious example of the static category Y; for example, "A cardinal is a bird," as opposed to, "An ostrich is a bird."[58] The participants were asked to respond simply by designating each statement as true or false. However, the true indicator relied upon by Rosch in the study was not whether the participants responded correctly, but rather *how long* it took the participants to respond. Rosch hypothesized that if categories possess essential elements, then there should be no

---

55 On the distinction between legal formalism and realism, see the next section.

56 Moskowitz, *Social Cognition*, p. 114.

57 Ibid.

58 See Eleanor Rosch, "Natural Categories," *Cognitive Psychology* 4 (1973), pp. 329–50, and "Cognitive representations of semantic categories," *Journal of Experimental Psychology* 104 (1975), pp. 192–233. These studies are described and analyzed in Moskowitz, *Social Cognition*, p. 115.

appreciable difference in response time as the variable X is revised. Every species X either is or is not a member of category Y, and if there is a certain set of essential characteristics that describes Y's membership, then cognitive processing time should be essentially equivalent across all Xs. The experiment consistently demonstrated, however, that there was in fact a meaningful time lag as the indicated species became a less typical representative of the category.

Rosch's and similar studies have caused an evolution in the way that cognitive psychologists view the nature of categories. Rather than conceptualizing categories as constituted by essential criteria, the absence of any of which precludes membership in the category, modern social cognition theory describes categories in more fluid terms. A category does indeed possess a set of "important," if not wholly "essential," characteristics that define its membership, but not every important or defining characteristic need be present for an accurate categorization to occur.

Moskowitz provides an illuminating illustration: "Your mental image of a chair is likely to have a back. But if you were to take away the back, the object would still retain its category membership. If you were to remove the arms, once again, the object would remain a chair."[59] Yet, as the object displays more of the important or defining categorical attributes, or as the object approaches the cognitive paradigm that may lie at its center, the accuracy of the categorization becomes more and more apparent. And, once again, as with categories of objects, so with categories of people. For instance, what traits must one display to be considered Asian? Clearly, physical attributes may play some role, but so might history, geography, language, culture, and so on. Hence, an individual, who lives in Minneapolis, born of a Korean mother and a Norwegian father, might accurately be described as "Asian," and so might the child of an Israeli mother and a Pakistani father, but surely there also exist other individuals more representative of the social category "Asian," at least in its American conception. The social category, that is, lacks essential characteristics, but as an individual displays or exhibits more of the important or defining categorical attributes, their membership in the category becomes more obvious.

It may seem strange, and even disconcerting, to speak of an individual as being constituted or defined by a social category in this way. Indeed, in subsequent chapters I intend to suggest that there is a serious moral cost in self-invention associated with legal constitutive processes that categorize and partially define persons. Nonetheless, the basic conception of individual human identity as partially a product of social forces is well recognized throughout the social sciences today.[60] As Joane Nagel indicates in her study of Native American ethnic

---

[59] Ibid., p. 116.

[60] See, e.g., Karen Cerulo, "Identity Construction: New Issues, New Directions," *Annual Review of Sociology* 23 (1997), pp. 385–409 (sociology); Kwame Anthony Appiah, *The Ethics of Identity* (Princeton, NJ: Princeton University Press, 2005), pp. 65–71 (political

identity: "We do not always choose to be who we are; we simply are who we are as the result of a set of social definitions; categorization schemes; and external ascriptions that reside in the taken-for-granted realm of social life."[61]

What is critical, however, and what will likely alleviate at least a certain amount of anxiety over the notion of individuals being socially defined, is two senses in which social categories are only *partially* constitutive of individual identity. First, every individual clearly will belong, to a greater or lesser extent, to a wide variety of social categories. It is not merely our nationality that describes us as social beings, but also our religion, or lack thereof, our gender, ethnicity/race, profession, age, political beliefs, associations, and so forth. The content of our social identities is composed of the various components or "building blocks" derived from our membership in such social categories, and at the center of all of our various constitutive social categories lies, always, a unique individual.[62] Second, since our concern in the present study is the influence of legal institutions on human identity, we are here interested primarily in the social or collective phase of human identity. Left largely unexplored in the present context are the personal dimensions of human identity, dimensions which, again, ensure the absolute uniqueness of each individual.[63]

Further attention will be paid to the nature of human social identity in the next chapter. Note here, though, the sense in which the more recent developments in cognitive psychology have demonstrated that *categories themselves* will be indeterminate, for this bears critically on the processes that give rise to such categories, including the processes that give rise to categories of human beings. As we move from the center of a category to its periphery, we encounter characteristics that are marginally less crucial to category membership. So, for example, the criterion "grows from a seed" is more central to and definitive of the category trees than is "bears fruit" or "has leaves," since we pretty clearly would want to both exclude tomato plants but include pine trees in the category trees. Yet both "bears fruit" and "has leaves" are helpful in filling out our description of the

---

philosophy); Rogers M. Smith, *Civic Ideals: Conflicting Visions of Citizenship in U.S. History* (New Haven, Conn.: Yale University Press, 1997) (political science, law); Joane Nagel, *American Indian Ethnic Renewal: Red Power and the Resurgence of Identity and Culture* (Oxford: Oxford University Press, 1996) (cultural studies); Dvora Yanow, *Constructing 'Race' and 'Ethnicity' in America: Category-Making in Public Policy and Administration* (Armonk, NY: M.E. Sharpe, 2003) (policy studies).

[61] Nagel, *American Indian Ethnic Renewal*, p. 26.

[62] See Karmela Liebkind, "Ethnic Identity—Challenging the Boundaries of Social Psychology," in Glynis M. Breakwell, ed., *Social Psychology of Identity and the Self Concept* (London: Surrey University Press, 1992), p. 164.

[63] On personal aspects of individual identity, see Anthony Appiah, "Identity, Authenticity and Survival: Multicultural Societies and Social Reproduction," in Amy Gutmann, ed., *Multiculturalism* (Princeton, NJ: Princeton University Press, 1994), p. 151.

category trees; they are peripheral rather than central category criteria.[64] This conceptualization of categories as possessing both central and peripheral criteria results in what is essentially a spatial metaphor, or a cognitive psychological mapping of categories, that reflects a social world of overlapping categories with relatively indistinct borders. As Moskowitz describes it:

> If each category contains some features that reside at the periphery, it is reasonable to assume that overlap of different categories is likely to occur, and that this will be especially likely to occur at the border between the categories, where the two peripheries meet and the less central features are shared. That is, each category has its boundaries, since it is defined by a set of properties that are more or less central. The qualities that define a category and the boundaries that limit membership in a category are 'fuzzy,' in that they lack discrete and clear demarcations.[65]

The categories remain within this conception, but their form becomes slightly more amorphous, their limits less definite. As a result, membership itself becomes less certain, or more in need of interpretation. Indeed, as presaged above, the modern conception in cognitive psychology of categories as "fuzzy sets" contrasts with the classical conception of categories as constituted by certain essential characteristics in a fashion that effectively parallels the distinction in American jurisprudence between legal formalism and legal realism.

Fuzzy Sets and Legal Indeterminacy

In brief, legal formalism stands for the proposition that particular legal controversies can often be resolved merely through reference to, and mechanical deduction from, authoritative legal resources. Legal realism, on the other hand, doubts that this is so, maintaining instead that most legal reasoning simply masks what are in fact controversial and indeterminate questions of moral value or public policy.[66] In other words, formalism describes legal analysis that moves easily, and determinately, from category to judgment, and legal realism is skeptical both of the existence of such categories and of the motivations for the judgments that result.

One well-known case provides a good illustration from which to appreciate the principal difference between these two perspectives on law. *United States v. E.C.*

---

[64] Moskowitz, *Social Cognition*, pp. 115–16.

[65] Ibid.

[66] This is, of course, the "sound bite" version of a distinction that has occupied generations of legal theorists. For a more detailed synopsis of what is involved in a claim of legal formalism, see Martin Stone, "Formalism," in Jules Coleman and Scott Shapiro, eds., *The Oxford Handbook of Jurisprudence and Philosophy of Law* (Oxford: Oxford University Press, 2002), pp. 166–205, and on legal realism, see Brian Bix, *Jurisprudence: Theory and Context*, 3d ed. (Durham, NC: Carolina Academic Press, 2004), pp. 177–87.

Knight was decided toward the end of the nineteenth century, during a period in which legal formalism was dominant in American legal thought.[67] In *E.C. Knight*, the Supreme Court decided that the Sherman Antitrust Act should be deemed inapplicable to a potential monopoly involved in the manufacture of sugar. The majority reasoned that, pursuant to the Constitution's Commerce Clause, the federal government had authority only to regulate "commerce" in sugar and not its "manufacture."[68] In so doing, the Court divided regulatory authority between the federal and state governments on the basis of a formalist, or categorical, analysis: activities that fell within the category "commerce" came within the control of the federal government, whereas conduct that could be classified merely as "manufacture" fell without "commerce," and so lied within the sphere of the several states.[69] Most critically, the Court treated its categorization of sugar refining as manufacturing rather than as commerce as if that conclusion simply followed mechanically from categorical criteria. "Commerce," the Court reasoned, "succeeds to manufacture, and is not a part of it."[70]

In contrast, a realist jurist might have noted the conspicuous, and indeed massive, impact that the American Sugar Refining Company's 98 percent monopoly in sugar refining would surely have on interstate commerce in that good.[71] The legal formalist majority in *E.C. Knight* sought to justify its decision by claiming that it was simply proceeding deductively from category to conclusion, whereas the realist perspective would regard both manufacturing and commerce not as precise categories but as "fuzzy sets," leaving a substantial degree of room for interpretation and policy-making.

Once we combine the idea that legal rights categorize persons with the understanding that social categories are themselves largely indeterminate, it is no great distance to see that legal institutions will at times play a substantial role in influencing aspects of our social identities. To see why this is so, let us return briefly to the Americans with Disabilities Act (the "ADA").[72] The ADA, you will recall, seeks to limit discrimination in the workplace and in the provision of public services and accommodations on the basis of an individual's disability. Above, we observed that the Act's investitive generality entails a collective aspect in the right; the right necessarily engenders a set of rights-bearers. Here, notice too that the set engendered by the ADA, composed as it is by, and of, individual human beings, is also a cognitive social category. According to the classical view of social

---

67 156 U.S. 1 (1895).

68 The Commerce Clause is contained in the U.S. Constitution, art. I, sec. 8, cl. 3.

69 *United States v. E.C. Knight*, 156 U.S. at 12: "That which belongs to commerce is within the jurisdiction of the United States, but that which does not belong to commerce is within the jurisdiction of the police power of the state."

70 Ibid.

71 See Bix, *Jurisprudence*, p. 179.

72 42 U.S.C. §12182.

categorization, there should be some essential criteria that describe the category of "disabled" persons. And, indeed, the Act contains investitive criteria that, in an effort to serve formal justice and legal generality, seek to describe the class of rights-bearers in specific terms. As we have seen, the ADA affords a right against discrimination to persons who exhibit "a physical or mental impairment that substantially limits one or more major life activities."[73] How successful is the right, then, in articulating determinate criteria?

In fact, all three aspects of the ADA's definition of disability clearly leave a significant amount of room for interpretation and further policy-making. Hence, HIV infection has been determined to constitute a "physical impairment," as has psoriasis and tendonitis, but a ruptured aortic aneurysm has not.[74] And sleeping, working, caring for oneself, and having sex have been deemed "major life activities," but awareness, driving to work, household cleaning, and reproduction generally have not.[75] And, further, whether any such major life activity is "substantially" limited by a confirmed physical or mental impairment remains an additional necessary inquiry, such that while, say, "remembering" might be a major life activity, the capacity to overcome mere "glitches" in thinking following a stroke would render that limitation too insubstantial to trigger the ADA's protections.[76]

Now, my intent here certainly is not to wade into the modern debate between legal formalists and legal realists over the indeterminacy of legal rules.[77] Nor is it even truly controversial, from either of these perspectives, that legislation will frequently be, at least in part, open-textured.[78] The point here is that although

---

[73] 42 U.S.C. §12102(2)(A).

[74] See *Bragdon v. Abbott*, 118 S. Ct. 2196 (1998) (HIV); *Cehrs v. Northeast Ohio Alzheimer's Research Ctr.*, 155 F.3d 775 (6th Cir. 1998) (psoriasis); *Chanda v. Engelhard/ICC*, 234 F.3d 1219 (11th Cir. 2000) (tendonitis); *DeJoy v. Comcast Cable Communs.*, 968 F. Supp. 963 (D. N.J. 1997) (aortic aneurysm).

[75] *McAlindin v. County of San Diego*, 192 F.3d 1226 (9th Cir. 1999) (sleeping; sexual relations); *Kidwell v. Board of County Comm'rs*, 40 F. Supp. 2d 1201 (D. Kan. 1999) (working; caring for oneself); *Deas v. River West, L.P.*, 152 F.3d 471 (5th Cir. 1998) (awareness); *Salamo Martinez v. Celulares Telefonica, Inc.*, 272 F. Supp. 2d 144 (D. P.R. 2003) (driving to work); *Marinelli v. City of Erie*, 216 F.3d 354 (3d Cir. 2000) (general housework and cleaning); *Zatarain v. WDSU-Television*, 881 F. Supp. 240 (E.D. La. 1995) (reproduction is not a "major life activity"), but see *Pacourek v. Inland Steel Co.*, 916 F. Supp. 797 (N.D. Ill. 1996) (reproduction is a "major life activity").

[76] *Hill v. Steven Motors, Inc.*, 228 F. Supp. 2d 1247 (D. Kan. 2002) (even if remembering is a "major life activity," mere glitches in thinking after suffering stroke deemed insubstantial).

[77] For modern explications of legal formalism, see, e.g., Frederick Schauer, "Formalism," *Yale Law Journal* 97 (1988), and Ernest J. Weinrib, "Legal Formalism: On the Immanent Rationality of Law," *Yale Law Journal* 97 (1988).

[78] See Hart, *The Concept of Law*, pp. 127–8

formal justice does indeed engender categories of persons, most of the time the social categories described by legal rules, including legal rights, will in fact be fuzzy sets. In light of the necessarily imprecise borders of social categories constructed through law, in light of the existence not only of essential but also numerous important peripheral investitive criteria for inclusion in the sets engendered by legal rights, legal actors will possess a significant degree of flexibility and influence in discerning similarities and differences among rights-claimants. And this will be true, of course, not only of the judicial and administrative actors charged with interpreting and applying legislative pronouncements, but also of the legislators themselves, in whom responsibility has been placed for setting, if not the precise boundaries of the categories of rights-bearers, then at least their more general outlines. As similarities and differences among rights-claimants are discerned by legal actors, and as the contours of social categories are influenced by legal institutions, the prospect for the legal constitution of social identity is raised.

Social Labeling and Law as an Agent of Socialization

In describing the nature of categories, we have said that there are not merely categories of objects but categories of persons as well. These social categories are well-known to us, and indeed play a substantial role in our everyday lives. Consider the following entirely ordinary conversation one might overhear at a neighborhood gathering:

> Neighbor 1: "We're planning to host a German exchange student next year."
> Neighbor 2: "Oh, that's a great idea. Last year two Israeli scouts stayed at our house while they worked at Camp Jaycee. The kids learned so much about the Jewish culture."
> Neighbor 3: "Oh, and guess what—the Chens sold their house. The real estate agent told me that a very nice gay couple purchased it. One is an artist and the other is apparently quite an athlete."

Within the space of approximately thirty seconds, we would have encountered two nationalities, one religion, three occupations (or perhaps avocations), and a sexual orientation; that is, seven social categories, or types of persons. That this sort of social classification is commonplace is beyond question, but what does it mean to say that there are different "types" of people? According to what social processes do these different types emerge? And, most critically, what role does law play in their emergence?

Recently, the first two of these questions have garnered considerable attention, particularly within cultural, identity, and lesbian and gay studies. Theorists writing from within these literatures suggest that the primary commonality among different types of persons is that each has been stamped with a particular *label*, or a social marker identifying an aspect of one's social identity. In his book, *The Ethics of Identity*, Anthony Appiah describes the structure of social identity by means of a three-part theory of social labeling.[79] According to Appiah's model, the first requirement for the construction of a collective social identity is the existence of a "social conception" about a particular collective of persons.[80] Such a social conception will only develop where there are "terms in public discourse that are used to pick out the bearers of the identity by way of criteria of ascription, so that some people are recognized as members of the group."[81] In other words, the first requirement for the presence of a meaningful social identity is a socially available and widely recognized social label that has been, or is in the process of being, attached to some collective of persons.

The social label may come from within the collective itself, as with certain religious or cultural groups, or it may develop around an external social consensus that the persons who fall within a particular class are alike in certain ways, either in terms of their appearance, their presumed behavior, or other socially detectable tendencies. These notions regarding classes of persons are, of course, stereotypes about the members of various groups, and the stereotypes are often inaccurate and can be tremendously injurious. Further, in the same way that we described the essential nature of social categories above as "fuzzy sets," social labels, to be meaningful, need not apply in any determinate fashion to any expressly defined set of persons. "For a social conception to exist, it is enough that there be a rough overlap in the classes ... so there need be no precisely agreed boundaries, no determinate extension; nor is it necessary that the stereotypes or criteria of ascription be identical for all users of the term."[82]

Hence, a social label may apply even where the social conception of the persons to whom the label is applied varies according to the bearers of the conception, perhaps in light of differences in social status or simply different life experiences leading to the development of different cognitive schema. For instance, one's conception of being Mormon or gay or African-American may entail very different meanings for the bearers of these labels than it would for persons outside these social classifications. There will also typically be a measure of disagreement regarding the content of the social label even *among* the bearers of any particular label.

As a brief thought experiment, imagine, for a moment, that you were asked to describe the artist Marc Chagall. Assuming the name is familiar, perhaps a colorful, somewhat surreal image of nineteenth- or early twentieth-century

---

[79] Kwame Anthony Appiah, *The Ethics of Identity* (Princeton, NJ: Princeton University Press, 2005).

[80] Ibid., p. 67.

[81] Ibid., pp. 66–7.

[82] Ibid., p. 67.

Russian-Jewish village life would flood your mind, or you might visualize some particularly vivid biblical or folkloric imagery. If you were like me—that is, if you shared my cognitive schema—probably you would begin by describing Chagall as one of the most famous Jewish artists of the modern era. Each of these four descriptive terms—famous, Jewish, artist, and modern—describes a type of person. Notice, though, that none has anything approaching a determinate meaning. There will rarely be uniformity regarding what it means to be famous, Jewish, an artist, or modern, even among persons to whom we might regularly attach these social labels. But neither this indeterminacy, or relative variation in the social conception of classes of persons, nor certainly their frequent derivation from inaccurate stereotypes, makes the social label itself any less potent or consequential. It simply means, first, that just as the sets of persons within society are best characterized as fuzzy, so too are the social labels used to describe them; and second, that social labels frequently function in an ascriptively inegalitarian fashion.

In conjunction with the development of a social conception with respect to some class of persons, and the application to that class of a social label, "the second element of a social identity," according to Appiah's model, "is the internalization of those labels as parts of the individual identities of at least some of those who bear the label."[83]

It is tempting to conceptualize Appiah's first two elements sequentially, such that a social conception, along with a social label descriptive of the conception, is developed first, and then subsequently internalized by those to whom the label is applied. This sequential conceptualization of the process of social identity formation, for example, is likely largely faithful to the social construction of racial identities. The social salience of a subordinated racial group, for example, probably does emanate at least initially from outside the group to whom the social label is attached, and only subsequently does the label and its (typically stigmatic) content become internalized.[84] Yet, the internalization of a social label need not follow in any precise way the development of a social conception with respect to that label; that is, Appiah's elements, at least as I interpret them, need not be sequential. Where the essence of a social label is derived internally, or constructed and then projected (intentionally or unintentionally) from within the collective itself, the internalization of a label ("we are X") may actually precede and may even instigate the development of a social conception ("you are X") regarding the collective. Again, the paradigmatic such collective, at least in the United States, would likely be a religious group. It seems unlikely, for example, that Amish practitioners' sense of their own social identity became internalized only once a more general social consensus regarding what it means to be Amish came to exist.

---

83 Ibid., p. 68.

84 See K. Anthony Appiah and Amy Gutmann, *Color Conscious: The Political Morality of Race* (Princeton, NJ: Princeton University Press, 1996).

Instead, the Amish identity springs primarily from the religious and traditional values that its members have come to affirm.[85]

Of course, the very existence of the Amish as a religious group in the United States is a result of broader social forces, particularly religious persecution that led to wide-scale emigration from Europe in the mid-sixteenth and early-seventeenth centuries.[86] Further, once a social conception regarding such a collective exists, its content, along with the meaning signified by its social label, may evolve in a way that leads also to an evolution in the substance of the identity characteristics internalized by the labeled members. Hence, what it means to be Amish within a broader heterogeneous society, even for the members of an Old Order sect, is subject to adjustment or even transformation as a result of changes in both internal collective and external social conceptions. The point, though, is that the broader process of constructing social labels, and the internalization of the content of those labels, most often proceeds interactively and in tandem rather than in a unilinear or sequential pattern.

As an individual to whom a social label has been attached internalizes the label, it becomes for them a part of who they are, an element of their identity that influences certain aspects of their social life. Recalling the idea of the artist as a social category, an individual so labeled may feel compelled, in light of their internalization of the social label, to act in the world *as* an artist; to support the arts, perhaps, or to attempt to be creative in other facets of their life. Similarly, a farmer might, in light of social norms associated with the label farmer, consciously seek to avoid appearing weak or lazy in public. Or perhaps she would come to the aid of a fellow farmer suffering drought merely because he is in need and he is a farmer. Firemen, especially after the events of September 11, 2001, are often perceived as brave and heroic; miners present a social image of struggle and loss; academics, an image of intelligence but impracticality. And returning once again to the Old Order Amish, the core of the religious group's value structure is grounded in a sense of *Gelassenheit*, or submissiveness. This value structure thus informs the Amish identity in ways that make a difference to their daily lives: the Amish are taught to be deferential, obedient, and content with simplicity and self-denial. "The religious meaning of Gelassenheit expresses itself in a quiet and reserved personality and places the needs of others above the self. Gelassenheit nurtures a subdued self—gentle handshakes, lower voices, slower strides—a life etched in modesty and reserve."[87] With the internalization of social labels, comes self-identification as labeled, and this self-identification helps to shape one's place in the world, and in the process even partially to define one's self.

---

[85] See, e.g., Donald B. Kraybill, *The Amish and the State* (Baltimore, Md.: John Hopkins University Press, 1993), pp. 7–15.

[86] Ibid., p. 6.

[87] Ibid., pp. 12–13.

"The final element of a social identity," Appiah suggests, "is the existence of patterns of behavior toward Ls [where L stands for labeled persons], such that Ls are sometimes *treated as Ls*."[88] This seems essentially the mirror opposite of Appiah's second, *identification-as*, element. Whereas the internalization of a social label reflects one's self-identification as labeled, the treatment-as element focuses upon the external social response to, and reinforcement of, that label.

As above, the relationship between this and the other elements in Appiah's model is best conceptualized as interactive and multi-linear rather than as sequential. Certainly, the third element may help facilitate the second; that is, treatment-as-labeled clearly may promote the internalization of a social label. And the third element might also influence the content of the first element, since treatment-as-labeled may stimulate movement in the underlying social conception itself, in either oppressive or progressive directions.

For example, the notion of treatment-as-labeled likely brings almost immediately to mind discriminatory social practices associated with an individual's race, gender, sexual orientation, nationality, etc. Hence, the discriminatory treatment of, say, a Muslim, specifically in light of her religious affiliation, might lead the person treated-as-labeled (element 3) further to internalize the Muslim aspect of her social identity (element 2). This sort of treatment-as-labeled (element 3) may also cause a transformation in the broader social conception of Muslims (element 1). This might happen, first, in a malevolent sense, by signaling one segment of the population's sense of how Muslims should be treated. But then, second, it might also cause a change in the underlying social conception of Muslims in a more benevolent sense, by shedding light on oppressive practices. Certain images broadcast of the treatment of civil rights protestors in the southern United States in the 1950s and 1960s seemed to have similar effects.

One way to conceptualize the core methodological idea of the sort of labeling theory explored here—the idea that the creation of a social label occurs simultaneously with the social invention of types of persons—is in terms of the approach that Ian Hacking has designated "dynamic nominalism."[89] In admittedly oversimplified terms, a nominalist would view our generalizing about various categories of objects and persons as entirely the result of human social thought; for example, the only true commonality among the objects in our category "trees," according to a thorough-going nominalism, is the fact that we have come collectively to describe all such objects as "trees." In contrast, a realist would point out that all of the objects that fall within our category trees do, in fact, emerge from a seed; realism views general categories as having an actual existence, or as being grounded in reality. Hacking, in describing a "dynamic

---

88 Appiah, *The Ethics of Identity*, p. 68.

89 Ian Hacking, "Making Up People," in Edward Stein, ed., *Forms of Desire: Sexual Orientation and the Social Constructionist Controversy* (New York: Routledge, 1992), pp. 69–88.

nominalism," seeks to provide an alternative both to conventional nominalism, to the extent that it envisions fixed or static categories, and to traditional realism. "The claim of dynamic nominalism," Hacking writes, "is not that there was a kind of person who came increasingly to be recognized by bureaucrats or by students of human nature but rather that a kind of person came into being at the same time as the kind itself was being invented."[90]

As an example of the way in which social categories or "kinds of persons" are constructed through a process of dynamic nominalism, Hacking points in particular to the idea that there is a social category of gay persons, or a homosexual type. Same-gender sexual activity, we know, has existed throughout recorded human history, but most commentators within gay and lesbian studies agree that homosexuality as a social category, as a type of person, developed only once individuals engaged in same-gender sexual behavior began to be labeled as such, or within the last century or so.[91] Clearly, the invention of the social label was in part a response to social forces, including extreme prejudice, and to the real existence of differences in social or sexual interaction, but the invention of the social label and category also simultaneously created a new way for people *to be*.[92]

In this respect, consider also the social category in the United States composed of Native Americans, as well as the derivation of the social label "American Indians." As Joane Nagel explains it:

> At the time of the earliest European contact with North America, there were no American Indians. The aboriginal inhabitants of North America encountered by European travelers spoke myriad languages; possessed a wide variety of cultures; displayed a broad diversity of social, economic, and political organization; and had no conception of themselves as a single "race," group or people.[93]

The Native American as a type of person, or as an aspect of one's social identity, is a product of the historical fact of two large, heterogeneous and previously removed populations, the European and the North American, converging, and the social classifications that resulted from those encounters.

Indeed, as most schoolchildren learn, the social label "American Indian" reveals more about the European explorers' true original objective (i.e., to locate a trade route to the East Indies), than it does about the ethnically diverse population to whom the label became attached.[94] Perhaps, had the European settlers perceived some incentive in differentiating among the hundreds of culturally, linguistically, politically, and geographically diverse tribes they encountered, the more general

---

90 Ibid., p. 78.

91 See especially the essays collected in Kenneth Plummer, ed., *The Making of the Modern Homosexual* (New York: Rowman Littlefield, 1981).

92 Hacking, "Making Up People," p. 70.

93 Nagel, *American Indian Ethnic Renewal*, p. 3.

94 Ibid.

social classification would have been less prominent and less constitutive of tribe members' social identities. However, from the settlers' perspective, and perhaps also from that of the indigenous inhabitants, the vast bulk of the social, economic, and military interaction between the populations was viewed through the single dimension of land and resource allocation.[95] Hence, consistent with Hacking's view of dynamic nominalism, the creation of the social category and cultural label, and the emergence of a collective identity, appears to have occurred simultaneously. Ever since, being Native American, either as a result of self-identification or as a consequence of external social ascription, or, as in Appiah's model, both, simply has become one of the many ways for persons to be in North America.

We have, then, a basic model of the processes by which social identity is constituted, and we have a sense of the interactive complexity of those processes. As Appiah says: "Where a classification of people as Ls [where, again, L stands for labeled persons] is associated with a *social conception* of Ls, some people *identify* as Ls, and people are sometimes *treated as* Ls, we have a paradigm of a social identity that matters for ethical and political life."[96] And it matters greatly, because an individual's social identity resonates both in one's self-perception, and during critical moments of social and political interaction.

Yet, what role does *law* play in the constitution of social identities such as those we've encountered? The idea that I would like to explore is that law should be viewed, in part, as an agent of socialization, or as a social medium through which ideas, including ideas about persons' social identities, can be constructed and spread throughout society. Although neglected, this idea is not a new one. Indeed, in his commentary on social life and politics in nineteenth-century America, Tocqueville may have been the first modern theorist to appreciate the constitutive influence of law:

> So legal language is pretty well adopted into common speech; the spirit of the law, born in schools and courts, spreads little by little beyond them; it infiltrates through society right down to the lowest ranks, till finally the whole people have contracted some of the ways and tastes of a magistrate. In the United States the lawyers constitute a power which is little dreaded and hardly noticed; it has no banner of its own; it adapts itself flexibly to the exigencies of the moment and lets itself be carried along unresistingly by every movement of the body social; but it enwraps the whole of society, penetrating each component class and constantly working in secret upon its unconscious patient, till in the end it has molded it to his desire.[97]

---

[95] Ibid.

[96] Appiah, *The Ethics of Identity*, p. 69.

[97] Alexis de Tocqueville, *Democracy in America*, ed. J.P. Mayer, trans. George Lawrence (New York: Harper Perennial, 1988), p. 270.

In this regard, consider again the social construction of the Native American as a type of person. American Indian ethnicity, as we have seen, arises as a general social category out of numerous, unique indigenous cultures, and the United States government has entered into hundreds of treaties with distinct, sovereign Indian nations. Despite this marked heterogeneity, legal institutions have viewed the different tribes and tribe members as similarly situated for purposes of a considerable number of their legal interests and obligations. This is neither surprising, nor necessarily disadvantageous. It is simply, as we have seen, the nature of law consistent with formal justice.

The law is general, and as a consequence persons are categorized according to characteristics deemed relevant by legal decision-makers. With respect to this particular legal category, it is the Native American status itself that has been deemed relevant. In the legislative arena, for instance, there is a general body of, and even a distinct Volume of the U.S. Code treating, federal Indian law.[98] Judicial decisions regarding individual tribes and tribe members, in light of their status as Native Americans, typically serve as general precedents for all other Native American tribes and individuals. There is within the U.S. government an administrative agency, the Bureau of Indian affairs, delegated by Congress general responsibility for regulating state interaction with Native American tribes. Even within the U.S. Constitution itself, Native Americans are accorded a distinct and, with respect to other tribes, undifferentiated status.[99]

It should, then, not be at all surprising that "American Indian" or "Native American" has come to be viewed as a way to be, or as a distinct type of person in American society, in ways that matter socially and politically. Why have so many of us come to believe that one's being Native American is an important aspect of the various tribe members' social identities? As Joane Nagel has indicated, "If informal ethnic categories and meanings can shape the everyday experiences of minority groups, formal or official ethnic labels are all the more powerful sources of identity and social experience because the carry the imprimatur of the state. When mandatory ethnicity is official, the power of the ethnic ascription is vastly reinforced."[100] The Native American social label, and its corresponding collective identity, has come so forcefully into view, at least in part, because the law categorizes indigenous cultures in this fashion, labels the collective "Indians," and indicates to every one of us that this is a distinction that will matter legally, politically, and socially.

Oddly, however, most sociologists and social psychologists who study the social construction of identity largely have failed to take note of law's constitutive influence. Admittedly, there are numerous other social institutions that serve as agents of socialization in a more immediate and powerful sense than do laws and

---

98 See Nagel, *American Indian Ethnic Renewal*, p. 8.

99 See, e.g., U.S. Const., art. I, sec. 2, cl. 3 (taxation).

100 Nagel, *American Indian Ethnic Renewal*, pp. 27–8.

legal institutions. Sociologists and social psychologists have focused primarily on the role of schools, the family, the media and popular culture, corporations and the market, and cultural, religious and peer groups in the social construction, delineation, and dissemination of social identity—but they have done so, without justification, almost to the complete exclusion of law.[101]

To be fair, though, the neglect has been mutual. Legal scholars interested in identity construction have been *at least* as inattentive to broader social institutions as sociologists and social psychologists have been to law. The growing literature on constitutive theory within the legal academy almost entirely neglects law's position *among* social institutions constitutive of human identity.[102] If pressed, however, it is doubtful that any serious legal commentator could believe that the law is as influential a socializing agent as, for instance, the educational system, the mass media, or the family. Schools regularly evaluate children in comparison to their peers, categorizing individual students according to academic, athletic, and other performance measures in ways that deeply influence the students' self-perceptions and social identities. As one study found, when "students perceive that teachers have labeled them as 'underachievers' or 'slow learners,' they may be more likely to behave in ways that corroborate that perception; by contrast, students labeled 'gifted' or 'intelligent' may more readily embrace academic performance as an activity boosting their self-concepts."[103] And the educational system socializes in a vast array of non-performance based directions as well; for instance, by teaching children, in ways both explicit and implicit (and for better or worse), that gender, nationality, ethnicity, and other collective identities are salient social differences.

Likewise, the proliferation and successful penetration in contemporary society of mass media and advertising has proven an effective instrument of socialization. Adolescent self-conceptions, in particular, are swayed, and to some extent intentionally manipulated, through newspaper and magazine images and articles, television shows, movies, and music.[104] Indeed, according to one researcher, individual adolescents serve as the audience for mass media an average of nearly

---

[101] See, e.g., Cerulo, "Identity Construction: New Issues, New Directions," p. 387; Allport, *The Nature of Prejudice*, pp. 211–12.

[102] See, e.g., Paul W. Kahn, *The Cultural Study of Law: Reconstructing Legal Scholarship* (Chicago: University of Chicago Press, 1999), but this is true of most of the work on constitutive theory cited *supra*, Chapter 1.

[103] Karen Lutfey and Jeylan T. Mortimer, "Development and Socialization through the Adult Life Course," in John Delamater, ed., *Handbook of Social Psychology* (New York: Kluwer/Plenum, 2003), p. 187, citing Robert Rosenthal and Lenore Jacobson, *Pygmalion in the Classroom* (New York: Holt, Reinhart, and Winston, 1968).

[104] Donna Eder and Sandi Kawecka Nenga, "Socialization in Adolescence," in Delamater, *Handbook of Social Psychology* (N.Y. Kluwer Academic/Plenum Publishers, 2003) pp. 173–4.

seven hours a day.[105] Even if this finding exaggerates the real degree of adolescent attention to media, clearly a significantly lesser extent still permits for fashion magazines to shape especially girls' self-images, sneaker advertisements to provide points of identity reference especially for boys, and popular music to construct entire youth sub-cultures.[106]

Moreover, even beyond the socializing effects of schools and the media, perhaps no social institution is as effectively constitutive of human identity as the most basic social unit, the family. Parents especially, but other relatives too, intensely influence childhood development in ways that extend well into adolescence and adulthood.[107] Our families determine, at least at the outset, our nationalities, our religious and other cultural affiliations (or our lack thereof), our social class, and even our life prospects and fundamental world-views. Though we may seek to distance ourselves from our native backgrounds in ways large and small, there is abundant evidence that social and cultural connections derived from familial sources remain persistent. As Michael Walzer has written, "identities are, mostly, the gifts of … parents."[108]

Hence, in comparison with other social institutions, law will generally play a secondary role in the socialization of persons and the construction of social identity. My intention in the next chapter, however, will be to demonstrate that, even as an admittedly lesser partner in the social constructionist project, legal institutions remain constitutive of human identity in ways that matter greatly. Law, we have seen, in the service of fairness, predictability, and freedom, and perhaps, on a deeper level, as a result of the fundamental processes of human social cognition, inherently categorizes persons. At a minimum, then, law functions in an institutionalizing and disseminating capacity, providing a mechanism for the entrenchment and further reinforcement of social group differentiation emanating from social institutions other than law.

Yet law's constitutive influence is not limited to so passive a role. Social categories, including those categories constituted by legal institutions, in light of their peripheral criteria and necessarily indistinct borders, are best conceptualized

---

[105] See Donald F. Roberts, "Media and youth: Access, exposure, and privatization," *Journal of Adolescent Health* 27 (2000), pp. 8–14.

[106] See Eder and Nenga, "Socialization in Adolescence," pp. 173–4; Melissa A. Milkie, "Social comparisons, reflected appraisals, and mass media: The impact of pervasive beauty images on Black and White Girls' self-concepts," *Social Psychology Quarterly* 62 (1999), pp. 190–210; Brian Wilson and Robert Sparks, "'It's gotta be the shoes': Youth, race, and sneaker commercials," *Sociology of Sport Journal* 13 (1996), pp. 398–427; Donna Gaines, *Teenage Wasteland: Suburbia's Dead End Kids* (Chicago: University of Chicago Press, 1991).

[107] See Lutfey and Mortimer, "Development and Socialization through the Adult Life Course," pp. 186–8.

[108] Michael Walzer, "On Involuntary Association," in Amy Gutmann, ed., *Freedom of Association* (Princeton, NJ: Princeton University Press, 1998), p. 65.

as fuzzy sets. This fuzziness, reflected also in the indeterminacy apparent in legal investitive criteria, creates additional room for the legal construction of social categories. In this way, law functions also in an interpretive and transformative capacity. Whenever a social category is to be institutionalized in law, it necessarily becomes subject to interpretation by legal institutions, both at the point of legislative entrenchment and, even more plainly, in the context of adjudication and administrative implementation.

Law, thus, not only provides an expedient means for the entrenchment and reinforcement of pre-existing social conceptions and social labels regarding the classes of persons sorted by law. It also serves, in its own right, as a source of further development of those conceptions and labels. Members of the society at large, consciously or unconsciously, take notice of the social conceptions and labels propagated through the law, and individual members of the categories reflected and further constituted by legal institutions internalize their differentiated status. In light of the social distinctions deemed relevant by legal actors, and also in light of the dissemination of these legal distinctions throughout society, individuals who fall within legally constituted classes will be treated as labeled. In this way, then, law indeed may be seen as constitutive of social identity. And this, as we shall see, will be especially true of legal rights.

Chapter 4

Rights and Social Groups

Rights and Identity

Do the rights that we have affect who we are? The standard liberal response holds that we should value rights for the freedom they afford us as individuals to chart our own life-courses. Rights permit us, so the claim goes, the liberty necessary to behave and believe in ways we choose. And in our dealings with others, rights allow us greater freedom to select our own associations. In this way, then, rights bring more closely together the will and the self; rights enable self-definitions. We are not (or need not be) preordained beings, but rather we invent and constitute our selves by choosing our particular paths, relations and attachments.[1]

Critics of liberalism typically suggest that this is a great problem. Human identity, they argue, is deeply rooted in social relationships, and liberalism's prioritization of rights therefore impedes essential self-discovery (as opposed to invention). Rights serve instead merely to atomize social life, and in the process to destabilize or even destroy various constituents of particular human identities. With such a profound emphasis on rights we become individuals first, and compatriots and friends and fellow believers only second—and then only, for the most part, when we choose to so join with others.[2]

---

1 See, e.g., John Stuart Mill, *On Liberty* (1859), Gertrude Himmelfarb, ed. (New York: Penguin, 1974), especially ch. 3; John Rawls, *A Theory of Justice* (Cambridge, Mass.: Harvard University Press, 1971); Ronald Dworkin, *Taking Rights Seriously* (Cambridge, Mass.: Harvard University Press, 1977).

2 See Michael J. Sandel, *Liberalism and the Limits of Justice*, 2d ed. (Cambridge: Cambridge University Press, 1998); Michael Walzer, *Spheres of Justice: A Defense of Pluralism and Equality* (New York: Basic Books, 1983), especially ch. 2; Charles Taylor, "Atomism," in *2 Philosophy and the Human Sciences: Philosophical Papers* (Cambridge: Cambridge University Press, 1985), pp. 187–211; Alasdair MacIntyre, *After Virtue: A Study in Moral Theory*, 2d ed. (Notre Dame, Ind.: University of Notre Dame Press, 1984); Roberto Mangabeira Unger, *Knowledge and Politics* (New York: Free Press, 1975). George Kateb has described the core of this critique of liberalism, albeit from a liberal perspective: "First, it is said that people need more *togetherness* than the individualist institutions and practices and general spirit of liberal society provide. Liberal society . . . cuts or weakens the habitual and unrationalized ties among people; it is indifferent or disrespectful to the past and to tradition; it fosters little or no attachment to anything outside oneself and one's circle; it makes personal identity a burden by making it paramount and by forcing it to be the willed

While they are helpful, these prevailing conceptions of the relationship between rights and human identity take us only so far. Taken together, the liberal and communitarian perspectives impose a false choice between conceptions of human identity as utterly self-determined or entirely collectively constituted.[3] But a meaningful conception of the self can ignore neither the reality of modern self-invention *nor* an account of social relations.[4] The strict dualism unravels, however, once the individualist assumptions of both rights-proponents and their critics are revealed as overdrawn. As described in the previous chapter, rights are strongly individualistic constructs, but under fundamental precepts of law and formal justice rights serve also inherently to relate persons one to another.

In this chapter, then, I want to describe an alternative approach to understanding the relationship between rights and identity, one that acknowledges the individualism of rights but also properly conceptualizes rights in social and relational terms. Rights are indeed the instruments of self-definition depicted by liberals and their critics, but they are also sources of social and self-meaning. What has been lost in most contemporary debates over rights and justice is an appreciation of the nature of law and its role in the process of defining social relations. Law and legally constituted relationships among persons inform social perceptions of identity, and social perceptions inevitably influence, and at times even dominate, self-understanding.[5] By obscuring the role of law in the process of defining social relations, the standard approaches have failed, therefore, to appreciate the more immediate impact that rights may have on human social identity. Human beings are never merely the product of preordained constitutive attachments, nor are we merely self-constituted. We are, in part and as well, constituted by rights.

---

creation of each individual . . ." George Kateb, *The Inner Ocean: Individualism and Democratic Culture* (Ithaca, NY: Cornell University Press, 1992), pp. 223–4.

3 Amy Gutmann observes this "duality" in "Communitarian Critics of Liberalism," *Philosophy & Public Affairs* 14 (1985), pp. 316–17.

4 See Unger, *Knowledge and Politics*, pp. 192–199; Charles Taylor, *Sources of the Self: The Making of the Modern Identity* (Cambridge, Mass.: Harvard University Press, 1989); Richard Dagger, *Civic Virtues: Rights, Citizenship, and Republican Liberalism* (Oxford: Oxford University Press, 1997), pp. 39–40.

5 For a general discussion of contemporary and historical social theoretical treatments of the self, see Craig Calhoun, "Social Theory and the Politics of Identity," in Craig Calhoun, ed., *Social Theory and the Politics of Identity* (Oxford: Blackwell, 1994). For more particular analyses of the impact of social perceptions on self-understanding, see Charles Taylor, "The Politics of Recognition," in Amy Gutmann, ed., *Multiculturalism* (Princeton, NJ: Princeton University Press, 1994); Steven Lukes, *Power: A Radical View* (London: MacMillan, 1974); John Gaventa, *Power and Powerlessness: Quiescence and Rebellion in an Appalachian Valley* (Urbana, Ill.: University of Illinois Press, 1980).

The Nature of Social Identity

In our contemporary, rapidly and continually evolving, pluralistic societies, issues concerning social identity have become increasingly prominent in public life and civic debate. It was not always this way, however. In earlier centuries, social life and group status were generally more constant, with one's social identity largely settled from birth, and with little space for meaningful self-invention thereafter. Our contemporary emphasis on social identity has often been linked to the sorts of epic social and political shifts, described by writers such as Tocqueville and Louis Hartz, from fixed statuses broadly to freedom of contract.[6] Yet analyses such as these tend to neglect the persistent nature of inegalitarian ascriptive statuses, including those manifestly at large at the time of both Tocqueville's and Hartz's writing, and continuing to restrain lives even today.[7] Perhaps, along with factors associated with the increasing heterogeneity of modern society, it has been the *promise* of freedom, the enhanced *possibility* of individual self-invention, even if it remains just out of reach, that has brought social identity so prominently to the fore in recent decades. Whatever its cause, the notion of social identity has come to dominate our contemporary conceptions of who and what we are, our most fundamental beliefs about our selves and our place among our fellow members of our societies.[8]

The modern notion of a collective identity has roots in nineteenth- and early twentieth-century sociological conceptions of collective social phenomena, such as Marx's evocation of a "class consciousness," Durkheim's suggestion of a "collective conscience," and Weber's methodological use of *verstehen*, or the need for a deeper, more contextual understanding of purposive human social behavior.[9] In these ways, the idea of collective identity emphasizes, in an extremely broad manner, essential connections and congruencies across persons within a given society, culture, or political system, connections that figure on virtually the deepest levels imaginable. More recently, however, these structural or essentialist accounts of collective identity have given way to narrower, and more socially variable, conceptions of collective identities as sources for the various constituent aspects of our social selves. Our collective identities today are still perceived as powerful constitutive agents, shaping social and self-perceptions in dramatic ways, but they

---

6 See Alexis de Tocqueville, *Democracy in America*, ed. J.P. Mayer, trans. George Lawrence (New York: Harper Perennial, 1988); Louis Hartz, *The Liberal Tradition in America* (New York: Harcourt Brace, 1955).

7 See Rogers M. Smith, *Civic Ideals: Conflicting Visions of Citizenship in U.S. History* (New Haven, Conn.: Yale University Press, 1997), pp. 20–26.

8 On the rise of interest in social identity more generally, see Judith A. Howard, "Social Psychology of Identities," *Annual Review of Sociology* 26 (2000), pp. 367–8

9 Karen Cerulo, "Identity Construction: New Issues, New Directions," *Annual Review of Sociology* 23 (1997), p. 386.

are also viewed more as social artifacts, or the product of interactive social forces, including law.

Law, in its most general instantiation, presumes that there is a universal human nature, marking an essential moral equivalence across all persons. It is partly on this basis that rights, variously termed natural, human, or general, may be said to be grounded. Yet, as we shall soon see, even such ostensibly universal rights are, upon further examination, far less so, and in this way contribute to the constitution of differentiated social identities. One approach to discerning the nature of social identity derives from this contrast between the innate characteristics of a purportedly universal human nature and the more fragmented aspects of our social selves. In this sense, our social identity is conceptualized as a sequence of symbolic components constructed atop, and supplementing, our common basic natures. Social symbols such as these, whether voluntarily adopted or imposed from without, serve in combination to distinguish us from most others. They signify to the world, and to ourselves, who and what we are in virtue of our membership in a variety of social groups. The sociologist Norbert Wiley, for example, describes the idea of social identity as representing "long-term, abiding qualities which, despite their importance, are not features of human nature as such. Identities individuate and allow us to recognize individuals, categories, groups, and types of individuals."[10]

Social identity has been studied most attentively from within the fields of sociology and psychology, and sociological and psychological conceptions of the idea differ in important ways. As one might expect, most fundamentally, the sociological perspective looks at the notion of social identity from the view of society, and focuses especially on the groups and categories that provide social labels for their members.[11] The psychological conception, on the other hand, focuses on the individual's social memberships from the individual's own perspective; that is, on the understanding one takes of and from one's membership in various social groups.[12] In the former conception, then, it is external social identification, and our reaction to such labeling, that is the predominant consideration. We are, on this view, the person we are *socially* acknowledged as being, though we may be at least partially successful in countering unwanted social definitions. In the latter conception, social identity is frequently appraised through

---

[10] Norbert Wiley, "The Politics of Identity in American History," in Craig Calhoun, ed., *Social Theory and the Politics of Identity* (Oxford: Blackwell, 1994), p. 130.

[11] See especially the seminal work of Erving Goffman, *Stigma: Notes on the Management of Spoiled Identity* (New York: Simon & Schuster, 1963); see also the helpful discussion in Timothy J. Owens, "Self and Identity," in John Delamater, ed., *Handbook of Social Psychology* (New York: Kluwer/Plenum, 2003), p. 224.

[12] Here, see especially the seminal work done by Henri Tajfel, *Human Groups and Social Categories: Studies in Social Psychology* (Cambridge: Cambridge University Press, 1981), also discussed in Owens, "Self and Identity," p. 224.

reference to one's "self-concept," with a particular emphasis on the ways in which the individual's *internal* self-conception is cognitively constructed in light of one's social memberships. At the same time, though, there is a significant degree of convergence between the two perspectives, especially in virtue of the mutually recognized influence that external social labeling has on the individual's internal self-concept. Indeed, it is at this point of convergence that law and legal rights will be seen most clearly as both enabling and frustrating self-invention.

Social identity is also usefully conceptualized in contrast to personal identity. Note, however, that by invoking "personal identity," we might be appealing to more than one conception of the idea. In its more dated connotation, roughly that generally in use prior to the second World War, and indeed still operative today within the discipline of the philosophy of mind, the idea of personal identity is concerned especially with the question of the continuity of the individual over time. This is consistent, of course, with one of the primary meanings of the term "identity," an essential sameness across different contexts. Hence, references to personal identity are sometimes intended to raise "the question of the sameness, or identity, of a substance, continuant, or thing, through different changes in time and space."[13] It is, though, an alternative sense of the term personal identity to which writers in political and social theory commonly make reference today. As Joseph Raz has written, "when talking of 'identity' I do not mean the term in the sense in which it fixes the limits of the continuity of an object, or an object of a kind: is this pile of timber which made up Theseus' boat Theseus' boat still? We mean the identity revealed in answers to the question who am I?"[14]

It is this latter sense of personal identity, this sense of identity as composed of elements of our larger selves rather than the sense of identity concerned with the endurance of an entity through time, that is most effective in providing the sort of contrast helpful in revealing the nature of social identity. As Anthony Appiah has suggested, "Each person's individual identity is seen as having two major dimensions. There is a collective dimension, the intersection of their collective identities, and there is a personal dimension, consisting of other socially or morally important features—intelligence, charm, wit, cupidity—that are not themselves the basis of forms of collective identity."[15] Appiah's reference here to the collective

---

[13] John Rawls, *Political Liberalism* (New York: Columbia University Press, 1993), p. 32, n. 34; see also Kwame Anthony Appiah, *The Ethics of Identity* (Princeton, NJ: Princeton University Press, 2005), p. 283, n. 6.

[14] Joseph Raz, *Value, Respect, and Attachment* (Cambridge: Cambridge University Press, 2001), p. 33.

[15] K. Anthony Appiah, "Identity, Authenticity and Survival: Multicultural Societies and Social Reproduction," in Amy Gutmann, ed., *Multiculturalism* (Princeton, NJ: Princeton University Press, 1994), p. 151. For a similar perspective, operative in social psychology, see Glynis M. Breakwell, ed., *Social Psychology of Identity and the Self Concept* (London: Surrey University Press, 1992), pp. 3–4: "Personal identity is that part of the self concept

dimension of an individual's identity is intended to elicit reflection upon those aspects of one's social identity—race, ethnicity, religion, gender, sexual orientation, for example—that figure so prominently in legal and political discourse today. The personal dimension of individual identity pertains to characteristics of that which we might more commonly designate our individual personalities, such as a person's penchant for being charming or witty. Put another way, social identity arises and is defined in virtue of our social memberships, whereas personal identity is composed of the sort of idiosyncratic traits that serve to differentiate us as individuals.[16] Hence, just as above, where social identity was seen to provide bases upon which our common human nature might be supplemented, thereby differentiating categories of persons in socially meaningful ways, personal identity ensures that members of collectivities, despite their common and deeply constitutive affiliations, nonetheless remain, always, differentiated and unique individuals. This, in combination with the realization that individual members commonly differ in their relations with even the most intensely constitutive social categories, ultimately belies essentialist conceptions of social identity.[17]

The notion that there exists a personal dimension to our identities is consistent with the way in which we've been understanding the concept of identity, for aspects of our personal identities, along with elements of our social identities, do indeed reveal who and what we are. The most significant difference between the personal and social dimensions of our identities, at least for present purposes, is that personal aspects are neither derivative of, nor do they delineate, membership in social groups. Certainly, there may exist a formal class of persons who are, say, jovial, but such a class is not marked by identity in a deep-seated or collective sense. Persons who exhibit joviality, wit, or charm might, in virtue of those traits, form a social category in the sense explored in the previous chapter.[18] But, as we shall see, social groups, as a particularly constitutive type of social category, tend to function as deep contexts, or entire frameworks that structure their member's lives across a broad range of prospects.

---

which is unique to the individual, a product of purposive action. Social identity, in contrast, is that part of the self concept derived from group and category memberships."

[16] On social identity as a cognitive schema, see Howard, "Social Psychology of Identities," pp. 368-9.

[17] See Karmela Liebkind, "Ethnic Identity—Challenging the Boundaries of Social Psychology," in Breakwell, ed., *Social Psychology of Identity and the Self Concept*, p. 159, noting that "people do not identify in an all or none fashion with the values and characteristics of various groups and individuals. They usually identify with some and dissociate themselves from others, i.e., they form only part-identifications with individuals and groups."

[18] Here, I differ from Appiah, who equates social categories and social groups. See Appiah, "Identity, Authenticity, and Survival," pp. 151-2.

Social Groups: Some Definitions and Ambiguities

In the previous chapter, we saw that, in virtue of formal justice, legal rights necessarily categorize persons and, in the process, engender sets of rights-bearers as well as sets of persons excluded from any given right. The remainder of this chapter will be concerned with showing when and how this relational aspect of rights serves also to constitute social groups and define self-meaning. Critical analysis of the justifications for these influences will be considered in the next chapter. Here, I seek merely to ascertain further the nature and function of rights in their relational and constitutive aspects.

Let us consider, then, in more precise terms what form the sets engendered by legal rights might take. For the charge might be leveled that the social categories engendered by legal rights are never truly *groups* at all but merely *aggregates*. Persons may be said to form an aggregate when they are categorized by virtue of some attribute.[19] Any attribute will do: hair color, dietary preferences, proximity to the sea, any of these may serve as a basis upon which people may be classified, or aggregated. As Tussman and tenBroek remarked in their classic article on equal protection, "To define a class is simply to designate a quality or characteristic or trait or relation, or any combination of these, the possession of which, by an individual, determines his membership in or inclusion within the class."[20] Certainly this is what the law does; the law sorts individual rights-claimants according to the degree of correspondence between their own particular situations (or attributes) and the investitive conditions described by any given legal right (more attributes). Those claimants able to demonstrate sufficient congruence with previously announced legislative and adjudicative criteria are classified as rights-bearers; those who fail to do so are excluded from the set.

Surely, then, the sets of rights-bearers constituted by legal rights are aggregates, but is this all they are? What is it that will distinguish mere aggregates from more robust social and cultural groups? Consider, in this regard, Iris Marion Young's influential definition of the concept of a social group: "A social group is a collective of persons differentiated from at least one other group by cultural forms, practices, or way of life . . . A social group is defined not primarily by a set of shared attributes, but by a sense of identity."[21] The first part of Young's definition

---

19 See the discussion by Iris Marion Young in *Justice and the Politics of Difference* (Princeton, NJ: Princeton University Press, 1990), p. 43.

20 Joseph Tussman and Jacobus tenBroek, "The Equal Protection of the Laws," *California Law Review* 37 (1949), p. 344.

21 Young, *Justice and the Politics of Difference*, pp. 43–4. On the concept of the social group more generally, see John C. Turner, et al., *Rediscovering the Social Group: A Self Categorization Theory* (Oxford: Blackwell, 1987); Larry May, *The Morality of Groups: Collective Responsibility, Group-Based Harm, and Corporate Rights* (Notre Dame, Ind.: University of Notre Dame Press, 1987).

suggests that groups can only exist in contrast with other groups; that is, in a society marked by social and cultural pluralism. The second part suggests that while specific objective attributes might serve as the initial basis for classification, the mere presence of such attributes is never a sufficient indication of the existence of a social group. The first part of the definition suggests the need, on the part of the members of any social group, for a substantial, collectively-felt difference; the second part requires that difference to amount not merely to an attribute but to a constituent of their identity. Membership in such a group, then, will affect individuals deeply and across a wide variety of social contexts. Examples of social groups are well-known, but tend in contemporary societies to correspond to ethnic, racial, sexual, gender, class, disability, and religious classifications.

On this basis, social groups should be distinguished from private associations, such as corporations, clubs, specific churches or other houses of worship (as opposed to religions), professional organizations, and political parties. Membership in a private association is both more voluntary and less extensively constitutive of identity than is membership in a social group. This is not to say that membership in a particular private association may not be required by employers or others, but individuals ordinarily *join* associations whereas people typically *find* themselves already living their lives as members of various social groups. As Young says, "Unlike associations, social groups are not explicitly constituted."[22] This also is not to say that membership in private associations does not affect individual identity. Clearly, an individual's affiliation with a particular political party, devotion to a given sports team, membership in a local Rotary Club, or employment by Microsoft, might very well constitute an important aspect of that individual's social identity. Yet, where membership in a private association might influence an individual's identity in a narrow and, often, a rather transitory sense, social groups tend to function on a deeper and more comprehensive level, influencing the very direction of one's life path. As Adeno Addis remarks:

> While those private associations are usually organized around one particular issue, one's affiliation to ethnic and cultural groups will tend to affect one's entire set of choices and options. In this sense, one could say that even though one's membership in various voluntary organizations contributes to one's identity, one's membership in a cultural or ethnic group provides the primary factor.[23]

Young comments similarly, "A person joins an association, and even if membership in it fundamentally affects one's life, one does not take that membership to define one's very identity, in the way, for example, being Navajo

---

[22] Iris Marion Young, *Inclusion and Democracy* (Oxford: Oxford University Press, 2000), p. 90.

[23] Adeno Addis, "On Human Diversity and the Limits of Toleration," in Ian Shapiro and Will Kymlicka, eds., *NOMOS XXXIX: Ethnicity and Group Rights* (New York: New York University Press, 1997), p. 124.

might."[24] After all, one becomes a member of an association specifically because one has an interest, of whatever sort, in that association. But one need not have any distinctive interest to be a member of an ethnic, gender, or other social group.

Indeed, it seems to fair to say that social group membership likely influences the very associations that individuals will join and leave behind throughout their lifetime. Were a person, call him Colin, to join a local squash association, for instance, this might enhance the extent to which Colin identifies himself, and is identified by others, as a squash player. That is, Colin might *be* more of a "squash player" as a result, or even a "squash pro," and he might then be recognized as such by others. Colin's membership in the association might, in that limited sense, influence his self concept and social identity. Yet, if Colin happens also to be British and of a certain socio-economic class, these broader social and cultural connections might go much of the way toward explaining Colin's disposition toward squash, since the sport tends to be played disproportionately by individuals of means and persons raised in Great Britain, as well as any number of other private associations of which Colin is a member. Our various associational affiliations not only run more shallowly through our lives and individual identities, but they also *derive*, in part, from deeper and more profoundly constitutive social group relations.

Consider also the relatively fleeting quality of these and most other associative identities. Our squash player, Colin, might of course switch his allegiance from squash to tennis far more efficiently than he might abandon his British background. Agnes might leave behind her job at Microsoft to work with Habitat for Humanity; Randy might become a far less active and identifiable member of the Rotary Club as she leaves to found a travel club; Sue might abandon the Green for the Democratic or even the Republican Party; and Eric (heaven forbid) might switch his allegiance from the New York Mets to the San Diego Padres. But, upon doing so, Agnes will remain African-American, Randy will retain her gender, and Sue will not be able so easily to cast off her disability. In these and myriad other ways, an individual's membership in a particular ethnic, religious or other social group will have ramifications for that individual's life opportunities and social identity that far outstrip those derived from associational affiliations.

This conception of that which constitutes a social group raises a number of issues that require clarification. First, in her more recent writings, Young herself has sought to recharacterize her conception of the essential nature of the social group, in part, it seems, to distance her claims from those associated with identity politics.[25] Young now claims that one's membership in a particular social group "positions" and "conditions" one's identity but does not constitute one's identity.[26] I interpret Young's more recent claim merely to mean that membership in a social

---

24 Young, *Justice and the Politics of Difference*, p. 46.

25 See Young, *Inclusion and Democracy*, pp. 87–107.

26 Ibid., pp. 99–102.

group never *fully* or *finally* constitutes one's identity, and not that legal rights are not, at least in part, constitutive of social identity.

The anxiety here appears to arise from the danger of essentializing human identity. Any time persons are categorized according to some characteristic deemed socially significant, and in particular according to some involuntary group affiliation, there is a risk of treating the group trait as essential, or of reducing the conception of any individual member of the group to that one trait. Of course, the reality is that all persons exist as complex entities with multiple, fragmented and even contradictory attachments and concerns.[27] A person who is, say, Jewish, is not merely Jewish, but might also be, among other things, a female citizen of France who practices law and plays the oboe. Given its generality, and its consequent proclivity for categorization, the law necessarily has but a limited capacity to acknowledge the full uniqueness of any given individual. Indeed, as indicated in the previous chapter, it may be impossible for human beings not spontaneously to categorize aspects of social life (including persons) in something approaching an essentialist form. Nothing in the present analysis, however, discounts the reality either of ultimately unique selves or the necessary intersectionality of group affiliations. Rather, the claim is precisely that rights play *a role* in the constitution of social life and human identity. That role will at times prove critical, but rights are never the only or even the central source of self-meaning. So while we do well to bear in mind Young's anxiety over essentialism, the basic claim that one may be constituted in part by social forces, including law and group membership, neither necessarily implies an essentialist conception of identity, nor disputes the possibility of resistive and re-inventive agency.[28]

A second potential ambiguity, within constitutive theory itself, bears mention. What does it mean to say that a legal right *constitutes* a social group? Certainly, reference to the constitution of social groups is not intended to suggest that such groups ever attain a status actually akin to a physical essence. Rather, groups attain a distinct ontological status in virtue of the relationships that come to exist among their individual members.[29] In addition, commonly, when we conceive of the constitution of some entity, we have primarily in mind its initial formation. Recall, however, that constitutive methodology in normative sociolegal theory reflects a quite different understanding.[30] Constitutive theory recognizes an enduring, interactive correspondence in which law affects society and society in

---

27 For a discussion of the complex and compound nature of human identity, see Calhoun, *Social Theory and the Politics of Identity*, pp. 27–9. See also the discussion on the nature of social identity in the previous section.

28 See, e.g., David M. Engel and Frank W. Munger, *Rights of Inclusion: Law and Identity in the Life Stories of Americans with Disabilities* (Chicago: University of Chicago Press, 2003), pp. 98–9.

29 On this aspect of the nature of groups, see May, *Morality of Groups*, p. 23.

30 See the discussion of constitutive methodology, *supra*, Chapter 1.

turn affects law. Hence, the claim that rights constitute groups may not be disproved simply by pointing to the prior existence of the group in question. It is obviously true, for example, that a social group composed of disabled persons existed prior to any given law that distinguishes among persons on the basis of disability; indeed, the legal proscription of discrimination on the basis of disability owes its existence in large part to the political activities of the members of that group.[31] Instead, the critical inquiry, from a constitutive perspective, is whether the character of that group, and so an aspect of its members' identities, has in some meaningful sense been *affected* post-right.[32]

Neither would an individual need actually to exercise a right for the right to have such constitutive effect. To take the same example as above, the very *existence* of a legal right against discrimination on the basis of disability might cause social actors to alter practices in ways that influence perceptions of disabled persons (positively or negatively).[33] For instance, in their study of the effects of the Americans with Disabilities Act on the lives of persons living with disabilities, David Engel and Frank Munger found that, "Although relatively few have actually asserted their rights by using the legal mechanisms made available under the ADA, many have found their lives and careers changed by the indirect, symbolic and constitutive effects of rights."[34] Further, a constitutive account of rights does not discount the prospect of human agency in the continuing construction of social identity; individual members or groups as social movements may resist constitutive legal categorization.[35] Hence, a right may be said to be constitutive of social groups and aspects of individual identities when the *existence of the right* contributes in some meaningful sense to the *ongoing construction* of the groups and identities in question.

Yet a third ambiguity raised by our definition of what constitutes a social group arises when the investitive criteria indicated by a given right coincide with the rights-bearers' culture. That is to say, what do we mean by "culture," and what is the relationship (semantically and otherwise) between social and cultural groups? Theorists who write in the area of multiculturalism typically have predominantly in

---

[31] See Doris Zames Fleischer and Fried Zames, *The Disability Rights Movement: From Charity to Confrontation* (Philadelphia: Temple University Press, 2001), pp. 88–93

[32] That a social group need not be initially formed in virtue of a legal rule for that rule to be considered constitutive of the group does not mean that there will never be instances in which a social group does owe its initial creation to law. For example, the U.S. Constitution might itself be deemed initially constitutive of the American citizenry.

[33] For examples of this type of influence, see Engel and Munger, *Rights of Inclusion*, p. 96.

[34] Ibid., p. 4.

[35] For examples of just this type of resistive self-invention, see ibid., pp. 98–9. For a more general discussion of the possibility of resistance to social definitions, see Young, *Inclusion and Democracy*, p. 101.

mind cultures associated with ethnic, religious and national groups.[36] As such, the rights evaluated by multicultural theorists are usually rights that have been granted to individual members of those specifically cultural groups, or to the cultural groups themselves as collective agencies. Theorists of the politics of identity and difference, however, commonly construe the notion of "culture" more broadly, and as a result tend to conflate the categories of cultural and social groups. Indeed, even Young's more recent conceptualization continues to define social groups in terms of differentiated "cultural forms [and] practices."[37]

This tendency toward conflation of social and cultural categories is far from surprising, and indeed makes a good bit of sense. For it coheres with one of the ways in which we commonly conceive of the idea of culture, as in the notions of "black culture" or "gay culture" or "the culture of disability."[38] But just as multicultural theorists in their treatments of cultural rights tend to ignore the full breadth of social groups, theorists of the politics of difference tend in their own analyses to discount the criticality of culture more narrowly construed.[39] Within the present study, I shall refer to the category "cultural group" in its more narrow sense, as one important type of social group. But it bears reiterating that legal rights respond broadly to the diverse ways in which persons in society may relate to one another. The specific nature of the collective entity constituted by a given right may be as variable as the investitive criteria used to distinguish rights-bearers from persons excluded from the right at issue.

Social Salience and Identity Types

The list of collective identity types is by now a common one. Throughout the literatures on identity in cultural studies, law, political science, religion, sociology, social psychology, etc., the list remains essentially the same: race, ethnicity, gender, sexuality, class, religion, age, nationality, and, more recently, disability. At times, depending upon the particular discipline and the author's specific

---

[36] See, e.g., Will Kymlicka, *Multicultural Citizenship: A Liberal Theory of Minority Rights* (Oxford: Clarendon Press, 1995), p. 19: "This is simply my stipulative definition of 'culture' and 'multicultural' . . . I am not including the sorts of lifestyle enclaves, social movements, and voluntary associations which others include within the ambit of multiculturalism. This is not because I think the issues raised by these groups and movements are unimportant. On the contrary, I take it as given that accommodating ethnic and national differences is only a part of a larger struggle to make a more tolerant and inclusive democracy."

[37] Young, *Inclusion and Democracy*, p. 90.

[38] See Kymlicka, *Multicultural Citizenship*, p. 18.

[39] For example, internal, partially self-governing national groups (e.g., Native Americans, Puerto Ricans) are rarely conceptualized as such. Ibid., p. 199, n.10.

predilections, identities related to social movements, geography, and even technology might enter the frame as well.[40]

Why these identity types? Why are we so likely to be identified, and to identify ourselves, in terms of our race, ethnicity, gender, and so on? Why not the size of our ear lobes, our eye color, or, for that matter, our weakness at the prospect of chocolate ice cream? What is it that makes socially salient human characteristics socially salient? As we shall see, not all rights are constitutive of social groups and human social identity; only those rights, the investitive criteria of which correspond to socially salient characteristics, may be said to be constitutive in a meaningful sense. Hence, attempting to decipher the enigma of social salience will be critical if we are to discern the basis for law's constitutive influence.

We saw in the previous chapter that categorization is an endemic aspect of human social perception and cognition. We categorize virtually all aspects of our social world, including characteristics exhibited by our fellow human beings. Experiments undertaken by cognitive psychologists have demonstrated that certain types of human characteristics are more likely to initiate social categorization—that is, to be socially salient—than others. Gordon Moskowitz describes the nature of the human characteristics that have a greater tendency to grab our attention, and the concept of social salience, in the following way:

> Some information is prominent in the perceptual field and seems to leap out from the background/context, making it figural and attention-grabbing. Its prominence in the context renders it able to capture attention and have a greater impact on our cognitive processing than stimuli (or features of stimuli) that are less prominent. Such information is said to be salient, or to have increased salience … The concept of salience informs us that there are features of the things we observe, the "data" in our social world, that are more powerful at directing our attention and influencing our responses than others.[41]

Further, that which we perceive to be the cause of some event or circumstance—including which person or group of persons we perceive to be the cause, and, as a consequence, blame, for some poor state of affairs—is often largely a function of cognitive processes operating in reaction to the presence of socially salient characteristics.[42] As Allport commented, "Even a fragment of visibility…focuses people's minds on the possibility that everything may be related to this

---

40 See Howard, "Social Psychology of Identities," pp. 374–84 (social movements; geography); Cerulo, "Identity Construction: New Issues, New Directions," p. 398 (technology).

41 Gordon B. Moskowitz, *Social Cognition: Understanding Self and Others* (New York: The Guilford Press, 2005), p. 53.

42 Ibid., p. 54.

fragment."[43] The potential for dangerous stereotypes, scapegoating, and group prejudice are, then, manifest, as we ascribe responsibility on the basis of social salience.

Human beings, we have said, mentally cannot process the entirety of our perceptual field. Out of the nearly limitless data points that we encounter in any given social interaction, we will in reality have the capacity to attend to very few. How then cognitively do we select among such a wealth of sensory information? And, in particular, how do we do so with respect to characteristics of our fellow human beings? Borrowing from long recognized research on the role of salience in object perception, social and cognitive psychologists have demonstrated that certain types of features exhibited by persons have a tendency to capture our attention and become socially salient.[44] These features include properties such as the relative intensity or vividness with which a characteristic is displayed or a behavior performed, the contextual novelty of such a characteristic, and the extent to which particular behavior is norm-violative, threatening or dangerous.[45] Further, the capacity of a stimulus to form a unit with other stimuli tends to increase perceived salience and causal attribution. For instance, a Catholic politician viewed praying in church might cognitively be categorized as a Catholic given the contextual salience of religion, but then later categorized as a politician when seen vigorously shaking hands with congregants after the service. In both such situations, either aspect of the individual's social identity might have been deemed salient, but that aspect that forms a unit with the individual's behavior will tend to become prominent and command attention.

The idea that we tend cognitively to categorize persons according to those characteristics that are most apt to capture our attention would seem to make sense of certain prominent social categories differentiated by marked, highly visual, physical traits. Skin color, which has long been taken as a basis for the social construction of racial classifications, is one obvious example.[46] Similarly, disabilities, differences in age and gender, and certain religious and ethnic customs, such as dress or patterns of speech, supply external, visual and aural physical distinctions that may capture attention and so trigger categorization.

Indeed, consider why it is that we are here able jointly to discuss and assess common social groups. This is possible only insofar as the categories that we

---

[43] Gordon W. Allport, *The Nature of Prejudice* (Reading, Mass.: Addison-Wesley, 1979, 1954), pp. 108–9.

[44] On the properties of objects that capture attention, see Leo Postman, Jerome S. Bruner, and Elliott McGinnies, "Personal Factors as Selective Factors in Perception," *Journal of Abnormal and Social Psychology* 43 (1948), pp. 142–54.

[45] On the relationship between object and person perception, and the social salience of human characteristics, see Moskowitz, *Social Cognition*, pp. 54–60.

[46] On the relationship between skin color and the construction of racial categories, see K. Anthony Appiah and Amy Gutmann, *Color Conscious: The Political Morality of Race* (Princeton, NJ: Princeton University Press, 1996), pp. 112–18.

come cognitively to construct may be shared across individuals within a given society or culture.[47] In part, this reflects the considerable role that physicality plays in the construction of social categories, since our external physical differences are available for all to see and (over)emphasize. Human physical characteristics, insofar as they are contextually novel, become cognitively salient, and thereby serve as the basis for social categorization that leads to the construction of social groups. Yet, while features like apparent contextual novelty might seem to explain the social cognitive salience of a physical trait like skin color, why then have social groups failed to form around other obvious physical differences, such as eye or hair color? Why is it that certain contextually novel human characteristics capture attention but not others? In fact, both lay and professional experimentation seem to have demonstrated the *potential* salience of virtually any apparent physical difference.

One well-known, and highly controversial, such experiment was conducted by Jane Elliott, an elementary school teacher in the small town of Riceville, Iowa, soon after the assassination of Martin Luther King, Jr.[48] In an effort to have her third grade students attempt to truly comprehend the nature of discrimination, Elliott divided her students into two groups differentiated according to the relatively meaningless criterion of eye color. Elliott then made that criterion socially meaningful. On alternate days, blue-eyed and brown-eyed members of the class were treated by Elliott and the rest of the class as either inferior or privileged categories of persons by, for example, segregating and "ghettoizing" the inferior set, marking the inferior set with special collars, permitting the privileged group to eat lunch first and denying the inferior group second servings, and otherwise suggesting that students who fell within the inferior category were of lesser intelligence and humanity than those in the superior set.

The impact on Elliott's students was quite powerful, dramatically altering their conceptions of themselves in relation to their fellow students. For instance, when asked to describe his feelings as a member, first, of the privileged category, student Raymond Hansen said, "I felt like a king, like I ruled them brown-eyes. Like I was better than them. Happy." And later, Hansen discussing his experience as a member of the inferior set commented, "I felt down, unhappy, like I couldn't do anything, like I was tied up and couldn't get loose."[49]

While her method was surely lacking in certain controls, the results of Elliott's classroom experiment seem rather compellingly to demonstrate the extensive capacity for human social construction of collective identity types on the basis of

---

[47] See Moskowitz, *Social Cognition*, pp. 117–19. Moskowitz's point, though, is that social categories are shared not merely as a result of our common perception of physical traits, but also in virtue of common cultural theories. This point is expanded on below.

[48] For a helpful depiction of Elliott's experiment, see William Peters, *A Class Divided: Then and Now* (New Haven, Conn.: Yale University Press, 1987).

[49] Ibid., p. 78.

highly apparent physical differences. Indeed, the social psychologists Judith Howard and Daniel Renfrow have suggested that Elliott's experiment effectively reveals the ways in which "characteristics that have no inherent social meaning can become meaningful in particular social configurations, and they then may be used to define groups of people and used in making attributions about the members of those social groups."[50]

Certain studies conducted by social psychologists themselves, concerning social cognition of physical differences, seem to have confirmed these findings. In one such study, two bearded men, one with red hair, the other with brown, were videotaped in conversation.[51] The researchers placed wholly unrelated photographs behind each of the men. Videotapes of the conversation were shown to participants in the study, and the participants were then asked to recall features of the images in the photographs. The researchers' theory was that since red hair is a relatively novel characteristic, participants' attention, all things equal, should be captured more by the man with the red hair than by the man with the brown hair. The man with the red hair, that is, would be cognitively more salient. As such, participants should be paying closer attention to the red-haired man and his surroundings and so should be more apt to recall aspects of the image in the photograph behind that man.

The obvious question, of course, is how the experimenters determined that it was the man's hair color, rather than simply the nature of the images themselves, that served as the source of salience. This the researchers attempted to control for by alternating whether the tape was shown in color or in black-and-white. They found that when the tape was shown in black-and-white, there were no significant differences in participants' recall of the images placed behind the two men; in other words, neither man or picture was especially salient. But when the tape was shown in color, participants indeed were able to recall features of the image placed behind the man with red hair with greater accuracy than the image placed behind the man with brown hair. The red-haired man's hair color was relatively novel, the researchers concluded, and on that basis cognitively more salient, leading participants to attend more closely to his surroundings.[52]

---

[50] Judith A. Howard and Daniel G. Renfrow, "Social Cognition," in Delamater, ed., *Handbook of Social Psychology*, p. 272.

[51] See Leslie Zebrowitz McArthur and Elise Ginsberg, "Causal Attribution to Salient Stimuli: An Investigation of Visual Fixation Mediators," *Personality and Social Psychology Bulletin* 7 (1981), pp. 547–53. In addition to the videotape with contrasting hair color, the researchers also created and used two other videotapes. In the first of these, one actor wore a boldly striped shirt while the other wore a plain grey shirt, and in the other, one actor wore a leg brace while the other did not. The findings on salience and causal attribution were comparable to those derived from the hair color video.

[52] See Moskowitz's discussion in *Social Cognition*, pp. 55–6. Surprisingly, no mention is made, either by Moskowitz or by the researchers themselves, of whether the

Experiments such as these appear to demonstrate that virtually any contextually novel and highly apparent physical human characteristic *might* become cognitively salient, serving as the trigger for social categorization, and in this way underlying, at least in part, the social construction of a collective identity group. The question that remains, however, is why it is that certain physical traits, such as skin color, have served as the basis for the identification of social groups, and other traits, such as eye or hair color, have not. This is the point at which, perhaps surprisingly, the theories involved in most of the literatures concerned with the nature and construction of social identity seem to come to an end. The question is a compelling one, however. Physicality, combined with contextual novelty, clearly might serve as a basis upon which persons may be cognitively categorized, but other social factors must be involved if we are to explain the obvious differential salience of racial, gender and other social groups. What, in combination with highly apparent physical traits, causes the construction of social groups?

Those who do consider the question point alternatively to power relations among persons in society, deeply embedded cultural norms, and, relatedly, a history which, to some extent, may have been lost to time. For instance, with respect to the influence of power arrangements on the constitution of social salience, there is a still developing sociohistorical literature in the constructionist vein that proposes the dominance of elites in the conception and manipulation of collective identities and associated schemas.[53] Similarly, social psychologists interested especially in the derivation of collective identities based upon supposed racial differences have suggested the criticality of racist ideology to the social construction of racialized groups.[54] The generation and sustainment of such ideology, they suggest, is a product of "power relationships and social practices that affect who is able to act on the basis of their category constructions, make them heard, and impose them on others."[55] Hence, where the superior resources enjoyed by members of dominant groups may enhance their own capacity for individual self-invention, that material and political superiority also provides the ascendant category with "the discursive power to define, locate, and order" the social identities of members of dominated groups.[56] Personal aspects of identity,

---

photographs themselves might have become more salient once they were shown in color. See McArthur and Ginsberg, "Causal Attribution to Salient Stimuli."

[53] For a review of this literature, see Cerulo, "Identity Construction: New Issues, New Directions," p. 390. Though it is not typically advanced in relation to collective identities, this theme would be consistent as well with much of the work published within critical legal studies. For an overview, see Mark Kelman, *A Guide to Critical Legal Studies* (Cambridge, Mass.: Harvard University Press, 1987).

[54] See, e.g., Nicholas Hopkins, Steven Reicher, and Mark Levine, "On the Parallels Between Social Cognition and the 'New Racism,'" *British Journal of Social Psychology* 36 (1997), pp. 305–29.

[55] Howard, "Social Psychology of Identities," p. 386.

[56] Howard and Renfrow, "Social Cognition," p. 273.

thus, may become more salient for members of privileged groups, but externally defined social group memberships remain most critical for socially subordinated persons, both in defining their social identities and their own self-concepts. In short, as Howard and Renfrow suggest, "power based upon social position has a major impact on social and self-categorizations."[57]

Beyond, or in combination with, physicality and power arrangements, history and culture may also be critical determinants of social salience. Above we noted that, in part due to our common perception of external physical traits, social categories tend to be shared. But such categories are also common across people in a given society or culture in virtue of the theories inculcated and the narratives taught to individuals by their cultures. Allport, for instance, tells the story of a small, remote Guatemalan community in which there existed an extreme, almost mythic, form of anti-Semitism, despite the fact that not a single resident of the community had ever come into contact with a Jewish person:

> How did the Jew-is-to-be-hated category grow up? In the first place, the community was strongly Catholic. Teachers had told the residents that the Jews were Christ-killers. It also so happened that in the local culture was an old pagan myth about a devil who killed a god. Thus two powerfully emotiónal ideas converged and created a hostile prejudgment of Jews.[58]

Whether or not Allport's tale is apocryphal, it illustrates the deep sense in which socially salient differences may be culturally constructed. If we find skin color, gender, nationality, religion, and the like, socially salient, this will be due in part to the presence of contextually novel physical differences among persons and power imbalances used to emphasize and exploit those differences. But it will also be due, in no small measure, to the myths and narratives, the structural and symbolic resources, of families, tribes, and broader cultural groups.

The cultural construction of social salience thus reflects the possibility of a collective form of self-invention, as any given ethnic, religious, or other cultural group, consciously or unconsciously, differentiates itself from broader social categories. Of course, cultural or collective self-determination is no guarantee of individual self-invention. With the socially constitutive capacity of culture comes the continued prospect of ascription and domination, now simply refocused at the cultural group level. Cultural elites or majorities, that is, often have the power to shape internally salient differences among group members, and in the process vulnerable individuals or sub-groups may be unfairly labeled and subordinated. Indeed, as liberal democratic political systems attempt simultaneously to protect cultural and individual autonomy, cultural vulnerability has proven an intractable problem, and one which we shall return to in the final chapter of this book. Here,

---

[57] Ibid.

[58] Allport, *The Nature of Prejudice*, p. 22.

though, the crucial point is that socially salient differences among persons are in significant part a consequence of culturally constructed theories and narratives.

Cultural differences that influence human perceptions of social salience may be based on relatively recent religious or political schisms or other social divarications, or they may derive from events and circumstances now lost to the haze of time. The historically more ancient bases for cultural variation are sometimes referred to as "deep history" or "deep culture," reflecting the long entrenched and seemingly innate cultural characteristics ingrained within language, certain religious beliefs, and views of the world and the nature of human existence.[59] Along these lines, the broad, and much remarked upon, distinction between Eastern and Western cultures offers an illustration. Suk Chang, for instance, describes Asian cultural conceptions of the self in far more relational terms than we are accustomed to in Western societies.[60] Where Western cultures tend to foster individualistic thinking and virtues, the socially salient aspects of human life in Eastern cultures tend more toward relations with families, communities, nature, and the universe. Indeed, the very notion of an individual human identity, in its Western conception, may be absent in Eastern and other cultural contexts.[61] Such far-reaching and deeply embedded differences as these arise primarily from an ancient past about which we can only speculate, and yet deep cultural differences continue to influence our contemporary perceptions of social salience in dramatic ways.

Within cognitive psychology, deep cultural differences, such as the Eastern-Western cultural divide referenced in the previous paragraph, are sometimes thought to result not merely in varied interpretations of social circumstances and human behavior, but, more fundamentally, in different cognitive styles through which those interpretations arise.[62] If this is the case, it may be that profound differences in culture result in materially different modes of human social cognition, thereby rendering even our most basic mechanisms for discerning social salience sensitive to cultural variation.

In a recent archival study, Michael Morris and Kaiping Peng suggest that Western cultures, with their powerful, nearly endemic emphasis on the democratic and autonomous nature of human beings, produce in their citizens cognitive orientations particularly sensitive to these values.[63] As a result, Morris and Peng contend, persons raised within a more individualistic cultural environment will be

---

[59] On the nature and effects of "deep culture," see Liebkind, "Ethnic Identity," p. 149.

[60] See Suk C. Chang, "The Self: A Nodal Issue in Culture and Psyche—An Eastern Perspective," *American Journal of Psychotherapy* 36 (1982), pp. 67–81.

[61] See Liebkind, "Ethnic Identity," p. 149.

[62] See Moskowitz, *Social Cognition*, pp. 117–19.

[63] Michael W. Morris and Kaiping Peng, "Culture and Cause: American and Chinese Attributions for Social and Physical Events," *Journal of Personality and Social Psychology* 67 (1994), pp. 949–71.

more likely to perceive individual traits and dispositions as the primary causes of human behavior. Individuals who develop cognitively within Eastern cultures, on the other hand, where social relations and collective virtues are more prominent, the researchers suggest, will acquire a more collectivist cognitive style, and so will tend to discern explanations for human behavior in social terms.

In an effort to discern the influence of cultural difference along these lines, Morris and Peng observed the ways in which acts of murder were described in two newspapers. The newspapers were based in the same city, but served different—American and Chinese—readerships. Where the American reporter's account of the murder emphasized the particular characteristics and nature of the individual murderer, the Chinese reporter's account focused more intently on the social circumstances surrounding the murder. According to Morris and Peng, the different emphases displayed in the newspaper reports reflect the way in which cultural differences may influcnce social cognition and attribution. Cognitive styles developed within different cultural contexts appear to alter the way in which human beings perceive, construe, and categorize the social world.[64] The cognitive schemas with which we approach and frame the world would seem to be, in significant part, a bequest from our religions, our cultures, and our ancestors.

Social salience, then, is a consequence of a number of complex and interrelated cognitive and social factors. Physicality, power relations, cultural differences, and deep history all may play a role in the construction of collective identity types. Moreover, social salience, and so social group membership, is, to a great extent, self-sustaining. Once a human characteristic becomes socially salient, the characteristic will then carry information that will be perceived as useful in drawing inferences and planning behavior within any given social system. If cognitively we operate by virtue of categorization and inference, then naturally we will have a tendency to focus on those features around which inferences abound. So, for instance, since skin color has been a socially salient characteristic for so long, and a great deal of social information (i.e., stereotypes) has therefore become attached to the characteristic, cognitively we will attend to differences in skin color much more regularly and with greater intensity than we will an information-poor trait such as eye or hair color. "Some features, such as race and gender," Moskowitz has written, "have natural informational value because of a rich history of stereotypes and beliefs and inferences that perceivers feel they can lean on."[65] Another way of putting this is that a socially salient feature's very utility as a socially salient feature will capture our attention, thereby reinforcing the feature's social salience. Where, as so often with skin color, the socially salient information is false and oppressive, a vicious cycle of subordination results.

By the time a social or cultural characteristic such as race or gender or disability is brought into service as a legally investitive criterion, the characteristic

---

64 Moskowitz, *Social Cognition*, p. 118.

65 Ibid., p. 64.

typically will have long been socially salient. Indeed, the embedment of a social or cultural characteristic within a legal right may be viewed as a long fought for achievement, as with certain cultural rights of recognition and rights granted to persons with disabilities. On the other hand, as we have seen, inegalitarian ascriptive labels have also found a too congenial home in law, and it has in many cases taken centuries to disengage an individual's legal status from these oppressive categories.

In both of these cases, however, legal actors and institutions have taken those characteristics that have become socially salient in light of physical differences and power relations among persons, and by virtue of cultural forces and deep history, and have reinforced their social salience by setting them down as legal rights and corresponding burdens; by making them, that is, legally salient. Further, as a social and cultural practice in its own right, the law functions also as an agent of socialization, as a social mechanism enabling the spread and further construction of social conceptions regarding the categories of persons described by rights. In the next section, then, we shall turn our attention to the socially constitutive influence of legal rights. We have said that, in virtue of formal justice and legal generality, the law necessarily categorizes persons. When, though, in categorizing persons, will legal rights also constitute social groups? As we shall see, the answer turns on the relative social salience of the investitive criterion at issue.

Legal Rights and the Constitution of Social Groups

Having discerned the nature of, and the predominant sources of salience for, collective social identities, we are now in a position to consider the role that law may play in the constitution of such groups and identities. Above we distinguished social groups from mere aggregates. Here, then, we might imagine an associational scale running roughly from one's status purely as an individual, to one's status as an affiliated but unintegrated part of some more general aggregation, finally to one's status as a member of a collectively conceptualized social group.[66] As we have seen, any set of individuals that has been taken

---

[66] A "community" would seem the next and perhaps the ultimate step on this scale. That notion is itself a rather slippery ideal, however. Community has been noted as a term with "a high level of use but low level of meaning." David Miller, ed., *The Blackwell Encyclopedia of Political Thought* (Oxford: Blackwell, 1987), p. 88. Jeremy Waldron has indicated something of the problem in defining the term: "One example of this difficulty is found in the way communitarians characteristically avoid the task of defining 'community.' What sort of entity is it that is supposed to have made us who we are, given us our character, endowed our lives with their particularity? For example, as we write these papers on the role played by 'community' in our moral reasoning about the law, are we talking about some neighborhood association in Berkeley, or about the People and State of California, or about the United States as a whole? Or are our perspectives even wider than that? Are we

together as an aggregate cannot proceed to the next higher associational level without something highly remarkable occurring. For the transition from aggregate to social group involves what might best be described as a virtually organic moment.[67] And that moment occurs only upon the creation of a group character or common status strong enough to define a socially salient aspect of each individual member's identity.[68]

This would seem a rare occurrence. We might suspect, therefore, that few legal rights classify individuals in such a way as to inform their very being. And we would be right in this suspicion. Imagine, for example, that we engage in a contract for the sale of wheat. You promise to sell and I promise to buy some number of bushels at so and so a price. Assume that upon delivery of my wheat I refuse to pay the agreed upon price. In all likelihood, I have breached our contract, and a competent court will find that you have a legal right to receive damages. The court will, perhaps unconsciously given how simplc the case is, relate your situation to the thousands of wronged promisees that have come before you, and it will conclude that you are relevantly like the previous claimants. Treating similar cases similarly, the court will classify you as one among the scores of sellers of goods to have been refused payment in the context of a valid agreement.

Now, post-right, will society's conception of you or your conception of yourself have been fundamentally altered? This seems doubtful. Will you march down the street screaming, "I am a seller of goods who has been refused payment, hear me roar!" Certainly not. Your status as a wronged vendor evinces little salience for any person beyond your particular commercial transaction. By affirming your right to receive damages on this basis the court will have inducted

---

talking about the common culture and civilization that makes it possible for a New Zealander trained at Oxford to write for the *California Law Review*?" Jeremy Waldron, "Particular Values and Critical Morality," in *Liberal Rights: Collected Papers 1981–1991* (Cambridge: Cambridge University Press, 1993), p. 194. Stephen Holmes has commented similarly: "Antiliberals invest this word [community] with redemptive significance. When we hear it, all our critical faculties are meant to fall asleep. In the vocabulary of antiliberals 'community' is used as an anesthetic, an amnesiac, an aphrodisiac . . . There is nothing it will not do for you once you expose yourself to its redeeming powers. But what is community?" Stephen Holmes, "The Permanent Structure of Antiliberal Thought," in Nancy L. Rosenblum, ed., *Liberalism and the Moral Life* (Cambridge, Mass.: Harvard University Press, 1989), p. 230. For one insightful and influential attempt at a definition, however, see Sandel, *Liberalism and the Limits of Justice*, p. 150, discussed *infra*, Chapter 5.

[67] I am grateful to Dennis Patterson for suggesting this formulation.

[68] It might be argued that some form of overt collective action beyond common social or cultural practices is required as well for a collection of persons to exist as a social group. But this condition fails to account for the possibility of a social group constituted repressively into (at least temporary) quiescence. See, e.g., Gaventa, *Power and Powerlessness*.

you merely into a very broadly conceived aggregate; no meaningful social group will have been engendered or further constructed.

Now, though, consider the same case with two critically important differences. Imagine now that it is one hundred or so years earlier, and imagine that you are a married woman. We have entered into an agreement, you have kept your side of the bargain, and I fail to pay. Under this second scenario a competent court might very well find that you have no right to receive damages. This is so because, in virtue of the complex interplay of physical (i.e., gender-related) differences, power relations, cultural theories, and historical artifacts that together determine social salience, a woman's marital status served at the time as a socially and legally salient distinction. Traditional common law principles, reflecting, reinforcing, and further refining this socially salient difference, considered women to have relinquished their separate legal identity upon marriage, including the capacity to enter into contracts.[69] A court might therefore correctly hold, on the basis of the governing law, that in our case no valid contract had ever been created, in which case I could not possibly be in breach. In rejecting your claim, the court formally still would be treating similar cases similarly, but in this second scenario the fact that you are a married woman has made you relevantly dissimilar. The court would thus exclude you from the class of rights-bearers on the basis of that ascribed characteristic.

Under this second scenario, then, you might very well feel differently about yourself post-decision. Social perceptions of you, of who you are in relation to the rest of the world, might also be altered, and these will in turn affect your self-conception.[70] In the first scenario, whether the court had accepted or rejected your claim, you would have been unlikely to have conceived of yourself, or to have been perceived by the world, in any significantly different way as a rights-bearer or as a person denied her claim. The legal decision simply would not have been socially salient. But under the second scenario a much more intrusive difference has been drawn. You are not a man, and you are not a single woman. You are different from those types of persons. Your status is that of a *married woman*, and the law makes that difference matter.

Fortunately, though, you are not alone. By virtue of the generality of the rule of law which has denied your claim, you necessarily have been sorted into a class of non-rights-bearers. You have been excluded from a set of rights-bearers on the

---

[69] See E. Allen Farnsworth, *Contracts* (Boston: Little Brown, 1982) p. 214; 2 S. Williston, *Contracts*, 3d ed., sec. 269, 269A (Boston: Little Brown, 1959). Most such restrictions were eliminated by statute during the nineteenth century, but some remained in effect even into the 1970s. See Martha Minow, *Making All the Difference: Inclusion, Exclusion, and American Law* (Ithaca, NY: Cornell University Press, 1990), p. 128. Similar restrictions have been applied to numerous other groups including, for example, prisoners and Native Americans. See Williston, *Contracts*, sec. 272.

[70] See Taylor, "Politics of Recognition."

basis of a characteristic shared by many other persons; as such, your exclusion is simultaneously an inclusion. You are now one of a group of persons unable to enter into and enforce valid agreements, one of a group of people denied their freedom, one of a *group of married women*. Of course, you were a married woman even before we entered into our invalid agreement, and even before you entered the courthouse. But now that status has taken on a further social and institutional dimension.[71] Now the status of being a married woman represents not just a legal and social arrangement between you and another person; now it also represents your lack of an individual legal identity, and in that sense your incapacity to be free. You have been related, by law, to a group of similarly situated people, and you have been further defined by law as one of *them*. A group consciousness has been further stirred by the law, and this time, you tell yourself, there shall indeed be a roar.

Constitutive Aspects of Special and General Rights

Above we were forced to resort to an historical shift to demonstrate that legal rights can indeed constitute social groups. There are still remnants of the incapacity doctrine in contract law, and elsewhere, and with them the institution of various social groups.[72] For the most part, however, individuals are free in private law to engage one another on a formally equal footing. But this does not mean that the constitutive aspect of legal rights is a mere relic of the past. It does mean, however, that the form of right that Hart termed "special" will today play only a minimal role in the constitution of social groups.[73]

Recall that special rights are those rights that arise as a result of particular transactions, such as our agreement to sell wheat above, or on the basis of some special relationship between individuals, such as the fiduciary relationship that exists between parent and child.[74] In contrast with special rights are "general

---

[71] See Neil MacCormick and Ota Weinberger, *An Institutional Theory of Law: New Approaches to Legal Positivism* (Dordrecht: Kluwer, 1986), pp. 49–76.

[72] See, e.g., Minow, *Making All the Difference*, discussing the status of persons deemed mentally incompetent.

[73] For an argument that private law nevertheless instantiates community, see Robert C. Post, *Constitutional Domains: Democracy, Community, Management* (Cambridge, Mass.: Harvard University Press, 1995). It might also be argued that special rights which arise on the basis of fiduciary relationships engender critical social relations. In that case, however, the social relationship would run across the rights equation, as between the individual whose interest was protected by the right and the individual(s) whose duty was thereby engendered. The social groups described in the text above instead consist of individuals on only one side, the interest side, of the rights equation.

[74] See H.L.A. Hart, "Are There Any Natural Rights?," in Jeremy Waldron, ed., *Theories of Rights* (Oxford: Oxford University Press, 1984), pp. 84–8; see the discussion, *supra*, Chapter 1.

rights," or those rights which implicate everyone, and which we commonly refer to today as human rights (e.g., the rights to freedom of speech and to the free exercise of one's religion). Whereas special rights protect the interests of, and impose obligations upon, only those particular individuals involved in a given transaction or relationship, general rights protect the interests of and impose obligations upon everyone. In what sense, then, might general rights constitute social groups?

We are said to possess general rights simply on the basis of our common humanity, deriving as they do from, in Hart's terms, "the right of all men to be free."[75] Given the seemingly universal character of such an investitive criterion, general rights would appear to engender the broadest conceivable class of rights-bearers, a sphere coextensive with humankind. Yet, to suggest that such a global sphere constitutes a social group would seem tautological. Such a suggestion would amount to something like the claim that a human being might conceive of herself as such simply because she exists as a human being. Indeed, our definition above suggested that a social group is discernible only against a background of difference; its existence is premised fundamentally on social contrast. So the idea of humanity serving as, and human rights constituting, such a vast and universal social group will not do. However, once we move from the realm of moral to legal rights, it becomes apparent that there is unlikely ever to be a truly universal class of positive rights-bearers. Generality in positive law is distinct from, for instance, the universality associated with physical laws, and so general rights devised and applied as positive legal rights necessarily function as a form of group-differentiated right.[76] To the extent that seemingly general rights are instituted as positive legal rights situated in a particular rather than a universal legal system, there will always be persons excluded from the set. I do not mean by this to suggest that positive rights may never extend extraterritorially, for surely they may. Positive legal rights might run to the border, so to speak, and they might for certain purposes extend beyond. But in the absence of something like a truly universal, and fully implemented, declaration of human rights, there will always, at the least, be persons outside a particular legal system excluded from a given legal right.[77]

There is thus one obvious sense in which general rights are constitutive and in which special rights are not. This is the sense in which a constitution, or any situated body of general rights, might constitute a "people," a nation, or a particular public culture.[78] Such a class of rights-bearers would be exceedingly

---

[75] Ibid., p. 88.

[76] On logical aspects of the law's generality, see Edwin W. Patterson, *Jurisprudence: Men and Ideas of the Law* (Brooklyn, NY: Foundation Press, 1953), pp. 106–16. Universal declarations of human rights come closest to uniting logical and positive legal generality.

[77] See Joseph H. Carens, "Aliens and Citizens: The Case for Open Borders," *Review of Politics* 49 (1987), p. 252; Veit Bader, "Fairly Open Borders," in Veit Bader, ed., *Citizenship and Exclusion* (New York: St. Martin's, 1997), pp. 28–60.

[78] See, e.g., Rogers M. Smith, *Stories of Peoplehood: The Politics and Morals of*

broad, and the character and constitutive influence of a given social group will only be as strong as the extent to which the defining characteristic of the group itself permeates each member's identity. Surely, though, there is a sense, often a very strong sense, in which the set of individuals that make up a particular nation may perceive themselves, and may be perceived by others, in terms of their nationality or public culture.[79] I need hardly stress the uncertain normative character of this form of social identity; there is, of course, no guarantee that the national or public cultural identity constituted by a given set of rights will reflect liberal democratic values. The point here is merely that the nationalist self-conception, whether in its liberal or a more threatening instantiation, may be constituted, in significant part, through law.

We have spoken thus far primarily of external exclusion from general rights, but, of course, no legal system is universally inclusive even viewed from an interior perspective. Once we set general rights in positive form, as for example in the U.S. Constitution, the central investitive criterion tends to be some conception of "personhood." In some contexts, as for example in the Due Process and Equal Protection Clauses, the investitive criterion of personhood is explicit; in others, for example the speech and religion clauses of the First Amendment, we arrive at the same criterion by way of negative inference.[80] But in either case the precise borders of the protected class are left for subsequent interpretation and deliberation.

At first glance, personhood would seem a simple criterion to apply. And yet history has demonstrated just how liberally (and so, in effect, how illiberally) the term may be construed. Indeed, all of the following categories of human beings have, at one time or another, and at least for certain purposes, been deemed non-persons: slaves, prisoners, sailors, lepers, excommunicates, Jews, Quakers, the terminally ill, the mentally disabled, children, persons born out of wedlock, and aliens.[81] In each of these instances, as in the case of married women above, a

---

Political Membership (Cambridge: Cambridge University Press, 2003); Post, *Constitutional Domains*; Joseph Raz, *The Morality of Freedom* (Oxford: Clarendon Press, 1986); Stephen Macedo, *Liberal Virtues: Citizenship, Virtue, and Community in Liberal Constitutionalism* (Oxford: Clarendon Press, 1990).

[79] See Kymlicka, *Multicultural Citizenship*, pp. 124–5: "Citizenship . . . is an inherently group-differentiated notion. Unless one is willing to accept either a single-world government or completely open borders between states—and very few liberal theorists have endorsed either of these—then distributing rights and benefits on the basis of citizenship is to treat people differentially on the basis of their group membership."

[80] Compare U.S. Const. amend. V: "nor shall any person . . . be deprived of life, liberty, or property, without due process of law," and amend. XIV, sec. 1: "nor shall any state . . . deny to any person within its jurisdiction the equal protection of the laws," with U.S. Const. amend. I: "Congress shall make no law . . . prohibiting the free exercise [of religion]; or abridging the freedom of speech."

[81] See *Dred Scott v. Sandford*, 60 U.S. (19 How.) 393 (1856), deeming slaves non-

particular physical or cultural characteristic, through the interactive operation of human social cognition, power relations, cultural narratives and deep history, has been rendered socially salient and has served as a basis upon which to exclude individuals from a general class of rights-bearers. In consequence, each such set has been formally, and sometimes physically, segregated from the general populace. Individuals bearing such socially salient characteristics have been further related, by law, to a class of similarly situated persons, and defined as "non-persons." In this way, sets of persons deemed non-persons have been further constituted by law as distinct social groups. In effect, in each of these cases, a seemingly general right has been interpretively transformed into a social group-differentiated right.

Let us consider one such case. For at least four years during the 1830s, Dred Scott resided in northern areas of the United States where slavery was illegal.[82] In prior and subsequent years, however, Scott lived as a slave in slave states. In 1853, Dred Scott brought suit against his owner in federal court, claiming that his prolonged residence in a free state had made him a free man. The federal court's jurisdiction over the case was premised upon diversity of state citizenship. On appeal, therefore, the Supreme Court needed as an initial matter to determine whether Scott could, under these circumstances, proceed for jurisdictional purposes as a "citizen." Chief Justice Roger Taney, however, stated the issue much more broadly:

> The question is simply this: Can a negro, whose ancestors were imported into this country, and sold as slaves, become a member of the political community formed and brought into existence by the Constitution of the United States, and as such become

---

persons; W.S. Holdsworth, *History of English Law*, Vol. 9 (London: Methuen, 1966), pp. 3–4, 91–9, cited in Minow, *Making All the Difference*, p. 127. These distinctions have mostly been eliminated. See, e.g., *Yick Wo v. Hopkins*, 118 U.S. 356 (1886), deeming a resident alien a constitutional "person" for equal protection purposes; *City of Cleburne v. Cleburne Living Center*, 473 U.S. 432 (1985), holding that while certain liberties might be withheld from mentally disabled persons, equal protection rights apply. Fetuses, too, have been deemed non-persons. See *Roe v. Wade*, 410 U.S. 113 (1973); *Planned Parenthood v. Casey*, 505 U.S. 833 (1992). But the status of a fetus as a person raises issues that the other categories of persons obviously do not. See, e.g., Ronald Dworkin, *Life's Dominion: An Argument about Abortion and Euthanasia* (London: Harper Collins, 1993), pp. 21–4. Corporations, on the other hand, often are considered persons. See, e.g., *Santa Clara County v. Southern Pacific*, 118 U.S. 394 (1886); *Chicago, M & St. P. Ry. v. Minnesota*, 134 U.S. 418, 456–7 (1890), deeming corporations "persons" under the Due Process Clause of the Fourteenth Amendment.

[82] Probably the most helpful account of the case is that contained in Don E. Fehrenbacher, *The Dred Scott Case: Its Significance in American Law and Politics* (New York: Oxford University Press, 1978); see also Smith, *Civic Ideals*, pp. 263–71.

> entitled to all the rights, and privileges, and immunities, guaranteed by that instrument to the citizen?[83]

Framed in this way, Taney conflated the investitive criterion of personhood with the clearly distinct criterion of citizenship. For according to the text, one need only be a "person" to assert most constitutional rights, and one need be a "citizen" only rarely.[84] Taney therefore raised not merely the procedural issue of the competence of a former slave to sue in federal court, but also the profoundly consequential issue of the legal status of persons of African descent in general.

Were the Court thus to determine that a person of African descent could not be a citizen, it would, under Taney's reasoning, entail the further conclusion that all such individuals were incapable of holding constitutional rights *at all*. And, of course, this is precisely what the Court held. Taney compared the status of persons of African descent, whether slave or free, at the time of the Constitution's drafting with that of acknowledged members of the political community, and he concluded that a relevant difference existed, a difference sufficient to justify distinct and discriminatory treatment.[85] All persons of African descent were thus excluded from the class of individuals deemed competent to hold rights. Even more, all such individuals were thereby legally defined as non-persons.[86] Taney's ruling thus reflected and further enhanced the social and legal salience of race in nineteenth-century America. The effect was the perpetuation and further construction through law of a minority social group, or in Taney's words for a majority of the Supreme Court, "a subordinate and inferior class of beings."[87]

There is a final sense in which general rights might constitute social groups and define aspects of persons. This occurs when general rights logically protect the interests of all persons but are interpreted and applied in light of group membership. For example, all "persons" in the United States have under the Equal Protection Clause a right against discriminatory governmental treatment. But any claim under that clause necessarily will be based on a characteristic shared by

---

83 *Dred Scott*, 60 U.S. at 403.

84 See Alexander M. Bickel, *The Morality of Consent* (New Haven, Conn.: Yale University Press, 1975), ch.2; see also Peter H. Schuck, "Membership in the Liberal Polity: The Devaluation of American Citizenship," in William Rogers Brubaker, ed., *Immigration and the Politics of Citizenship in Europe and North America* (Lanham, MD: University Press of America, 1989), p. 54, indicating a handful of ways in which citizenship matters.

85 Taney simply ignored the fact, conveyed in Justice Benjamin Curtis's dissenting opinion, that at the founding free blacks had voting rights in a number of states. *Dred Scott*, 60 U.S. at 572–6 (J. Curtis, dissenting). Paul Finkelman makes this point in *Dred Scott v. Sandford: A Brief History with Documents* (New York: St. Martin's, 1997), p. 35.

86 As Alexander Bickel noted, "It has always been easier, it always will be easier, to think of someone as a noncitizen than to decide that he is a non-person, which is the point of the Dred Scott case." Bickel, *Morality of Consent*, p. 53.

87 *Dred Scott*, 60 U.S. at 404–5.

some class of persons. The critical interpretive question then becomes whether distinctions drawn according to that sort of characteristic are considered legally suspect. And, not coincidentally, the criteria for determining the suspect nature of such classifications turn on the presence of socially salient distinctions in the law at issue. For the most part, only when individuals are classified according to collective identities (e.g., race, religion, ethnicity, and gender) are those classifications deemed presumptively invalid. Moreover, certain "discrete and insular minorities," distinguished by their historical lack of political influence, are granted special protection as "suspect classes," and are on that basis further constituted as social groups.[88]

Indeed, many rights which are ostensibly general in form are far less so in practice. We might consider in this category the "Violence Against Women Act," which despite its particularistic title nevertheless grants rights to "*all persons* within the United States . . . to be free from crimes of violence motivated by gender."[89] Legislative enactments which grant civil rights to all persons, or which increase penalties for "hate crimes," are similarly logically general, but are nonetheless clearly intended and commonly interpreted to protect members of vulnerable social groups. Even the right to the free exercise of one's religion, a (supposedly) paradigmatic general right,[90] is in obvious ways reliant on one's membership in a particular religious group, and, on that basis, constitutive of social groups and self meanings. But, as we have seen, the constitutive aspect of each of these logically general rights must first overcome an additional interpretive hurdle. For the rights themselves fail to indicate, in other than an inferential sense, the particular character of the group(s) to be constituted.

---

[88] For a classic justification of this doctrine, see John Hart Ely, *Democracy and Distrust: A Theory of Judicial Review* (Cambridge, Mass.: Harvard University Press, 1980). For arguments that equal protection analysis should be conceptualized as group-oriented, see Owen M. Fiss, "Groups and the Equal Protection Clause," *Philosophy & Public Affairs* 5 (1976); Vernon Van Dyke, "Justice as Fairness: For Groups?," *American Political Science Review* 69 (1975); Patricia Williams, "Metro Broadcasting, Inc. v. FCC: Regrouping in Singular Times," *Harvard Law Review* 104 (1990); Cass R. Sunstein, "Casuistry," in Robert Post and Michael Rogin, eds., *Race and Representation: Affirmative Action* (New York: Zone Books, 1998). For arguments contrary, see Paul Brest, "In Defense of the Anti-Discrimination Principle," *Harvard Law Review* 90 (1976); Charles Fried, "Metro Broadcasting, Inc. v. FCC: Two Concepts of Equality," *Harvard Law Review* 104 (1990).

[89] 42 U.S.C. §13981(b) (emphasis added). The Age Discrimination in Employment Act is similarly intended to benefit a particular class of persons (i.e., the aged) but grants rights to employees generally. 29 U.S.C. §623(a).

[90] Hart, "Are There Any Natural Rights?," p. 87.

Constitutive Rights

Consider now, though, a different sort of right. Consider a form of right that straightforwardly includes only some while obligating many. Rights such as these defy Hart's categories from the outset; they are neither fully special nor even hypothetically general. Indeed, it is this expressly differentiated form of right that most intriguingly constitutes social groups. Intriguingly, because the constitutive effect is, at once, immediate, conspicuous and innate.

The sorts of rights mentioned in the previous section are constitutive in the sense that they serve further to construct social groups, and thereby inform aspects of human identity, but they are not constitutive in the direct sense applicable here. The constitutive influence of rights is premised fundamentally on social contrast. In each case in which special and general rights constitute social groups and self-meaning, the differentiation engendered remains contingent on a first-order interpretive decision regarding the status of classes of persons. Recall first that special and general rights may project contrast by excluding persons according to characteristics interpretively determined. Special and general rights that are constitutive in this sense are only contingently constitutive since the social contrast may change as social views and legal interpretations shift.[91] Now recall that general, though not special, rights may project contrast in a second way. General rights may logically be granted to persons merely as such but in effect be applied differently depending on group membership. Again, however, such general rights, by definition, designate no particular social group for special protection. The differentiation produced thus remains contingent on a supplemental particularization of a logically universal class, though the interpretation is not always complicated.[92]

In contrast, the constitutive effect of the pure form of constitutive right is direct and inherent. Unlike special and general rights that may interpretively reflect and further construct social categories, constitutive rights intrinsically project social contrast. This is so because differentiation is inherent in the structure of the right itself; constitutive rights openly grant benefits only to some. Indeed, in part for this reason, there are often stringent limitations placed on such rights. This is so, first, because any right that specifies a particular class of persons for benefits must, at least ostensibly, pass the test of formal justice; sufficient reasons must be

---

[91] That is not to say that in those instances where special and general rights are constitutive they are only meekly so. On the contrary, we have seen just how powerful their exclusionary effect can be. The constitutive force of any right depends less on the form a right takes than on the extent to which its defining characteristic permeates human consciousness.

[92] This is not to suggest that directly constitutive rights are self-interpreting. My point is simply that whereas general rights entail interpretation of a logically universal class, directly constitutive rights merely require construction of a particular social group.

advanced to justify such disparate treatment. And second, directly constitutive rights face limitations because a discrete segment of society must have the social and political influence necessary to impose legal obligations on the mass of society. But when reasons, sufficient or otherwise, are provided and accepted, and such rights are devised and politically implemented, the constitutive effect of this most direct form of group-differentiated right can be most compelling.

In this vein, consider again the Americans with Disabilities Act (the "ADA"), the legislation in which Congress prohibited discrimination in the workplace, and in the provision of public services and accommodations, on the basis of disability.[93] Recall that to fall within the protections of the ADA, one must be "disabled" within the meaning of the Act, which means that one must have a "physical or mental impairment that substantially limits one or more of the major life activities of such individual."[94] Above we explored the way in which this right, in virtue of its legislative generality, necessarily engenders a class of rights-bearers. Here let us consider the nature of that class so that we may discern the right's constitutive influence.

The set of persons engendered under the ADA will be composed exclusively of persons whose lives have been constrained in some significant way by physical or mental impairments. The legislation turns then on the presence of physical and mental distinctions rendered socially salient in virtue of the complex processes of human social cognition, power relations, cultural theories, and historical conditions. The individuals included within the legislation will be legally, and in that sense further socially, differentiated from the mass of society. That is, such rights-bearers will be further constituted by law as members of a social group of "disabled" persons.

The recent case of *Bragdon v. Abbott*, in which the Supreme Court recognized a significant new claim under the ADA, vividly elucidates the Act's constitutive impact.[95] In *Bragdon*, Sidney Abbott, a pre-symptomatic HIV-infected patient, sued her dentist when he refused to treat her.[96] Ms. Abbott claimed that, pursuant to the ADA, the dentist's refusal constituted unlawful discrimination on the basis of disability. As an initial matter, then, the Court needed to determine whether Ms. Abbott's condition was encompassed within the ADA's investitive criteria. In characterizing prospective rights-bearers under the ADA, Congress had borrowed almost verbatim its definition of "disability" from the Rehabilitation Act of 1973—prior legislation concerning "handicapped individual[s]"[97]—and it specifically

---

[93] 42 U.S.C. §12182.

[94] 42 U.S.C. §12102(2)(A).

[95] *Bragdon v. Abbott*, 118 S. Ct. 2196 (1998).

[96] Ibid. at 2201.

[97] See ibid. at 2202, discussing derivation of definition of "disability" from the Rehabilitation Act of 1973.

directed interpretation of the ADA to cohere with that previous standard.[98] Even more, the prior Rehabilitation Act carried with it a list of presumptive disabilities.[99] HIV, however, could not possibly have been included in the list because the virus had not yet been identified as the cause of AIDS at the time of the earlier legislation. *Bragdon* thus presented the Court with a novel issue: whether to extend the ADA to encompass within its protections persons who have been infected with HIV but who have not yet developed symptoms. The Court needed to determine whether the statutory definition of "disability" might encompass the earliest stages of AIDS. In effect, the Court needed to determine whether Ms. Abbott was "disabled."

To make this determination, the Court needed to relate the patient's, Ms. Abbott's, condition to the statutory criteria and to the circumstances of prior claimants deemed disabled.[100] Though her condition was yet pre-symptomatic, the Court reasoned that HIV nevertheless affects the body on the cellular level and so constitutes a "physical impairment."[101] And though Ms. Abbott could still bear children, the Court held that the risk that any such child might be born infected with HIV was sufficient to demonstrate that she was "substantially limited" from engaging in the "major life activity" of human reproduction.[102] By thus granting the plaintiff her claim, the Court in *Bragdon* expanded, and in the process further constructed, the social group of disabled persons depicted in the legislative right. And notice too the specific constitutive impact on the plaintiff herself. For Ms. Abbott no longer exists simply as a woman with a potentially life-threatening disease. She is now, in the eyes of the law, and in the eyes of society, and perhaps even in her own eyes, "disabled."[103]

---

[98] 42 U.S.C. §12201(a).

[99] See *Bragdon*, 118 S.Ct. at 2202–3.

[100] The Court's statement in *Sutton v. United Airlines, Inc.*, 119 S. Ct. 2139, 2147 (1999) that, based on its statutory definition, the ADA calls merely for an "individualized inquiry" should not be misconstrued as contrary to the provision's relational character. Rather, the Court's somewhat misleading point was simply that, given the statutory definition, what causes the right to attach to a given individual is not the particular type of impairment but the effect the impairment has on the individual. Hence, the ADA does not engender particular sub-groups categorized according to impairment, but the statute does constitute a broader social group composed of "disabled" persons. In addition, what the Court failed to mention is that there surely will be certain impairments that inherently limit major life activities, but technically it remains the limitation and not the impairment that causes the right to attach.

[101] *Bragdon*, 118 S. Ct. at 2203–4.

[102] Ibid. at 2204–6.

[103] On HIV and disability as an aspect of identity, see Simi Linton, *Claiming Disability: Knowledge and Identity* (New York: New York University Press, 1998), p. 12. On "disability" as a marker of identity more generally see also the essays collected in Tom Shakespeare, ed., *The Disability Reader: Social Science Perspectives* (New York:

Rights that attach on the basis of group membership can in this way strongly impact social relations and aspects of human identities. Indeed, it is precisely because the scope of rights is so highly variable that we need to be especially attuned to questions of justice in evaluating group-differentiated rights. Formally, a right's scope is constrained only by the investitive conditions defined by the right itself and the promise of formal justice that like cases must be treated alike. Formal justice forces government officials publicly to advance reasons for disparate treatment, but there remains no guarantee of substantive legitimacy. As we have seen, the group-differentiated form of right arises not merely in virtue of directly constitutive rights but also where differentiated rights are carved interpretively, and hence categories of persons are excluded, from logically general rights.

From a liberal perspective, this constitutive influence is highly significant. This is so because the nature of the social groups to which one is deemed to belong will crucially affect how one is perceived in society, and often how one perceives oneself.[104] As we have said, an individual's status as a member of a social group described by a legal right will constitute a meaningful aspect of that individual member's identity.[105] And yet, as we have also said, a basic commitment of liberal justice is to individual human agency in the construction of one's self. Hence, from a liberal perspective special attention is warranted because to the extent persons are categorized and identities are constructed by law, rather than in accordance with individual volition, we face a potentially serious loss of individual autonomy. At the same time, however, constitutive rights may provide a basis for the recognition of meaningful social and cultural differences among persons, and they may afford otherwise burdened or unpopular groups with legal protections conducive to fairness and substantive equality. Persons defined by law as disabled may be subject to a moral cost from the perspective of liberal justice, but they may also, in light of that same construction, live their lives free from discrimination.

For these reasons, the constitutive aspect of rights is itself normatively ambiguous. In the final chapter of this book, we will explore in greater detail the processes by which social groups and aspects of human identities are constituted by rights. Both group-differentiated rights that arise by exclusion from general rights, and constitutive rights that directly differentiate among claimants according

---

Continuum, 1998).

[104] On the impact of social perceptions on self-understanding, see Taylor, "The Politics of Recognition"; see also Berlin, "Two Concepts of Liberty," p. 155: "some, perhaps all, of my ideas about myself, in particular my sense of my own moral and social identity, are intelligible only in terms of [my] social network."

[105] On the constitution of individual identity by group membership, see Young, *Justice and the Politics of Difference*, p. 45; Joseph Raz, "Multiculturalism: A Liberal Perspective," in *Ethics in the Public Domain: Essays in the Morality of Law and Politics*, rev. ed., (Oxford: Clarendon Press, 1994), p. 178.

to group membership, will be characterized in light of constitutive theory and evaluated in a contextual setting. First, though, we shall need to construct a standard against which to assess such rights. Group-differentiated rights do not merely acknowledge or recognize attachments individuals derive from membership in various social and cultural groups. Such rights also transform and confer membership, constituting aspects of social and personal identities by further constructing individuals as members of social groups. In order adequately to assess group-differentiated rights, then, we shall need to draw upon a deeper understanding of the idea (and the ideal) of membership. And in order to evaluate such rights from a liberal perspective we shall need to derive from that concept, and in light of liberal principles, a liberal conception of membership. This will be the subject of the next chapter.

Chapter 5

Liberal Membership

Membership is essential and inescapable. Even the would-be hermit may, at a minimum, be considered a member of that group of persons especially eager for social isolation. Membership is also critical to who we are as individuals. As we have seen, it is true both that every individual is unique and that all persons share their common humanity. But in addition to being unique and to being human, some of us are also Hindu and some are not; some of us are members of the middle-class and some of us are more or less well off; some of us are musicians while others of us are tone deaf. Ultimately, a significant part of what distinguishes each of us as individuals is the sum of our various memberships. Membership serves as our connection to the social and cultural structures that inspire and help shape our values, norms, and world-views. Within, or, as in the case of the hermit, even without, society, our memberships, both those that are voluntary and those that are imposed upon us, come partially to define our social identities and self-concepts.

Membership, or its lack, can also dramatically impact life prospects. Consider, as just one example, the case of Julia Martinez, a full-blooded member of the Santa Clara Pueblo tribe of Native Americans. As a young woman, Martinez married a Navajo man, and the couple had several children. Martinez's children grew up on the Santa Clara reservation, lived there as adults, and learned to speak Tewa, the tribal language. Yet, a Santa Clara tribal rule restricts membership in the tribe to persons whose fathers had been Santa Claran. As a result, not only were the Martinez children excluded from tribal offices and elections, they also were excluded from inheriting Martinez's interest in the tribe's communal property, which meant that they would be forced to leave the reservation upon Martinez's death. Julia Martinez, along with her daughter Audrey, brought a legal challenge to the Santa Clara tribal rule excluding them from membership. In *Santa Clara Pueblo v. Martinez* (1978), however, the Supreme Court upheld the tribal exclusion.[1] The presence of a Native American tribe, considered in critical respects a sovereign nation, seriously complicates the moral and legal questions presented in a case like *Santa Clara Pueblo*, and I do not seek here to parse the wisdom or legal propriety of the Court's decision. Clearly, though, the ruling, and the gender-biased membership criterion upon which the ruling is based, demonstrates that contests over the shape of group membership can affect

[1] *Santa Clara Pueblo v. Martinez*, 436 US 49 (1978).

individuals in the deepest and most pragmatic possible senses. It also demonstrates that questions of membership are themselves often closely tied to questions of justice.[2]

My aim in this chapter will be to arrive at a liberal conception of membership, a perspective largely missing in the theoretical literature on law, politics, and culture, and one from which we might assess the legitimacy of group-differentiated rights. John Rawls's theory of liberal justice explicitly neglects the question of membership, simply assuming instead the existence of a closed society. As Rawls writes, "I shall simply proceed on the idea that we may reasonably begin with the basic structure of one society as a closed and self-sufficient system of cooperation."[3] And, indeed, following Rawls, few liberal theorists have concerned themselves with the idea of membership *per se*, though later in this chapter we shall encounter some who have touched upon its underpinnings. Liberalism's general neglect of membership from a theoretical perspective may be partly why membership has been so often uncritically conceptualized as an exclusively communitarian ideal. But it is surely not the full reason, for membership does indeed denote social attachment, and communitarian perspectives stress the importance to human virtue of collective forms of social life. Yet, while a communitarian *conception* of membership may be well engrained in our thinking and in our literature regarding rights, social identity and justice, there is nothing necessarily (indeed, there is necessarily nothing) communitarian about the *concept* of membership.

The Concept of Membership

Concepts and Conceptions

When we make reference to a *concept*, we make reference to the meaning of an idea taken at a highly general level of abstraction. A *conception* is a particular

---

[2] For treatments of the *Martinez* case, see Joane Nagel, *American Indian Ethnic Renewal: Red Power and the Resurgence of Identity and Culture* (Oxford: Oxford University Press, 1996), p. 30; Ayelet Shachar, *Multicultural Jurisdictions: Cultural Differences and Women's Rights* (Cambridge: Cambridge University Press, 2001), pp. 18–20; Judith Resnik, "Dependent Sovereigns: Indian Tribes, States, and the Federal Courts," *University of Chicago Law Review* 56 (1989).

[3] John Rawls, "Kantian Constructivism in Moral Theory," *Journal of Philosophy* 77 (1980), p. 524; see also John Rawls, *Political Liberalism* (New York: Columbia University Press, 1993), p. 12. Further, while Rawls acknowledges the fact of immigration, he nonetheless puts that fact to one side for purposes of his theory of justice. Ibid., p. 136, n.4. Rawls does, however, explicitly raise the question of immigration in his later work, see John Rawls, *The Law of Peoples* (Cambridge, Mass.: Harvard University Press, 1999), which is treated later in this chapter.

interpretation of a concept; it offers a perspective on that concept from a more narrow degree of abstraction.[4] As Ronald Dworkin has noted: "At the first level agreement collects around discrete ideas that are uncontroversially employed in all interpretations; at the second the controversy latent in this abstraction is identified and taken up."[5]

Take for example our concept of a *book*. Considered at a highly abstract level, a book, we might say, is a literary composition. This much is largely uncontroversial. But there may then be any number of distinct interpretations of the general idea that a book is a literary composition. For instance, we might ask whether a literary composition must be published to constitute a book. Must it be published in print form, or is an electronically published work still to be considered a book? Must it contain a certain minimum number of pages to be a book? Must it be bound? What is literary? And so on. How one responds to controversial questions regarding the particular concept at issue will determine one's conception of that concept.

Now consider again the more complicated concept of justice: like cases are to be treated alike, and different cases are to be treated differently.[6] The concept of justice, says Rawls, is largely uncontroversial. "Men can agree to this description of just institutions since the notions of an arbitrary distinction and of a proper balance, which are included in the concept of justice, are left open for each to interpret according to the principles of justice that he accepts."[7] But the concept is uncontroversial, then, only because the distribution with which it is concerned is described almost entirely in the abstract. Nothing in the concept of justice itself determines specifically justifiable allocations or suitable recipients for this distribution; that we must treat similar cases similarly begs the question of criteria for determining difference and similarity. Hence, in order to resolve any genuine dispute we would need in addition to discern appropriate principles in light of which we might identify relevant similarities and differences among claimants. Any given set of such principles would then reflect a distinct interpretation, or a discrete conception, of the concept of justice.[8]

---

4 Ronald Dworkin, *Taking Rights Seriously* (Cambridge, Mass.: Harvard University Press, 1977), p. 135; Rawls, *Political Liberalism*, p. 14, n.15.

5 Ronald Dworkin, *Law's Empire* (Cambridge, Mass.: Harvard University Press, 1986), p. 71.

6 H.L.A. Hart makes this point in *The Concept of Law* (1961), 2d ed. (Oxford: Clarendon Press, 1994), p. 160: "justice is far more complicated . . . because the shifting standard of relevant resemblance between different cases incorporated in it not only varies with the type of subject to which it is applied, but may often be open to challenge even in relation to a single type of subject."

7 John Rawls, *A Theory of Justice* (Cambridge, Mass: Harvard University Press, 1971), p. 5.

8 See, e.g., ibid. (justice as fairness); Joseph H. Carens, *Culture, Citizenship, and Community: A Contextual Exploration of Justice as Evenhandedness* (Oxford: Oxford

In assessing specifically the coherence of group-differentiated rights with liberal justice, we need by way of standard a substantive conception of membership reflective of liberal values.[9] Constructing such a liberal conception of membership is, thus, the aim of this chapter. First, though, we need to distinguish the concept of membership itself from the prevailing communitarian conceptions of that idea.

Membership

With his seminal work on the relationship between membership and justice, Michael Walzer is, perhaps, the theorist most responsible for initiating our contemporary understanding of the idea of membership. In the sense in which Walzer invoked the idea, "The primary good that we distribute to one another is membership in some human community."[10] What type of good, then, is membership? Plainly, membership is a relational good; membership provides an individual with a connection to some number of others, or in Walzer's conception, to "some human community." The particular community Walzer had foremost in mind, however, was distinctly political in character, or that of the sovereign nation:

> At stake here is the shape of the community that acts in the world, exercises sovereignty, and so on. Admission and exclusion are at the core of communal independence. They suggest the deepest meaning of self-determination. Without them, there could not be communities of character, historically stable, ongoing associations of men and women with some special commitment to one another and some special sense of their common life.[11]

On Walzer's interpretation, then, the distribution of the social good of membership in the national political community should reflect the values of those who are already members, or citizens. Walzer's treatment of the concept of membership is, in this sense, derivative of his more generally relativistic view of justice. Recall Walzer's conviction that a political society should be judged according to norms

---

University Press, 2000); Brian Barry, *Justice as Impartiality* (Oxford: Clarendon Press, 1995).

[9] For an argument that principles of impartiality and equal concern and respect mandate the application of a uniform standard across different types of groups, see Thomas W. Pogge, "Group Rights and Ethnicity," in Ian Shapiro and Will Kymlicka, eds., *NOMOS XXXIX, Ethnicity and Group Rights* (New York: New York University Press, 1997), pp. 187–221.

[10] Michael Walzer, *Spheres of Justice: A Defense of Pluralism and Equality* (New York: Basic Books, 1983), p. 31.

[11] Ibid., p. 62. Walzer's depiction of the nation-state as a "community" is itself a troublingly broad usage. See the discussion, *supra*, Chapter 4, n. 66.

derived from the shared values of those who inhabit the particular society.[12] Hence, just as the members of a political community should, on Walzer's reckoning, be the authors of the principles that determine what is just in their society, so should they also define the contours of the community itself, or its political membership. Tentatively, then, we might say that Walzer's conception of membership is best described as *political inclusion and exclusion according to contingent internal norms.*

Walzer is surely correct to see in his claim a semblance of self-determination, at least in the sense that democratic forms of governance instantiate political liberty. But the self in this species of self-determination is explicitly posited as a collective rather than an individual agency.[13] Just as it is, in Walzer's conception, the community that is acting in the world and exercising sovereignty and the like, it is the community that collectively determines its own membership boundaries. From the perspective of *an individual* inside the society being constructed, though, this is far from suggesting the deepest meaning of self-determination. And, of course, for those at the gates the political community's powers of admission and exclusion do not suggest, but patently constrain, self-determination.

In truth, however, Walzer's treatment does temper communal self-determination in at least two significant ways. First, immigration decisions, though subject in the first instance to the judgment of political majorities, are at the same time morally constrained according to the external principle of mutual aid.[14] In consequence of this principle, Walzer's conception would require the liberal granting of political asylum, at least to necessitous persons not too ideologically removed from the political culture of the host country, even where such a policy might otherwise be rejected according to democratic decision procedures.[15]

Second, even simply within the political sphere of membership that is his subject, Walzer remains cognizant that the concept of membership must engage not merely the external question of the contours of a nation's boundaries, but also the internal question of whether a given nation sanctions forms of differentiated citizenship. That is, in addition to issues regarding immigration, external exclusion, and relations with those outside national borders, the concept of membership also subsumes critical questions of inequality and differentiated political status within any particular nation. Does the state, at least as a formal

---

[12] As David Miller puts it, Walzer "see[s] justice as the creation of a particular community at a particular time." David Miller, "Introduction," in David Miller and Michael Walzer, eds., *Pluralism, Justice and Equality* (Oxford: Oxford University Press, 1995), p. 2.

[13] Indeed, Walzer's theory of self-determination is in this sense rather Rousseauian. See Jean-Jacques Rousseau, *On The Social Contract* (1762), trans. Donald A. Cress (Indianapolis, Ind.: Hackett Publishing, 1983) Bk. I, ch. 6, pp. 24–5, describing the concept of the general will.

[14] Walzer, *Spheres of Justice*, pp. 33–4. On the principle of mutual aid as a natural duty, see also Rawls, *A Theory of Justice*, pp. 114–17, 338–9.

[15] Walzer, *Spheres of Justice*, pp. 48–51.

matter, afford all members of its national community the same political freedoms and opportunities? Is citizenship even open to all members? Or is full political membership reserved for some established elite or other distinctive segment of society, as it was, for example, in the ancient city-states of Greece, as well as for much of the history of modern western liberal democracies, including the United States?[16]

Though his treatment here remains limited to the political realm (as opposed to broader differentiated policies that may affect social and cultural groups in disparate ways, more on which below), Walzer is plainly concerned with internal restrictions on democratic participation, and in particular with the plight of temporary guest workers. Indeed, Walzer derides the practice of admitting, but denying even the prospect of citizenship to, guest workers, even despite democratically expressed, shared understandings supporting such exclusionary practices.[17] This, Walzer maintains, contravenes the principle of political justice, which requires "that the processes of self-determination through which a democratic state shapes its internal life, must be open, and equally open, to all those men and women who live within its territory, work in the local economy, and are subject to local law."[18] Hence, our statement of Walzer's conception of membership should be amended to account for the constraints he would impose on the processes of collective political self-definition. Membership, thus, is conceptualized by Walzer as *political inclusion and exclusion according to contingent internal norms, subject to the principles of mutual aid and political justice.*

Now, it may appear as if this infusion of liberal principles represents a significant universalizing influence on Walzer's otherwise relativistic conception of membership. Note, however, that political justice is rendered by Walzer exceedingly narrowly, such that it may constrain majoritarian decision procedures purely with respect to internal exclusions from full citizenship. The principle of political justice apparently is intended to have no force when viewed from an

---

16 For discussion of differentiated citizenship in ancient Athens, see the essays collected in Virginia Hunter and Jonathan Edmondson, eds., *Law and Social Status in Classical Athens* (Oxford: Oxford University Press, 2000).

17 Walzer, *Spheres of Justice*, pp. 52–61.

18 Ibid., p. 60. Joseph Carens comes to a similar conclusion, though from an explicitly liberal perspective, in Joseph H. Carens, "Migration and Morality: A Liberal Egalitarian Perspective," in Brian Barry and Robert E. Goodin, eds., *Free Movement: Ethical Issues in the Transnational Migration of People and of Money* (University Park, PA: Penn State University Press, 1992), pp. 29–30. In contrast, Yasemin Soysal, writing on the treatment of temporary guest workers in Europe, suggests the presence of a movement toward a "postnational" conception of membership, based not on citizenship at all but on a fully universalized model grounded in personhood. See Yasemin Nuhoglu Soysal, *Limits of Citizenship: Migrants and Postnational Membership in Europe* (Chicago: University of Chicago Press, 1994).

external perspective. Neither is the principle of mutual aid an exceptionally demanding restraint on collective decision-making regarding membership. Beyond mandating the limited provision of asylum to politically repressed, and sufficiently like-minded, refugees, the principle of mutual aid is considered by Walzer too indeterminate a criterion reliably to settle broader questions of political membership.[19] Beyond the manifest problems associated with its relativism, however, as an interpretation of the idea of membership, Walzer's conception appears incomplete along two dimensions: first, it fails to account satisfactorily for the sense in which membership constitutes critical aspects of human identity; and second, it remains unduly narrow, limited as it is exclusively to the question of membership in the political realm.

Along the first dimension, note that the way in which Walzer introduces and dramatizes the plight of temporary guest workers is by drawing an analogy to the status of metics, or resident aliens, in ancient Athens. Metics, like contemporary guest workers, lacked full political membership, and thus rights of political participation, in a sense contrary to the principle of political justice as Walzer has articulated it. The constitutive influence of the metics' legally constructed status, though, is almost entirely ignored in Walzer's treatment. As far as I can tell, the only reference Walzer makes to the effect their legal status had on the metic social identity is a fleeting recognition that "these exclusions both expressed and enforced the low standing of the metics in Athenian society."[20] Even more, Walzer wholly eschews consideration of the third legally constituted social class in Athenian society, that of slaves, suggesting, "I shall not focus on them, since the injustice of slavery is not disputed these days, at least not openly."[21] This choice is reasonable on Walzer's part, insofar as his subject is the application of political justice narrowly to temporary guest workers, the contemporary analogue to the Athenian metics. As an explication of the idea of membership, however, it seems an opportunity squandered, for the status of both slaves and metics, as distinguished from that of citizens, in ancient Athens provides a favorable window on the relationship between legally constructed membership and social identity.

As Jonathan Edmondson has written: "Status groups, whether citizens, resident aliens, or slaves, were defined at least in part juridically, by the manner in which they were treated by Athenian law and judicial practice."[22] Indeed, Edmondson

---

[19] Walzer, *Spheres of Justice*, p. 34. Though he does not imagine the principle of mutual aid determining political membership beyond the context of political asylum, Walzer does suggest that in extreme cases the principle could necessitate the transfer of land or other resources. See ibid., p. 46–8, discussing the debate over the "White Australia" immigration policy.

[20] Ibid., p. 53.

[21] Ibid.

[22] Jonathan Edmondson, "Preface," in Hunter and Edmondson, *Law and Social Status in Classical Athens*, p. vi.

suggests that though contemporary research has focused predominantly on the three primary social classes of citizen, metic, and slave, the classical Athenian polis in fact was composed of an even richer mosaic of social identities, including citizens, disenfranchised citizens, bastards, transient foreigners, resident metics, and public, private, and manumitted slaves, all of which were reflected in Athenian law.[23] While attention to the full diversity of ancient Greek social life clearly lies beyond the confines of either Walzer's or the present study, even brief consideration of the three primary social orders helpfully illuminates the interrelationship between law, membership, and social identity. For each of the Athenian social orders was constructed and sustained, in part, in virtue of differentiated legal rights and obligations, privileges and disabilities.

Consider, for instance, that Metics were not merely excluded from political office and participation, they also, among other disabilities, were required to be sponsored by a citizen (a *prostates*), pay a special annual poll tax (the *metoikion*), and were prohibited from owning real property (unless granted *enktesis*) or marrying Athenian citizens. In fact, a violation of this final proscription was punishable by sale into slavery, a penalty that citizens never faced.[24] Legal disabilities such as these served to mark metics as members of a particular, and particularly less worthy, social class. Indeed, differentiated legal penalties for essentially similar crimes were quite common in Athenian law. For instance, although one convicted of murdering a citizen would be subject to the death penalty, murder of a metic would result merely in banishment.[25] Such differential penalties were rooted deeply in Athenian perspectives of the relative worth of, and relationship between, citizen and metic. For, though both crimes involved the killing of another person, the two murders would have been viewed as crucially different crimes, with the killing of the citizen deemed the far greater affront, thereby further degrading the metic social identity.

Of course, such differential treatment would only have been more stark, and its constitutive influence magnified, with respect to slaves. The severe liabilities attached to, indeed virtually complete civil and political incapacity associated with, the status of the slave in Athens perhaps render the law's influence on the slave's social status obvious, even palpable. Consider, nonetheless, the effect of such differential treatment within just one realm of Athenian law, again, that of its penal law. Where citizens and metics were routinely fined, though often in differing amounts, for violations less egregious than murder, slaves were almost uniformly whipped for apparently equivalent crimes. Now, the obvious rationale for such a marked differentiation in sanctions is, of course, the seeming inability of slaves to pay a fine. Yet, as Virginia Hunter has pointed out, there were slaves who had

---

23 Ibid., p. v.

24 Virginia Hunter, "Status Distinctions in Athenian Law," in Hunter and Edmondson, *Law and Social Status in Classical Athens*, pp. 16–19.

25 Ibid., p. 18.

accumulated significant wealth, and even they suffered the whip. Something both more ominous and more constitutive than a simple, pragmatic acknowledgement of the slave's lack of economic resources would appear to be reflected in this sort of differential punishment. "I would suggest," Hunter writes, "that we are dealing with something structural in the nature of slavery that required the public acknowledgement of status distinctions through representations and symbols."[26] The whip, indeed, may have served not merely as an effective instrument of punishment, but also as a further marker of the slave's denigrated social status.

Trevor Saunders's remarkably comprehensive analysis of Plato's penology in the *Laws*, though articulated for Plato's ideal state of Magnesia rather than any actual Greek city-state, would appear to lend credence to Hunter's view. Across most of the twenty-one different offenses characterized by Plato, citizens typically receive the lightest penalty, followed by a moderately more severe penalty for metics, with whipping or death typically reserved for slaves.[27] Perhaps even more telling, though, Plato imagines three offenses for which citizens should be subject to a more extreme sanction than either metics or slaves. These include the offenses of: (a) sacrilege; (b) theft of public property; and (c) unscrupulous pleading. Slaves and metics convicted of these crimes might be whipped, fined, or exiled, depending on the circumstances of the case. Under each of these three offenses, however, citizens alone would be put to death. Why, in these three instances, a more severe sanction for citizens than that administered to members of the other social classes? The answer, it turns out, only further buttresses the claim that the law reflected and substantially reinforced the notion of the citizen as a socially and morally superior being. For even these comparatively stiffer penalties carry with them constitutive meanings that favorably construct the social identity of the citizen. Sacrilege committed by a citizen is deemed a greater social loss than the same offense committed by a mere metic or a slave. Theft of public property is considered an offense to the notion that citizens should be above greed. And, similarly, unscrupulous pleading is regarded as an act beneath the citizen. In this way, as Saunders suggests, "Plato's penal code is absolutely drenched in considerations of status."[28]

With membership in the various primary orders of Magnesian or Athenian society, came differentiated legal and social status, and with differentiated status comes social identity. The tendency of group membership to influence aspects of individual identities, though perhaps obliquely hinted at, remains largely absent from Walzer's conception. Membership, though, is never merely a question of political inclusion and exclusion; it also fundamentally concerns, in fact defines, aspects of human identity. Further, recognition of the constitutive nature of

---

[26] Ibid., p. 13.

[27] Trevor J. Saunders, *Plato's Penal Code: Tradition, Controversy, and Reform in Greek Penology* (Oxford: Clarendon Press, 1991), pp. 336–7.

[28] Ibid., p. 342.

membership reveals a related problem in Walzer's conception of the idea. Although Walzer explicitly describes membership as a distributional "good," and though its possession clearly *can* be of substantial benefit to its bearers, we have already seen that membership is not a reliably desirable property. As depicted in previous chapters, every person's social identity is the product of numerous social forces, and some number of these external forces categorize and construct individuals in harmful ways. With inclusion comes exclusion, and too frequently the characteristics that serve as the basis for exclusion simultaneously constitute social memberships of an ascriptive and inegalitarian character. As a result, in contrast to Walzer's neglect of membership's constitutive influence, and his depiction of the idea as a seemingly invariable social good, the concept of membership constructed below will reflect, in a central way, membership's critical effect on human identity as well as its conceptual status as a value-neutral property.

The second sense in which Walzer's conception of membership is contestable relates to its limited scope. For Walzer's conception concerns only membership in the political sphere. Citizenship, in itself, however, is obviously an important but hardly the only meaningful species of membership with which we need to be concerned. As Larry Chartrand explains: "There are very real and important distinctions between the two concepts. Membership is a broad ideal and theoretically includes an unrestricted notion of belonging, which can legitimately apply [to] many groups ... Whereas, citizenship has 'come to signify rights and privileges, duties and responsibilities in a political community.'"[29] Individuals, as we have seen, are never merely citizens (or non-citizens) but are also commonly members of various social and cultural groups, corporations and private associations, smaller geographic regions and units, and families. Yet, in Walzer's account, institutions such as these receive attention only to the extent they further understanding of the particular nature of political membership.[30]

Of course, it remains true that, in certain times and places, political membership has been intimately connected with membership in specifically identifiable religious, ethnic, and linguistic communities. In particular, nineteenth- and early twentieth-century German society has been characterized as a prominent

---

[29] Larry Chartrand, "Métis Identity and Citizenship," *Windsor Review of Legal and Social Issues* 12 (2001), p. 37, quoting David Elkins, "Aboriginal Citizenship and Federalism: Exploring Non-Territorial Models," *Report Prepared for Royal Commission on Aboriginal Peoples* (1994), p. 5. Although Chartrand is specifically interested in differences that exist between the notions and practices of citizenship and membership in the context of a particular Canadian aboriginal group, the Métis people, on a conceptual level the distinction he draws is one of general applicability.

[30] See Walzer, *Spheres of Justice*, pp. 35–42, assessing social clubs, neighborhoods, and families as part of an effort to discern, through analogy, the character of political membership.

western example of this type of cultural-political conjunction.[31] Yet, cultural homogeneity as an aspect of liberal democratic nationality is increasingly rare today. Such states tend instead to be marked by formally egalitarian constitutional provisions amid varying degrees of cultural pluralism. As such, ethnic, religious and other cultural forms of membership have been formally, and to a great extent practically, dislodged from the political realm.[32] Such forms of membership therefore require distinct treatment. In addition, whether as a result of involuntary ascription or more emancipatory self-association, modern political communities encompass spheres of social membership of enormous variation. As a result, any meaningfully inclusive conceptualization of membership must accommodate not merely political but also, more broadly, the prospect and import of social and cultural group affiliation. Indeed, in this regard, legal systems, in distributing group-differentiated rights, distribute membership on multiple levels, and so not just political and constitutional membership are at stake in such rights, but also membership in a broad array of social and cultural groups.

In contrast to Walzer's more narrowly political conception, then, we might consider as well the more expansive conception of membership, though also broadly from a communitarian perspective, apparent in Michael Sandel's interpretation of "community":

> [T]o say that the members of a society are bound by a sense of community [means] . . . that they conceive their identity—the subject and not just the object of their feelings and aspirations—as defined to some extent by the community of which they are a part. For them, community describes not just what they *have* as fellow citizens, but also what they *are*, not a relationship they choose (as in a voluntary association) but an attachment they discover, not merely an attribute but a constituent of their identity. In contrast to the instrumental and sentimental conceptions of community, we might describe this strong view as the constitutive conception.[33]

Although presented as a definition of community *per se*, Sandel's constitutive conception is in fact directed most forcefully to what he perceives as an intrinsic

---

[31] In their classic collaborative work in social philosophy, Stanley Benn and Richard Peters characterize nationhood of this sort as grounded in an "organic" as opposed to a classically liberal contractualist foundation. See S.I. Benn and R.S. Peters, *Social Principles and the Democratic State* (London: George Allen & Unwin Ltd., 1959), pp. 247–51.

[32] On the evolution of the conception of political membership from a traditional basis in kinship and ethnic ties to its modern conception as a "complex, variegated, multipurpose idea," see Peter H. Schuck, "Membership in the Liberal Polity: The Devaluation of American Citizenship," in William Rogers Brubaker, ed., *Immigration and the Politics of Citizenship in Europe and North America* (Lanham, MD: University Press of America, 1989), p. 64.

[33] Michael J. Sandel, *Liberalism and the Limits of Justice*, 2d ed. (Cambridge: Cambridge University Press, 1998), p. 150.

relationship between the character of a particular community and the identities of its individual members; that is, to what it means to be a *member* of a "constitutive community." For Sandel, community properly forges the social aspects of individual human identity, and communal membership therefore furnishes and nurtures a person's genuine nature. In this way, Sandel's conception of communal membership is fundamentally reliant upon his conception of the nature of the self. In contrast to the liberal (deontological) conception of the person as existing prior to its ends,[34] Sandel contends that persons exist naturally encumbered by particular attachments derived from the social and cultural communities of which they are members.[35] Along this same vein, in his more recent articulation of the antecedence of communal membership, Sandel writes, "Unless we think of ourselves as encumbered selves, already claimed by certain projects and commitments, we cannot make sense of ... indispensable aspects of our moral and political experience."[36]

Hence, where Walzer views membership as fundamentally concerned with communal self-definition, Sandel theorizes membership as communal definition of the self. And where Walzer's perspective is unduly constricted by a narrow focus on citizenship, Sandel's conception embraces national citizenship but moves beyond the political realm to encompass attachments generally. In contrast, then, to Walzer's more limited political conception, membership under the Sandelian view is conceptualized as *constitutive attachment.*

The Sandelian conception is persuasive, insofar as it captures an aspect apparently missing from Walzer's analysis, but nonetheless central to the idea of membership. This is so, as we have seen, because our various memberships do indeed tell us something also about our selves, about *what*, and in that sense *who*, we are. Just as an individual's status as a member of the citizen, metic, or slave social order came, virtually unavoidably, to inform the individual's social identity in ancient Athens, so too will one's status as a member of a religious or other cultural group, ethnically or racially identified social group, private association or political organization, and so on, come to constitute an aspect of the modern individual's social identity today. As Hannah Arendt suggested: "The moment we want to say who somebody is, our very vocabulary leads us astray into saying what he is; we get entangled in a description of qualities he necessarily shares with others like him . . . his specific uniqueness escapes us."[37]

---

[34] Rawls, *A Theory of Justice*, p. 560: "For the self is prior to the ends which are affirmed by it; even a dominant end must be chosen from among numerous possibilities."

[35] Sandel, *Liberalism and the Limits of Justice*, pp. 152–4. For a similar argument, see also Alasdair MacIntyre, *After Virtue: A Study in Moral Theory*, 2d ed. (Notre Dame, Ind.: University of Notre Dame Press, 1984), pp. 204–5.

[36] Michael J. Sandel, *Democracy's Discontent: America in Search of a Public Philosophy* (Cambridge, Mass.: Harvard University Press, 1996), p. 14.

[37] Hannah Arendt, *The Human Condition* (Chicago: University of Chicago Press,

Yet, crucially, neither is this essentially constitutive aspect of membership lost on core, even canonical, liberal thinkers. Isaiah Berlin, for instance, thought similarly:

> When I ask myself what I am, and answer: an Englishmen, a Chinese, a merchant, a man of no importance, a millionaire, a convict—I find upon analysis that to possess these attributes entails being recognized as belonging to a particular group or class by other persons in my society, and that this recognition is part of the meaning of most of the terms that denote some of my most personal and permanent characteristics.[38]

Indeed, the mere recognition that social and cultural membership is partially constitutive of human identity is not, in itself, an overt challenge to liberalism. Though communitarian thinkers, following Sandel, may fetishize, or at least be overly preoccupied, with constitutive attachments in themselves, there is nothing necessarily anti-liberal in the unadorned idea that group membership may play a role in the constitution of individual life and identity. As we shall see later in this chapter, a number of liberal theorists, particularly those concerned with cultural pluralism, have characterized the availability of a wide variety of social contexts within which individuals may define and revise aspects of their social identities as not merely conducive, but perhaps even essential, to individual well-being.[39] As Joseph Raz has commented, to acknowledge the role of group membership in constituting individual identity is not to privilege "mystic collective entities at the expense of concern for humans. It is [to] recogni[ze] the dependence of personal identity and personal meaning on people's membership of, and identification with, a wide range of groups, national, religious, professional, and more."[40] What is crucial, on the liberal view, is not denying the importance of social group membership in the construction of individual identity, but ensuring, consistent with other liberal values, a maximal role for the individual in the process of that self-construction. This essential human agency, rather than the bare constitutive influence of membership, is the fundamental difference separating the Sandelian and liberal perspectives on membership.

At the same time, though, that we acknowledge, with Sandel, the real potential for social group membership to supply various components of our individual identities, we need bear in mind the strong sense in which the self at the center of all of our various attachments persists. We are, so to speak, more than simply the

---

1958), p. 181.

38 Isaiah Berlin, "Two Concepts of Liberty," in *Four Essays on Liberty* (Oxford: Oxford University Press, 1969), p. 155.

39 See, e.g., Will Kymlicka, *Multicultural Citizenship: A Liberal Theory of Minority Rights* (Oxford: Clarendon Press, 1995), pp. 82–4, and Carens, *Culture, Citizenship, and Community*, pp. 69–77.

40 Joseph Raz, *Value, Respect, and Attachment* (Cambridge: Cambridge University Press, 2001), p. 35.

sum of our parts. Moreover, while it is true, as Arendt says, that a person's particular uniqueness may escape us, that is true at least in part because we are not them. In their now classic study of human personality, the cultural anthropologist Clyde Kluckhohn and psychologist Henry Murray pronounced: "Every man is in certain respects (a) like all other men (b) like some other men (c) like no other man."[41] Kluckhohn and Murray's maxim neatly captures the essential commonality of the human species, our natural proclivity for social attachment, but also the ultimate distinctiveness of every individual. For at the core of any person's complex and varied attachments and cross-cutting allegiances remains the individual self. As Walzer has commented, "At its center, the self is what it is, 'perdurable,' as Lionel Trilling liked to say, though its configuration changes over the course of its endurance."[42] This is at least partly why even Sandel is careful to indicate that constitutive ends define human identity only "*to some extent*." Joseph Raz has similarly said, albeit from a very different perspective than that of either Sandel or Walzer, "one's culture constitutes (*contributes to*) one's identity."[43]

There is, thus, a fair degree of common ground between the Sandelian and the liberal multicultural conceptions of communal membership. Both perspectives concede and even, albeit to varying extents, positively affirm an integral role for social membership in the constitution of human identity. Moreover, neither view falls prey to the cardinal fallacy of essentialism. Yet, as indicated above, from the liberal perspective, the Sandelian conception remains contestable in another, and perhaps an even deeper, sense. The problem concerns the teleologic foundation apparent in Sandel's conception of individual identity as antecedently constituted by collective ends. As an empirical matter, not only are people constituted by a plurality of ends, but people can and also do change, even in the deep, constitutive sense that Sandel has in mind.

Indeed, recent empirical work within the fields of sociology and social psychology lend credence to the view that constitutive ends are subject to rational revision. While many of the sociological and social psychological studies concerning the unsettled nature of human identity have focused on shifts in collective identity types brought about through changes in broad historical cultural configurations, increasingly empirical studies have concentrated more narrowly on the mutability of individual social identity within particular social circumstances.

---

41 Clyde Kluckhohn and Henry A. Murray, eds., *Personality in Nature, Society and Culture* (New York: Knopf, 1948), p. 35; see also Stephen Mennell, "The Formation of We-Images: A Process Theory," in Craig Calhoun, ed., *Social Theory and the Politics of Identity* (Oxford: Blackwell, 1994), pp. 176–80.

42 Michael Walzer, *Thick and Thin: Moral Argument at Home and Abroad* (Notre Dame, Ind.: University of Notre Dame Press, 1994), pp. 100–101.

43 Joseph Raz, "Multiculturalism: A Liberal Perspective," in *Ethics in the Public Domain: Essays in the Morality of Law and Politics*, rev. ed. (Oxford: Clarendon Press, 1994), p. 179 (emphasis added).

For example, in their study of identity reconstruction in the context of life transitions, David Karp, Lynda Holmstrom, and Paul Gray "report a great deal of interpretive effort by high school seniors preparing to leave home for college, as they anticipate affirmation of some identities, creation of new identities, and discovery of unanticipated identities."[44] While, for most college-bound individuals, there may be no time when one is more susceptible to, or capable of, identity reconstruction than during the transition from the parental home to the quasi-independence of university social life, nonetheless the potential for identity instability remains a reality throughout one's life span, and this remains true even with respect to core commitments. Rational revisability of ends and attachments is not only conducive to, even constitutive of, individual autonomy, and on that ground morally essential, it is also an empirically established fact of social life

Of course, limitations on our capacity to revise attachments do exist. As we have seen, some attachments are imposed from without. We may no sooner change the color of our skin, nor the social meanings ascribed to that characteristic, than we may alter the course of the seas. Nor can we turn back the clock and adjust the circumstances of our births, including our parents' religious affiliation (or lack thereof), socioeconomic class, and so on. Yet, as clearly, we may, as we mature, determine that it is necessary to strive against social conceptions that depend upon skin color. We may critically assess and, though it may not come easily, revise our religious and other cultural affiliations. And though certainly not every social attachment will be a matter of choice, many such attachments surely will be a product of how we decide to live our lives.

In the course of life, old attachments are severed, new attachments established. As a consequence of this life process, inevitably, we may change aspects of who we are and see our lives take on different meanings. In light of external changes and events, new circumstances, or even simply the passage of time and the natural evolution of human life and society, individuals revise their perceptions of the good, their relationships with others, and, in the process, aspects of their social identities and self concepts.[45] Hence, in contrast to Sandel's conception of membership as constitutive attachment, the alternative deontological assumption of individual *constitutive autonomy* will serve as an integral element in the construction of a liberal conception of membership. Before we can begin to build a liberal conception, however, we need finally to isolate the heart of the concept of membership itself.

---

[44] Judith A. Howard, "Social Psychology of Identities," *Annual Review of Sociology* 26 (2000), p. 374, reviewing the results of David A. Karp, Lynda Lytle Holmstrom, and Paul S. Gray, "Leaving Home for College: Expectations for Selective Reconstruction of the Self," *Symbolic Interaction* 21 (1998): 253–76.

[45] See Kymlicka, *Multicultural Citizenship*, p. 91: "No end is immune from such potential revision;" see also Rawls, Political Liberalism, pp. 30–3.

There are, of course, critical differences between Walzer's relativistic and narrowly political and Sandel's more comprehensive constitutive conceptions of membership. Indeed, Sandel has recently attempted to distance his own views from those of other theorists broadly classified as communitarian, including Walzer's theory in particular.[46] Nonetheless, both Walzer's and Sandel's conceptions of membership invoke aspects critical to the very idea of membership. Integral to any sound understanding of the idea of membership are the processes, described by Walzer, by which persons are excluded from or included in some class of persons. Similarly essential is the notion, invoked by Sandel, that particular attachments may come to constitute aspects of our social identities. Hence, once we strip away Walzer's relativism and Sandel's teleology, we may discern a sense of membership sufficiently abstract to constitute its conceptual core: *Membership is a property, distributed exclusively to a particular class of persons, that describes an aspect of each member's social identity.*

Liberal Multiculturalism: Autonomy and Toleration

In what then consists a liberal conception of membership? In his own exploration of the relationship between membership and justice, Walzer suggests that "[t]he distribution of membership is not pervasively subject to the constraints of justice."[47] This might indeed hold true of membership as an abstract concept. But a liberal conception of that idea would consist in a particular interpretation of the concept, an interpretation specifically reflective of liberal values. By definition, a liberal conception of membership would constrain the distribution of membership according to the principles of liberal justice.[48]

Within the context of differential treatment of categories of persons, liberal principles have received sustained examination particularly within contemporary debates in multicultural theory. The more interesting of these debates today rarely concern the essential justice of culturally-differentiated policies. Rather, recent discussions have tended to accept as an initial premise that official differential treatment is made necessary by state bias toward particular conceptions of the good, and so have focused instead on the appropriate extent of, and occasions for,

---

[46] See Sandel, *Liberalism and the Limits of Justice*, p. x: "Insofar as 'communitarianism' is another name for . . . the idea that rights should rest on the values that predominate in any given community at any given time, it is not a view I would defend."

[47] Walzer, *Spheres of Justice*, p. 61.

[48] Joseph Carens characterizes the relationship between liberalism and immigration policy in a similar vein: "People live in communities with bonds and bounds, but these may be of different kinds. In a liberal society, the bonds and bounds should be compatible with liberal principles." Joseph H. Carens, "Aliens and Citizens: The Case for Open Borders," *The Review of Politics* 49 (1987), p. 271.

such differential treatment.[49] Indeed, with the more recent exposure of ethnocultural neutrality as fantasy, cultural rights have in recent years found a rather congenial resting place directly in the heart of liberal theory.[50] Yet questions regarding just how far liberal society should go in acknowledging and accommodating the claims of minority cultural groups have been answered variously depending principally upon how respondents regard the fundamental nature of the liberal justification for differential rights. That is to say, while debates over multiculturalism have now largely become debates *within* liberal theory, they have also evolved into debates fundamentally *about* liberal theory, or about the nature and principal commitments of liberalism and the liberal state.[51]

The prevailing point of view in the recent multicultural literature has taken autonomy as the fundamental value in liberal theory.[52] The predominance of the autonomy perspective in liberal multicultural theory is due in no small measure to its obvious association with, indeed partial derivation from, the classical conception of liberalism put forth by John Stuart Mill, as well as the more recent conceptions of Rawls and Raz.[53] What this emphasis has meant for multiculturalism is that, far from resting claims for cultural recognition and accommodation on communal interests, culturally-differentiated rights are now substantially more likely to be defended as essential to individual well-being.[54]

---

49 But see Brian Barry, *Culture and Equality: An Egalitarian Critique of Multiculturalism* (Cambridge, Mass.: Harvard University Press, 2001), discussed *infra*, Chapter 6.

50 Indeed, Rawls himself has recast his theory to account for private attachments. See Rawls, *Political Liberalism*.

51 Proponents of both of the broadly defined perspectives on liberalism described below urge a fundamental reconceptualization of liberal society as deeply plural. See Joseph Raz, "Multiculturalism," *Ratio Juris* 11 (1998), p. 197: "We should learn to think of our societies as consisting not of a majority and minorities, but as constituted by a plurality of cultural groups."; Chandran Kukathas, "Cultural Toleration," in Ian Shapiro and Will Kymlicka, eds., *NOMOS XXXIX: Ethnicity and Group Rights* (New York: New York University Press, 1997), p. 84: "we should think of the public realm as an area of convergence of different moral practices." For an alternative view, criticizing liberalism as an authoritative basis for discerning the propriety of cultural policies on the ground that liberalism is itself "embedded in a particular culture," see Bhikhu Parekh, *Rethinking Multiculturalism: Cultural Diversity and Political Theory* (Cambridge, Mass.: Harvard University Press, 2000), p. 338.

52 See especially Raz, "Multiculturalism: A Liberal Perspective"; Kymlicka, *Multicultural Citizenship*.

53 See John Stuart Mill, *On Liberty* (1859), Gertrude Himmelfarb, ed. (New York: Penguin, 1974); Rawls, *A Theory of Justice*; Rawls, "Kantian Constructivism in Moral Theory"; Joseph Raz, *The Morality of Freedom* (Oxford: Clarendon Press, 1986).

54 See Raz, "Multiculturalism," p. 178, for an argument that cultural groups' "moral claim to respect and to prosperity rests entirely on their vital importance to the prosperity of individual human beings." See also Kymlicka, *Multicultural Citizenship*, p. 105, arguing

To appreciate just how comfortable the relationship between cultural rights and a robust individualism may be, consider again that liberalism of the sort advanced here remains committed, at its deepest levels, to individual self-invention. Yet one of the principal ways in which persons may define themselves is through social attachments. "For most people," as Joseph Raz has written, "membership in their cultural group is a major determinant of their sense of who they are; it provides a strong focus of identification; it contributes to what we have come to call their sense of their own identity."[55] Hence, insofar as membership in a particular cultural group may constitute an aspect of one's very identity, rights that respect such cultural attachments serve rather directly to protect crucial individual interests. Further, as we have seen, in contrast to communitarian conceptions of the self, liberal theorists envision even constitutive ends and attachments as subject to critical reflection and revision.[56] This is why official recognition and accommodation of diverse cultural attachments is increasingly recognized as essential to liberal individualism. Cultural associations are said to provide the critical "contexts of choice" within which we as individuals may define and revise aspects of our selves.[57] According to the autonomy perspective, then, cultural rights are conceived of as (some of) the instruments of liberal self-invention.

At the same time, there remain significant differences among adherents to the prevailing autonomy perspective in liberal multiculturalism, particularly regarding which types of cultural groups should receive differential treatment. For example, Will Kymlicka, who has done perhaps more than any other theorist to frame the current debate, draws a critical distinction between indigenous minority national groups (e.g., Native American and Alaskan tribes), that have been collectively and coercively incorporated into a broader "multination" state (like the United States), and ethnic immigrant groups, composed of persons who have been incorporated on

---

that cultural membership enables individual choice. For a contrary argument, see Chandran Kukathas, "Are There Any Cultural Rights?," *Political Theory* 20 (1992), p. 107, suggesting that liberalism's "emphasis on individual rights or individual liberty bespeaks not hostility to the interests of communities but wariness of the power of the majority over minorities."

[55] Raz, "Multiculturalism," p. 178; see also Berlin, "Two Concepts of Liberty," pp. 155–7.

[56] See John Rawls, "Justice as Fairness: Political not Metaphysical" (1985), in Samuel Freeman, ed., *John Rawls: Collected Papers* (Cambridge, Mass.: Harvard University Press, 1999), pp. 404–5, suggesting that "our conceptions of the good may and often do change over time, usually slowly but sometimes rather suddenly." See also Kymlicka, *Multicultural Citizenship*, p. 91: conceptions of the good change "even for those people who think of themselves as having constitutive ends."

[57] See Will Kymlicka, *Liberalism, Community, and Culture* (Oxford: Clarendon Press, 1989), p. 166, suggesting that "the cultural structure [be] recognized as a context of choice"; Kymlicka, *Multicultural Citizenship*, pp. 82–4, describing "societal culture" as a critical "context of choice"; Carens, *Culture, Citizenship, and Community*, pp. 69–73, discussing multicultural "contexts of choice."

an individual or familial, and to some extent volitional, basis.[58] Members of incorporated national groups, Kymlicka argues, arrive (though, of course, they have never truly left) still firmly entrenched in their own "societal culture," with its distinct institutions and social practices.[59] Members of ethnic immigrant groups, on the other hand, may bring with them certain aspects of their former lives, such as language and collective historical narratives, but will of necessity have left behind the institutionalized practices that formed the core of their previous societal cultures.[60] Since Kymlicka considers access to a societal culture a precondition of liberal justice, this distinction matters greatly. Indeed, for Kymlicka it justifies affording more extensive cultural rights to members of minority national groups, who require continuing access to their own societal cultures in order to live autonomous lives, than to members of ethnic immigrant groups, who may more readily achieve autonomy within the societal culture of the dominant national group.[61]

Unsurprisingly, there is considerable disagreement even among liberal multicultural theorists of the autonomy perspective both over the viability of the notion of a "societal culture" itself and over the propriety of the distinctions Kymlicka draws between different types of cultural groups on the basis of that construct. Joseph Carens, for instance, has noted that Kymlicka's conception of access to a single societal culture as a precondition of liberal justice, combined with his willingness to fold immigrants within the dominant societal culture, leads logically to a blanket preclusion of distinctive cultural rights for ethnic immigrants.[62] Carens adheres to the basic notion of culture as an essential context of choice for autonomous individuals, but conceives of the sources of cultural meaning as "multiple, varying and overlapping," rather than as homogenous Kymlickian societal cultures. Rather than drawing categorical lines between different types of cultural groups, we serve justice best, argues Carens, by being more attentive to the full context of particular cultural claims.[63]

Another group of liberal commentators, even more interested in protecting cultural identities, have sought to challenge the prevailing autonomy perspective itself. Theorists such as William Galston and Chandran Kukathas have argued that liberalism, properly conceptualized, is rooted not in the notion of autonomy but

---

[58] Kymlicka, *Multicultural Citizenship*, pp. 10–12.

[59] Kymlicka defines "societal culture" as "a culture which provides its members with meaningful ways of life across the full range of human activities, including social, educational, religious, recreational and economic life, encompassing both public and private spheres." Ibid., p. 76.

[60] Ibid., pp. 77–8.

[61] Ibid., pp. 82–4.

[62] Carens, *Culture, Citizenship, and Community*, p. 57.

[63] Ibid., pp. 72–7; see also Jeremy Waldron, "Minority Cultures and the Cosmopolitan Alternative," in Will Kymlicka, ed., *The Rights of Minority Cultures* (Oxford: Oxford University Press, 1995), critiquing Kymlicka's notion of a homogenous "cultural structure."

ultimately in the ideals of toleration and diversity.[64] Galston and Kukathas both relate their alternative perspectives to a vigorously libertarian view of the state. Galston, for example, suggests: "The heart of the tolerance a liberal society needs is the refusal to use state power to impose one's way of life on others."[65] And Kukathas maintains: "For each social union to have any significant measure of integrity, it must *to some extent* be impervious to the values of the wider society."[66] Yet what is most critical in understanding the arguments offered by these theorists of the toleration perspective is precisely that *extent*, or the degree to which each theorist is willing to take their distrust of state authority in the realm of culture. For the foundational similarity in their approaches to justifying cultural freedom on the grounds of toleration and diversity belies an even more fundamental difference in their conceptions of liberal society and the political state.

For instance, although Galston at various points claims both instrumental and intrinsic virtue in diversity, he appears ultimately most concerned with respecting diversity as a means toward achieving social stability, or a fair *modus vivendi*.[67] Kukathas, on the other hand, defends toleration as an independent value, one constitutive of public reason.[68] Whereas Galston remains committed to diversity and mutual toleration "[w]ithin a framework of civic unity," Kukathas would, without reservation, sacrifice social unity for toleration.[69] And where Galston continues to conceptualize the liberal state as constructed broadly for the attainment of "shared liberal purposes," Kukathas conceptualizes the public realm as the "convergence of different moral practices" including, but not limited to,

---

[64] See William A. Galston, "Two Concepts of Liberalism," *Ethics* 105 (1995), p. 524: "Rather than taking autonomy or critical reflection as our point of departure, what we need instead is an account of liberalism that gives diversity its due;" Kukathas, "Cultural Toleration," p. 99, arguing that "at the core of liberalism is the idea of toleration." The recent distinction between what I have termed above the autonomy and tolerance perspectives arose in the context of a series of articles and responses between Kymlicka and Kukathas. See Chandran Kukathas, "Are There Any Cultural Rights?," *Political Theory* 20 (1992), p. 120; Will Kymlicka, "The Rights of Minority Cultures: Reply to Kukathas," *Political Theory* 20 (1992); Chandran Kukathas, "Cultural Rights Again: A Rejoinder to Kymlicka," *Political Theory* 20 (1992), p. 680: "The differences [between Kymlicka and myself] stem, ultimately from two views of liberalism."

[65] Galston, "Two Concepts of Liberalism," p. 524.

[66] Kukathas, "Are There Any Cultural Rights?," p. 127.

[67] See Galston, "Two Concepts of Liberalism," p. 527, maintaining diversity as instrumentally and intrinsically valuable; ibid., p. 519: "All too often the alternative to finding a way of living together—a modus vivendi—is cruel and bloody strife."

[68] See Kukathas, "Cultural Toleration," p. 83: "Toleration is not important because it promotes reason . . . toleration is important because if toleration is forsaken then so is reason."

[69] Galston, "Two Concepts of Liberalism," p. 526; Kukathas, "Cultural Toleration," p. 99.

liberalism.[70] In practical terms, these conceptual differences matter dramatically; Kukathas's cultural libertarianism becomes far more radical than Galston's. For example, while Galston's conception of liberalism as toleration would nonetheless urge a "vigorous" liberal civic education and "strong prohibitions . . . against the use of coercion to prevent individuals from leaving such groups," Kukathas's conception would sustain "communities which bring up children unschooled and illiterate" and exclude intervention "[e]ven in cases where there is clear evidence of terrible practices."[71] Hence, the toleration perspective on liberalism exhibits a certain degree of diversity of its own.

Recent liberal multicultural theory has thus been marked by two major stances, the autonomy and toleration perspectives on liberalism. Moreover, there has not only been a significant range of disagreement between the two but also within each perspective. Yet on one issue the views of all of the above commentators converge. Theorists of the autonomy and toleration perspectives commonly presume an inevitable clash between the collective interests of any given cultural group and the individual interests of certain of its members. Adherents of both the autonomy and toleration perspectives generally countenance what Kymlicka has called "external protections," or differentiated policies designed to "protect a particular ethnic or national group from the destabilizing impact of the decisions of the larger society."[72] These sorts of protections—for example, conduct exemptions granted to members of particular religious groups, or rights to the use of particular languages or natural resources—seek to achieve a fair degree of equality between different groups in society. Where the perspectives differ, however, is with respect to what Kymlicka terms "internal restrictions," or cultural group claims "to restrict the liberty of [group] members in the name of group solidarity."[73] These sorts of claims, ranging from constraints on criticism of group customs to practices involving mutilation and arguably torture, seek collective freedom to preserve and implement traditional practices even at the expense of individual freedom and equality within particular groups.[74]

With respect to claims for internal restrictions, theorists who take autonomy as the fundamental commitment of liberalism would privilege individual over collective freedom. Theorists who conceive of toleration as the core of liberalism would more readily sacrifice intra-group individual liberty to cultural tradition.

---

[70] Galston, "Two Concepts of Liberalism," p. 525; Kukathas, "Cultural Toleration," p. 84.

[71] Galston, "Two Concepts of Liberalism," p. 528; Kukathas, "Cultural Toleration," pp. 87, 89.

[72] Kymlicka, *Multicultural Citizenship*, p. 37.

[73] Ibid., p. 36.

[74] See Amy Gutmann, "The Challenge of Multiculturalism in Political Ethics," *Philosophy & Public Affairs* 22 (1993), p. 195, suggesting that "clitoridectomy may qualify as a form of torture."

Indeed, this point of divergence, as described here by Kukathas, serves as the essential presupposition of the contemporary liberal-multicultural debate:

> My contention here is that we are faced with a fundamental conflict between two irreconcilable aspirations: on one hand, to leave cultural communities alone to manage their own affairs, whatever we may think of their values; and, on the other hand, to champion the claims or the interests of individuals who, we think, are disadvantaged by their communities' lack of regard for certain values. Unfortunately, one cannot have it both ways.[75]

There are roots of both branches of the autonomy-toleration dispute stretching back for centuries. In this sense, Galston describes the autonomy perspective as essentially reflective of Enlightenment values, and the toleration perspective as derivative of the post-Reformation project.[76] However, once the latter perspective is exploited to justify even "terrible practices,"[77] it becomes difficult, perhaps impossible, to conceptualize in liberal terms. In practice, certain of the traditional beliefs and customs for which cultural groups seek toleration will directly contravene the liberal rights of individual group members, even to the point of being radically repressive. This is so, in part, because the vulnerability of particular categories of persons, in particular women and children, is often deeply encoded in cultural traditions. Hence, the state, through its toleration of such practices, thus becomes complicit in the cultural repression of vulnerable group members.

Ayelet Shachar's treatment of the problem of cultural toleration as it arises in the context of family law helpfully demonstrates the ways in which the costs of such toleration are often disproportionately borne by women.[78] Shachar describes family law as the social arena in which toleration of traditional cultural practices often "hits hardest."[79] Indeed, even absent cultural toleration, there is perhaps no realm more commonly conceptualized as private than that of the family, and collective privacy has been shown to breed personal vulnerability.[80] As Shachar points out, such vulnerability becomes even more acute as authority over the regulation of family life is devolved from the state, which is somewhat more likely to intervene to protect at-risk individuals, to the leaders of the family's cultural group, the traditional precepts of which may *explicitly prescribe* personal and sub-group vulnerability. Moreover, since so many cultural groups define the contours

---

[75] Kukathas, "Cultural Rights Again," p. 678.

[76] William A. Galston, *Liberal Pluralism: The Implications of Value Pluralism for Political Theory and Practice* (Cambridge: Cambridge University Press, 2002), pp. 24–6.

[77] See Kukathas, "Cultural Toleration," p. 89, discussed *supra*, this section.

[78] See Shachar, *Multicultural Jurisdictions*.

[79] Ibid., p. 11.

[80] See Susan Moller Okin, *Justice, Gender, and the Family* (New York: Basic Books, 1989), pp. 134–69.

of their communities according to familial lineage and marital status rules, group leaders are more likely to demand jurisdiction in the context of family law than in virtually any other legal arena. "A *nomoi* group's membership rules, encoded in family law, thus provide the bonds which connect the past to the future, by identifying who is considered part of the tradition."[81] Indeed, in the absence of authority over the rules, and so bounds, of group membership, a cultural community's capacity to preserve and further construct it's collective identity must to some extent be sacrificed. And this will be particularly true of non-territorial cultural groups, or "imagined communities," the membership boundaries of which can only be constructed socially.

The freedom collectively to cultivate a cultural identity, enjoyed by virtue of state accommodation of cultural traditions, is not without its costs, however. And this will be particularly true for female members of traditional cultural groups. As Shachar suggests, women are often deemed to "occupy a special position in constituting collective identities," since they are "the bearers of legitimate children and [the] primary socializers of the young."[82] Yet, ironically, the strong biological and social roles women occupy in the preservation and extension of cultural identities serve also to rationalize severe limitations on their life options. For example, since many cultural groups view control over marriage and birth as critical elements in the demarcation of membership in their communities, such groups may seek to prescribe "how, when, and with whom women can give birth."[83] Further, women may be denied educational and employment opportunities, and, in the event of divorce, inequitable property distribution rules may be applied, in an effort specifically to prevent women from abandoning their roles as bearers of the group's *nomos*.[84]

Indeed, the practical reality of threats to individual members of cultural groups from state toleration of traditional practices has been exposed in many contexts. Kymlicka has noted that some cultural groups "are concerned with controlling internal dissent, and seek group-differentiated rights in order to impose internal restrictions on their members."[85] And Kukathas readily admits that "significant harms can be inflicted (by the dominant powers in the group) on the most vulnerable members of a minority community."[86] The point here is not that

---

[81] Shachar, *Multicultural Jurisdictions*, p. 46. Shachar's reference to cultural groups as "*nomoi* groups" is derived from Robert Cover's use of the Greek *nomos* to describe a discrete legal culture, or a collection of persons joined in virtue of a particular set of group-generated prescriptions and unique narratives. See Robert M. Cover, "The Supreme Court 1982 Term: Forward: Nomos and Narrative," *Harvard Law Review* 97 (1983).

[82] Shachar, *Multicultural Jurisdictions*, pp. 50, 55.

[83] Ibid., p. 52.

[84] Ibid., p. 56.

[85] Kymlicka, *Multicultural Citizenship*, p. 38; see also Susan Moller Okin, "Feminism and Multiculturalism: Some Tensions," *Ethics* 108 (1998).

[86] Kukathas, "Cultural Toleration," p. 88.

cultural rights fail utterly to serve liberal purposes. As we have seen, cultural rights can be vital instruments of self-invention. The critical point here is that once cultural rights are detached from, and so no longer constrained by, the principle of autonomy, the practical consequence is often a form of cultural oppression that is difficult to harmonize with liberal principles.

The Liberal Self: Constitutive Autonomy

In constructing a liberal conception of membership for use in assessing group-differentiated rights, I shall therefore draw foremost upon that branch of liberalism that conceptualizes human beings as fundamentally equal and autonomous agents. This view of liberalism, robustly Millian in its conception, holds that individuals must remain free, consistent with an equal freedom for all, to act in accordance with their own rationally and independently chosen sense of what is good and valuable in life.[87] In *A Theory of Justice*, Rawls famously revived examination of this capacity for the free and rational invention and revision of one's ends and attachments with his claim that "the self is prior to the ends which are affirmed by it; even a dominant end must be chosen from among numerous possibilities."[88] And in his subsequent reply to certain critical treatments of *A Theory of Justice*, Rawls made this notion even more plain: "free persons conceive of themselves as beings who can revise and alter their final ends and who give first priority to preserving their liberty in these matters."[89]

The relationship between personal autonomy of the sort here depicted and Kantian moral autonomy is a matter of some controversy, and I shall not engage that contemporary debate in any depth within these pages.[90] Speaking in very general terms, however, moral autonomy is commonly thought not merely a matter of self-direction, but also a question of one's moral relationship with one's fellow human beings. Persons are said to act autonomously, in the Kantian moral sense,

---

[87] See Mill, *On Liberty*, especially ch. 3; Rawls, "Kantian Constructivism in Moral Theory."

[88] Rawls, *A Theory of Justice*, p. 560.

[89] John Rawls, "Reply to Alexander and Musgrave" (1974), in Samuel Freeman, ed., *John Rawls: Collected Papers* (Cambridge, Mass.: Harvard University Press, 1999) p. 240; see also Rawls, "Kantian Constructivism in Moral Theory," pp. 521–2: "as free persons, they think of themselves not as inevitably tied to the pursuit of the particular final ends they have at any given time, but rather as capable of revising and changing these ends on reasonable and rational grounds."

[90] For sustained examination of the relationship between personal and Kantian moral autonomy, see especially Gerald Gaus, "The Place of Autonomy within Liberalism," and Jeremy Waldron, "Moral Autonomy and Personal Autonomy," in John Christman and Joel Anderson, eds., *Autonomy and the Challenges to Liberalism: New Essays* (Cambridge: Cambridge University Press, 2005), pp. 272–306, 307–29.

when they are capable of guiding (i.e., they are free rationally to guide) their actions in accordance not only with their own ends but also constrained by universalized attention to the interests of others. In this project, as indicated above, I am primarily concerned with a form of personal autonomy, or the virtue inherent in deciding for oneself one's own beliefs and direction in life. To be a liberal self, an autonomous self, in the sense articulated, is to engage in sustained rational exploration of one's self and one's relationship to social life. It is to live in enduring (though surely not constant) dialogue with oneself, as if Socrates himself might be accommodated within the mind of each individual.

In the context of this discussion concerning the relationship between rights and human identity, however, I shall refer to this central liberal virtue not as personal but as *constitutive* autonomy.[91] In part, this choice is strategic. With the idea of constitutive autonomy, I seek to create a more explicit link between constitutive and liberal theory, and thereby bridge an unfortunate disciplinary divide. On a more substantive level, too, I think the choice of term better reflects the sense in which an autonomous person is a maximally self-defined person, a person free to the greatest possible extent to constitute one's self and one's life path in virtue of one's own beliefs regarding appropriate sources of value.[92] "Autonomy," Raz has

---

[91] Here I use the idea of "constitutive autonomy" to refer to the autonomous construction of the human self. This sense of "constitutive autonomy" is distinguishable from another sense in which the term has prominently been used. Rawls labeled as "constitutive autonomy" the Kantian view that the moral order of values is constituted through the activity of practical human reason, in contrast with the "doctrinal autonomy" that attends Rawls's own political constructivism. See Rawls, *Political Liberalism*, pp. 99–100. "Constitutive autonomy" is sometimes also invoked in the context of confederative, especially consociational, systems of government to signify the reservation or devolution of local authority to constitute (i.e., design) governmental structures and institutions. See, e.g., *Core Document Forming Part of the Reports of States: Belgium, U.N. International Human Rights Instruments*, ¶ 50, U.N. Doc. HRI/CORE/1/Add.1/Rev.1 (1995), discussing institutional "constitutive autonomy" in Belgium; Arend Lijphart, *Democracy in Plural Societies: A Comparative Exploration* (New Haven, Conn.: Yale University Press, 1977), pp. 41–4, describing institutional "constitutive autonomy."

[92] See Raz, *Morality of Freedom*, pp. 369–73; George Kateb, "The Value of Association," in Amy Gutmann, ed., *Freedom of Association* (Princeton, NJ: Princeton University Press, 1998), p. 48: "to be a self-defined self is an end in itself". For judicial invocation of a self-definitional conception of liberty, see *Roberts v. United States Jaycees*, 468 U.S. 609, 620 (1984), suggesting that associative freedom "safeguards the ability independently to define one's identity that is central to any concept of liberty"; *Bowers v. Hardwick*, 478 U.S. 186, 205 (1986) (Blackmun J., dissenting): "individuals define themselves" through freely chosen relationships; *Planned Parenthood v. Casey*, 505 U.S. 833, 851 (1992): "At the heart of liberty is the right to define one's own concept of existence, of meaning, of the universe, and of the mystery of life."; *Lawrence et al. v. Texas*, 123 S.Ct. 2472, 2478 (2003): substantive commitments to liberty "should counsel against attempts by the State, or a court, to define the meaning of the relationship or to set its

suggested, "is an ideal of self-creation."[93] Indeed, Mill claimed that the absence of this sort of freedom would render us something less than human:

> [I]t is the privilege and proper condition of a human being, arrived at the maturity of his faculties, to use and interpret experience in his own way . . . to conform to custom merely *as* custom does not educate or develop in him any of the qualities which are the distinctive endowment of a human being. The human faculties of perception, judgement, discriminative feeling, mental activity, and even moral preference are exercised only in making a choice . . . He who lets the world, or his own portion of it, choose his plan of life for him has no need of any other faculty than the ape-like one of imitation.[94]

In this sense, liberalism envisions individual constitutive autonomy as essential to the fulfillment of basic human dignity. Exercising constitutive autonomy, on this view, is what it means to be free, to be human.

But, of course, it may be objected, one can never truly constitute oneself entirely independently of social forces. "The completely autonomous person is," as Raz has also said, "an impossibility."[95] We are constrained and constructed in numerous ways beyond our choosing, and this condition is inescapable. We may neither choose to live our lives harming others in horrible ways, nor know entirely when our choices are our own and when the product of social relations. In a similar vein, George Kateb has suggested, "The mere fact that we are not born as adults makes this subject elusive, probably forever."[96] Still, the ranges of social and individual construction of the self are not fixed absolutes. They are, in part, subject to the public culture, as well as the form and reach of legal institutions, within which individuals interact and coexist. All things equal, the liberal self will be more likely to flourish within a society that seeks to constrain social forces constructive of the self and instead promotes conditions conducive to individual constitutive autonomy.

Rawls has more recently recast his theory of justice to account for non-public attachments, and in the process he has conceptualized the liberal self as fundamentally divided.[97] Rawls's political liberalism recognizes that the divergent world views held by persons in heterogeneous liberal democratic societies will

---

boundaries absent injury to a person or abuse of an institution the law protects."

93 Raz, *Morality of Freedom*, p. 370.

94 Mill, *On Liberty*, pp. 122–3.

95 Raz, *Morality of Freedom*, p. 155.

96 George Kateb, *The Inner Ocean: Individualism and Democratic Culture* (Ithaca, NY: Cornell University Press, 1992), p. 18.

97 See Rawls, "Justice as Fairness: Political not Metaphysical," pp. 404–5, and see generally Rawls, *Political Liberalism*; see also Stephen Macedo, *Diversity and Distrust: Civic Education in a Multicultural Democracy* (Cambridge, Mass.: Harvard University Press, 2000), pp. 212–28.

preclude reasoned agreement on certain issues. He thus aims, in his latter work, to "construct a conception of justice that takes deep and unresolvable differences on matters of fundamental significance as a permanent condition of human life."[98] The construction of a just and stable society, in light of deeply conflicting comprehensive views, depends upon the development of fair terms of cooperation, or the aspiration toward an "overlapping consensus" representing agreement among reasonable persons concerning the basic structure of a just society.[99] This overlapping consensus is achieved in part by conceptualizing persons as divisible into public and non-public selves.[100] It is the public, the institutional self that participates in Rawls's political consensus. The non-public, non-political aspect of the individual, on the other hand, reflects various attachments and convictions derivative of the individual's cultural, religious, philosophical or moral life and associations.

Indeed, Rawls in his political liberalism acknowledges that individuals often envision such attachments as final, as ultimately constitutive.[101] "These convictions and attachments help to organize and give shape to a person's way of life, what one sees oneself as doing and trying to accomplish in one's social world."[102] Yet, both the value placed on, as well as recognition of the empirical reality of, constitutive autonomy survives Rawls's more recent appreciation of deep cultural and philosophical pluralism. With respect to an individual's non-public self, Rawls maintains, "our conceptions of the good may and often do change over time, usually slowly but sometimes rather suddenly."[103] We are, hence, likely to think of ourselves, and to be perceived by others, differently as our cultural, moral, and philosophical attachments and beliefs shift. In consequence, the non-public aspects of our selves, of our social identities and self concepts, evolve. And yet, according to Rawls, a stable, ongoing, and just political consensus remains possible because our public selves survive. "For example, when citizens convert from one religion to another, or no longer affirm an established religious faith, they do not cease to be, for questions of political justice, the same persons they were before. There is no loss of what we may call their public identity..."[104] In this way, then, the liberal self, divided, may in its public phase enable political justice,

---

[98] Rawls, "Kantian Constructivism in Moral Theory," p. 543.

[99] See Rawls, *Political Liberalism*, Lecture IV.

[100] Rawls, "Justice as Fairness: Political not Metaphysical," p. 405.

[101] Rawls writes: "Citizens may have, and normally do have at any given time, affections, devotions, and loyalties that they believe they would not, and indeed could and should not, stand apart from and objectively evaluate from the point of view of their purely rational good." Ibid.

[102] Ibid.

[103] Ibid.; see also Rawls, *Political Liberalism*, p. 31.

[104] See Rawls, "Justice as Fairness: Political not Metaphysical," pp. 405–6; Rawls, *Political Liberalism*, p. 31.

while in its non-political aspect continuing to aspire toward individual constitutive autonomy.

Interestingly, in his more recent work, Walzer too calls for something like constitutive autonomy with reference to a divided self. Walzer suggests three ways in which the individual self differentiates itself. The self divides according to its different social roles (e.g., as a citizen, doctor, teacher, or parent); the self divides among its different identities (e.g., in light of attachments to family, nation, religion, or gender); and the self divides among its ideals, principles and values.[105] Given the persistently pluralist theme apparent throughout Walzer's thought, the first two (overlapping) aspects of self-differentiation are hardly surprising. The third division, however, envisions the self as subject to "internal reflection and debate," and in that sense engaged in a "moral enterprise."[106] This aspect of the divided self presents the prospect of a self standing apart from itself, with the goal of critique and reform. Indeed, to explain the division of the self in philosophical terms, Walzer makes reference to Sartre's account of the "self-creation" of the intellectual, the guardian of values who through self-reflection aspires to rise above his "petty-bourgeois conditioning."[107] Walzer is critical of this aspiration, both for its failure to appreciate the utter complexity of the self (he says it is too "thin") and for its elitism, but notably not for its emphasis on self-reflection and revision.

Notice, then, how, in emphasizing the essential (and essentially democratic) human capacity for constitutive revision, Walzer approaches Mill and Rawls. Of course, the approach is merely that. Walzer remains interested not merely in freedom and pluralism, but largely in an essentially relativist and collectivist conception of freedom and pluralism. "Societies," Walzer continues to believe, "have a particular, and a rightly particular, shape because their members have particular selves."[108] Yet the liberal vision of the self as rationally revisable is now instrumental to Walzer's thought as well. Membership remains relative to and contingent upon collective self-determination for Walzer, but we now see that this collective self-determination is, in significant part, the product of the constitutive autonomy of a society's individual members.

---

[105] Walzer, *Thick and Thin*, p. 85.

[106] Ibid., p. 86.

[107] Ibid., p. 90; see Jean-Paul Sartre, "A Plea for Intellectuals," in *Between Existentialism and Marxism*, trans. John Matthews (New York: Pantheon, 1975), pp. 259–63.

[108] Walzer, *Thick and Thin*, pp. 102–3. And further: "I am inclined to say, of course, that thick, divided selves are the characteristic products of, and in turn require, a thick, differentiated, and pluralist society." Ibid., p. 101.

Constitutive Autonomy and Value Pluralism

This capacity for the free and rational invention and revision of one's ends and attachments, this constitutive autonomy, must serve as a guiding principle in the construction of any meaningfully liberal standard for the assessment of group-differentiated rights. Liberal membership thus places priority on securing the conditions conducive to individuals living an autonomous life. At the same time, however, a liberal conception of membership must reflect a range of human values, even values to some extent in tension with constitutive autonomy. Isaiah Berlin famously suggested a conflict among ultimate values, and so the inevitability in liberal society of choosing among incommensurable ends. "What is clear," Berlin wrote:

> is that values can clash . . . liberty, without some modicum of which there is no choice and therefore no possibility of remaining human as we understand the word—may have to be curtailed in order to make room for social welfare, to feed the hungry, to clothe the naked, to shelter the homeless, to leave room for the liberty of others, to allow justice or fairness to be exercised.[109]

The thought here is that critical human values, such as liberty and equality, may conflict such that a gain in one will, at times, lead to loss in the other. "We are doomed to choose, and every choice may entail an irreparable loss."[110] Conflicts such as these are ever-present, operating between societies, between groups within societies, between individuals within groups, even within individuals themselves. One cannot be both wholly spiritual and worldly-wise at once; you may seek self-possession where I wish to cast off inhibition; a gain in public welfare or security will often necessitate a cost in individual liberty. Absolute freedom for the wolves is death to the lambs, and so on.[111]

Value pluralism of this sort operates on (at least) two levels. First, values may conflict in a moral sense; that is, ideals themselves may be in conflict, to the point where a moral judgment of the sort noted above is required for resolution. We might thus refer to this sort of conflict as an instance of moral value pluralism. The second sense in which values may conflict is on a social level. This second sort of value conflict, call it social value pluralism, arises in light of the heterogeneous nature of society. Different persons, groups, communities, nations will have divergent conceptions of the good. Social and cultural conflicts thus will

---

[109] Isaiah Berlin, "The Pursuit of the Ideal" (1988), in *The Proper Study of Mankind* (New York: Farrar, Straus and Giroux, 1997), p. 10–11. See also Berlin, "Two Concepts of Liberty," p. 168: "The world that we encounter in ordinary experience is one in which we are faced with choices between ends equally ultimate, and claims equally absolute, the realization of some of which must inevitably involve the sacrifice of others."

[110] Berlin, "The Pursuit of the Ideal," p. 11.

[111] Ibid., p. 10.

arise in virtue of the ultimately incompatible ends encompassed within a given society or community. There is obviously, then, a strong degree of overlap between social and moral value pluralism. Moral value pluralism serves as a portion of the foundation for social value pluralism; it is partially in virtue of the possibility of moral conflict that social value pluralism becomes real.

Critically, the fact of moral value pluralism should not be mistaken for moral relativism. Berlin did not believe that human beings could determine objectively correct answers to all moral questions, but neither did he mistake evil for good. Of course, the relation between pluralism and relativism becomes one of degree, and for Berlin the range of moral truth may have been too narrow. Specifying the appropriate extent of this range is not part of the present project, but we can say that while within human experience there are not always objective answers to fractious moral questions, nonetheless reason will often lead to truth. Indeed, within political society, even where the result will not prove acceptable to all, the search for reasonable justifications will itself often be conducive to legitimacy.

The fact of value pluralism, however, may also promote individual constitutive autonomy. This is so because value pluralism forces us to make choices, indeed often the most difficult of choices, in order to proceed in our personal lives and social relations. Berlin, indeed, considered "[t]he necessity of choosing between absolute claims . . . an inescapable characteristic of the human condition."[112] The prospect of living an autonomous life is enlarged by, even contingent upon, the presence of meaningful options from which individuals might construct aspects of their lives and selves. A substantial range of options, both moral and social, is essential to the exercise of reflective deliberation and rational choice.[113] Indeed, self-creation may be at an extreme where individuals are forced to choose among incommensurable ends. What choice, after all, could be more telling, or more radically self-constructive, than a choice between values utterly in conflict? Pluralism thus enables constitutive autonomy by providing the circumstances under which persons may identify with alternative values and pursue diverse modes of life.

We have seen that, in light of value pluralism, an individual's liberty may be curtailed in order to ensure equality or fairness or some other critical value to others, and we have further noticed that the presence of options engendered by pluralism nonetheless serves constitutive autonomy in an important sense. Ensuring the presence of options through law, however, will also at times exact a sacrifice in constitutive autonomy, often only in a temporary or minimal sense but sometimes more firmly. For instance, an individual's options might be curtailed in light of discriminatory practices or other social conditions that fail to treat persons

---

[112] Berlin, "Two Concepts of Liberty," p. 169.

[113] See Stephen Macedo, *Liberal Virtues: Citizenship, Virtue, and Community in Liberal Constitutionalism* (Oxford: Clarendon Press, 1990), pp. 234–40; Raz, *Morality of Freedom*, pp. 398–9.

as equals. Where a particular category of persons systematically has been denied equal treatment, a common solution is to afford to such persons a legal right to be free from such discrimination. At times even a right to an affirmative legal remedy (e.g., remedies commonly associated with programs of affirmative action) may be deemed necessary or appropriate. Yet, as we witnessed in the previous chapter, inclusion within such a class may also have the effect of constructing an aspect of the identities of persons subject to the right. To the extent that rights construct individuals as members of groups, constitutive autonomy is, to a certain extent, sacrificed. Again, this is not to say that such a sacrifice necessarily will be illegitimate, or that we are wrong to advance such rights. Indeed, as we shall see in the final chapter, it may be that the options generated by the right enable substantial opportunities for constitutive autonomy in other spheres. We can draw no conclusions in the abstract; whether a constitutive loss exacted by a particular right is warranted remains contingent upon the context within which the right is invoked.

Further, even while the freedom to define one's self remains the prime commitment of liberal justice, human identity itself remains deeply rooted in social relationships. Liberalism may conceptualize persons as capable of subjecting even constitutive ends to rational reflection, and yet simultaneously recognize that such attachments often resonate powerfully in individuals' private lives.[114] Cultural freedom is, in this sense, a condition of liberal self-invention, even while it is accomplished in part by excluding oneself from more general social attachments and obligations. Prioritizing autonomy in deriving a liberal conception of membership neither compels nor even recommends abandonment of the liberal values of toleration and diversity. Rather, multiple avenues for the expression of toleration and diversity are essential to the project of autonomy, and prioritizing autonomy ensures that toleration and diversity will be constrained to serve liberal purposes. "Liberal persons," Stephen Macedo has written:

> are distinguished by the possession of self-governing reflective capacities. Further developing these reflective capacities leads one toward the ideal of autonomy and that ideal is the source of other liberal virtues. A political regime that makes the respect for rights its core value and which encourages the spread of diversity and toleration, provides ample opportunity and stimulation for the exercise of the capacities that enable people to channel and constrain their own projects so as to respect the rights of others, and actively to exercise their freedom of choice, to achieve self-mastery and self-control.[115]

---

[114] See Rawls, "Justice as Fairness: Political not Metaphysical," pp. 404–5, and "Kantian Constructivism in Moral Theory," pp. 543–55; Kymlicka, *Multicultural Citizenship*, p. 91.

[115] Macedo, *Liberal Virtues*, p. 269.

Indeed, we have already suggested that it is *only* within a society marked to some extent by a plurality of ideals that one may live an autonomous life.

Clearly, then, in assessing group-differentiated policy, a liberal conception of membership must mediate among diverse and at times conflicting demands—demands for constitutive autonomy and demands for cultural toleration, demands for broad inclusion in, and demands for self-exclusion from, various social groups. Recognizing the fact of liberal value pluralism, however, does not lead us back to a relativistic conception of membership. We may affirm the truth of the liberal conception of membership but at the same time acknowledge that a liberal conception will encompass a plurality of at times conflicting values.

Liberalism, Membership, and Exclusion

Our consideration of the concept of membership originated in the political sphere, with an assessment of Walzer's seminal treatment of membership in the context of national borders, immigration, and the naturalization of resident aliens. We have since ranged far beyond the sphere of political membership, but we come now full circle in order to consider the particular application of the principles of liberal membership to the critical questions of citizenship and exclusion that were of special concern to Walzer. Is citizenship, and are national borders, special? That is, should the application of liberal values to alienage status and immigration decisions differ in some qualitative sense from the application of those same values in the context of sub-national borders or the constructed bounds of other social and cultural group membership? What is the relationship between liberal and political membership, and how does that relationship influence public policy at the borders of a liberal democratic nation? Are there specifically *liberal* grounds on which borders may be closed and persons excluded?

Walzer, as we have seen, maintains that the regulation of national borders, as a matter of justice, must be subject to the nation's current membership. On this view, the political membership should be permitted to determine its own membership policy, in roughly the same sense that a private club is empowered to select its own members, qualified only by observance of the principles (discussed above) of mutual aid and political justice.[116] This is, according to Walzer, an essential aspect of the process of democratic and collective self-definition. It also serves several purposes that Walzer deems particularly vital.

First, Walzer argues that the process of communal self-determination yields internal cohesion, in the form of felt communal obligation and shared meaning. Upon this basis, the interests and culture of the governed will most closely approximate, and so occupy a privileged place among, those who govern; for "only

---

[116] See Walzer, *Spheres of Justice*, p. 40, drawing an analogy between private club and national political membership.

if there are members as well as strangers [would] state officials ... have any reason to worry about the welfare of their own people (and of *all* their own people) and the success of their own culture and politics."[117] Second, reserving membership decisions for members furthers, indeed on Walzer's view it fundamentally enables, cultural particularity: "The distinctiveness of cultures and groups depends upon closure and, without it, cannot be conceived as a stable feature of human life."[118] Third, and most generally, placing the power of exclusion within the largely unrestricted domain of the current membership "serves to defend the liberty and welfare, the politics and culture of a group of people committed to one another and to their common life."[119] Hence, from Walzer's perspective, exclusion is essential to the perpetuation of culture, while at the same time safeguarding the moral and economic interests of those who are already members. Upon further consideration, however, each of Walzer's claims appears, at least presumptively, dubious.

Patriotism, or the development of a general national spirit and sense of obligation to one's country and fellow citizens, might indeed be a natural result of the presence and defense of national borders. Yet, Walzer's further notion that communal cohesion might align the interests of the governors with the governed, on a national level no less, seems a stretch of reality. After all, interests among such a broad group of persons would reflect an enormous heterogeneity, and a vast array of political and other social institutions stand ready at all times to distort the relationship between state officials and the citizenry. What might be true for a small, tightly-knit cultural group cannot be extended without loss to a collectivity the size of a modern nation-state. Further, cultural particularity, Walzer's second rationale for an internally contingent membership policy, is not the exclusive province of a relativistic communitarianism. As Joseph Carens has suggested, "Open immigration would change the character of the community but it would not leave the community without any character."[120] Indeed, a more inclusionary perspective on immigration policy would better reflect a liberal democratic society's underlying public political culture of freedom, equality of opportunity, and toleration of difference.

Moreover, if: (a) communal cohesion and cultural particularity are indeed to be overriding considerations; (b) cultural particularity really is dependent upon closure; and (c) such particularity becomes more intense when concentrated, why then would Walzer's conception not emphasize the importance of internally contingent membership policies reflecting collective self-definition at more local levels? Why would the principles Walzer articulates be applicable only with respect to national border policy, and not also extend to smaller political entities, such as states, counties, and even towns? Why, on Walzer's account, should a

[117] Ibid., pp. 37–8.

[118] Ibid., p. 39.

[119] Ibid.

[120] Carens, "Aliens and Citizens: The Case for Open Borders," p. 271.

particular village not be authorized to exclude classes of persons as part of a supposed democratic effort at collective self-determination, subject only to the narrowly construed principles of mutual aid and political justice? Would not a smaller political sphere be both more internally cohesive and culturally distinctive, and so have greater potential as a "community of character?"

Walzer appears to recognize the seeming arbitrariness, even perversity, of concentrating his conception of membership at the level of national borders, but his response is vague and appears half-hearted. He argues, in essence, that closure is needed someplace, that open local borders are dependent upon the prospect of closed nations, and that local openness best serves liberty: "Since individual choice is most dependent upon local mobility, this would seem to be the preferred arrangement in a society like our own. The politics and the culture of a modern democracy probably require the kind of largeness, and also the kind of boundedness, that states provide."[121] Notice, though, the slide that takes place here, in justifying an emphasis on national borders, from the values of communal cohesion and cultural distinctiveness to liberty and democratic political culture.

From a liberal perspective, on the other hand, a perspective that prioritizes constitutive autonomy, equality of opportunity, and cultural toleration, membership policies at all levels of government should be as open as possible. Closed borders preclude a central avenue of individual self-determination and self-definition, place essential opportunities outside the reach of the many who fail the constrictive tests of mutual aid and political justice, and express at best disregard, but more likely contempt, for diverse social and cultural groups. On the liberal view, then, the *presumptive* position must be for more open borders, and thus for individual self-determination of political membership. As Joseph Carens has concluded, "Liberal egalitarianism entails a deep commitment to freedom of movement as both an important liberty in itself and a prerequisite for other freedoms. Thus the presumption is for free migration and anyone who would defend restrictions faces a heavy burden of proof."[122]

The presumption is a rebuttable rather than a conclusive one, however. To see why, we might consider again Rawls's position. We have seen that Rawls in both his comprehensive and political accounts of liberal justice prioritizes individual constitutive autonomy. At the same time, however, and consistent with his purpose of describing the basic structure of a just society, Rawls's theory is premised on the idea of society "as a closed and self-sufficient system of cooperation."[123] Hence, most of the critical issues of membership and immigration policy with which we are here concerned are simply put to one side for purposes of

---

[121] Walzer, *Spheres of Justice*, pp. 38–9.

[122] Carens, "Migration and Morality," p. 25.

[123] Rawls, "Kantian Constructivism in Moral Theory," p. 524; see also Rawls, *Political Liberalism*, p. 12.

Rawls's theory of justice.[124] In *The Law of Peoples*, Rawls's more recent work applying the principles of political liberalism on the level of international law and relations, Rawls is more explicit in his treatment of these questions but ultimately almost as indeterminate.[125] His approach is, first, to identify a number of the dominant causes of immigration, ranging from religious persecution to mass starvation to population pressures. Then, Rawls's second step is to "suggest that [these causes]," in light of the operation of his theory of justice on the international level, "would disappear in the Society of liberal and decent Peoples."[126] And hence: "The problem of immigration is not, then, simply left aside, but is eliminated as a serious problem in a realistic utopia."[127]

Now, this is fine for ideal theory, but it of course reveals little in the way of guidance for the practical application of liberal values to the crucial questions of immigration policy. Yet, even as his ideal theory cites the virtual end of problematic immigration issues, Rawls does acknowledge both the need for a people, through the agency of their government, to regulate land use and population size, and the continuing need for national boundaries, even if they are to a certain extent arbitrary or simply the result of historical circumstance.[128] Moreover, Rawls in an intriguing footnote intimates "that a people has at least a qualified right to limit immigration," and seems even to endorse one aspect of Walzer's rationale for limiting immigration, namely that of preserving a people's "political culture and constitutional principles."[129] Of course, the vigor of any qualified right is inversely proportional to the extent of its qualifications, and Rawls rather quickly notes that he will "leave aside what these qualifications might be."[130]

Rawls, thus, appears in *Law of Peoples* to countenance restrictions on immigration, though this is in part premised upon the elimination of the direst causes of immigration and also upon some number of yet unnamed qualifications. Given these conditions and unknowns, the interests or other circumstances capable of rebutting the liberal presumption in favor of freedom of movement and individual constitutive autonomy remain largely elusive. Perhaps, though, another course may be at hand. Perhaps we can glean, indirectly, something of the nature of the membership limitations Rawlsian liberalism would countenance, or even require, from the narrow limitations Rawls would impose internally on intolerant

---

[124] See ibid., p. 136, n.4.

[125] John Rawls, *The Law of Peoples* (Cambridge, Mass.: Harvard University Press, 1999).

[126] Ibid., p. 9.

[127] Ibid.

[128] Ibid., pp. 38–9.

[129] Ibid., p. 39, n. 48.

[130] Ibid.

sects. Reaching back to *Theory of Justice*, on the subject of liberal toleration of the intolerant, Rawls writes:

> Suppose that, in some way or other, an intolerant sect comes to exist within a well-ordered society accepting the two principles of justice. How are the citizens of this society to act in regard to it? Now certainly they should not suppress it simply because the members of the intolerant sect could not complain were they to do so … A more stringent condition is required: there must be some considerable risks to our own legitimate interests. Thus just citizens should strive to preserve the constitution with all its equal liberties as long as liberty itself and their own freedom are not in danger … when the constitution itself is secure, there is no reason to deny freedom to the intolerant.[131]

With respect to intolerant groups, thus, Rawls's theory of justice would limit their freedom only to the degree necessary to preserve the constitution of equal liberty itself. In the absence of a genuine risk to liberal institutions, preservation of liberty and toleration of difference are called for. Moreover, in view of the "natural strength of free institutions" and the "inherent stability of a just constitution," justifiable restrictions on the intolerant will be quite rare.[132] On this point, Rawls's view is that free institutions will be inherently stable in virtue of their tendency to convert critics of liberal justice into devotees of expansive freedom. Over time, Rawls suggests, principally as a matter of human psychology, persons living under and advantaged by free institutions will become attached to them.[133] In consequence, the freedom afforded an intolerant sect "should be restricted only when the tolerant sincerely and with reason believe that their own security and that of the institutions of liberty are in danger."[134]

We might extrapolate from the conditions Rawls imposes within his theory of liberal justice on restricting the freedom of intolerant sects to the restrictions liberalism might countenance on immigration decisions and national political membership. For the contexts for decision are, in an important sense, analogous, and the underlying principle would seem apposite. The presumption should be in favor of individual determination of membership, subject to rebuttal on the basis of genuine threats to liberal institutions or current members' security. Indeed, this construction well matches Rawls's more recent, seemingly enigmatic statement,

---

[131] Rawls, *A Theory of Justice*, pp. 218–19.

[132] Ibid., pp. 219–20.

[133] "The liberties of the intolerant," Rawls writes, "may persuade them to a belief in freedom." *A Theory of Justice*, p. 219. On the psychological principle, see also ibid., pp. 473–4. A similar psychological principle is at work in Rawls's argument for tolerating "decent" nonliberal peoples. See Rawls, *The Law of Peoples*, pp. 61–2, arguing that liberal toleration will cause nonliberal peoples to recognize the advantages, and to evolve internally in the direction, of liberal institutions.

[134] Rawls, *A Theory of Justice*, p. 220.

considered just above, that exclusion may be warranted to protect a people's "political culture and constitutional principles."[135] To the extent that a liberal democratic society's public culture and constitution truly would be threatened by immigration—to the extent that its core institutions really would be placed at risk—exclusion may be warranted. Liberalism, as a theory of government, need not be construed as self-defeating.

Notice the strength of this condition, however. We might quite sensibly presume, on this reasoning, that justifiable exclusions will be exceedingly rare, for few immigration decisions may realistically be taken as genuine threats to a liberal constitution. Furthermore, it is not too substantial a leap from Rawls's acknowledgment that reasonable security concerns may provide a ground for restrictions on intolerant groups to the recognition of a similar concern for security at the level of national borders. Of course, extreme care is required to avoid undue expansion of this rationale, for clearly the notion of security as a ground for closure might cloak what is actually jingoistic exclusionary sentiment. And the prospect for this sort of reaction has only become heightened in the current political climate, with anxiety over international terrorism influencing public perspectives in numerous policy areas. But that said, surely no rational theory of government, liberal or otherwise, could sensibly be read to countenance the ready admission of, for instance, a hostile invasionary force.[136] The limits to a justifiable exclusionary policy on the ground of national security are, indeed, all important, but the basic compatibility of liberalism with this *type* of limitation should not be in question.

In his illuminating discussion of the liberal presumption of freedom of movement, Joseph Carens adds the maintenance of public order and (on grounds somewhat removed from those offered by Walzer) the preservation of particular indigenous cultures to the list of conditions on open borders potentially consistent with liberal principles.[137] The "public order problem" consists in the recognition that abruptly throwing open national borders could, in light of resource disparities among populations, and the consequent potential for a sudden and sizable influx of persons from resource poor nations, overwhelm a host country's ability to manage its affairs in a just and equitable manner. The potential for substantial disorder, even the temporary collapse of public order, then, is suggested by Carens as a legitimate ground for modest restrictions on immigration. To the extent that such civic chaos would restrict members' liberty and equality, it is a ground consistent also with liberal values.

Carens is careful, however, to avoid an expansive interpretation of what might constitute risks to the public order, arguing in particular that an increased draw on the welfare state would not raise a public order problem. On Carens's reasoning, then, a state may not restrict immigration on the ground that new arrivals will sap

[135] Rawls, *Law of Peoples*, p. 39, n. 48.

[136] See Carens, "Migration and Morality," p. 28.

[137] Ibid., pp. 28–34, 36–40.

the nation's economic resources. From a liberal perspective, this narrowing construction of the public order problem makes sense in most instances, since equality of opportunity remains a core commitment of liberal justice. Yet it also seems conceivable that a nation might retain the capacity to maintain law and order, and so on Carens's reckoning not have a public order problem, and yet simultaneously face so sizable a drain on public resources that liberty and basic welfare become threatened. In other words, the potential threat to liberal values that Carens views as justification for reasonable restrictions on immigration might arise not just based on a breakdown in law enforcement but also, at least in an extreme case, from a failure of other public resources. Given the historical, and indeed the contemporary, proclivity toward expansive construction of the rationales for limiting immigration, however, Carens's reluctance to embrace a broader conception of the public order problem is, perhaps, understandable.

A final ground, arguably consistent with liberal principles, on which immigration might be restricted, draws heavily on those segments of the liberal tradition that privilege toleration and cultural diversity. If it is indeed the case, as many liberal-multicultural theorists contend, that cultures provide the contexts of choice in which individuals define aspects of their selves, and in that way express their autonomy, would the preservation of culture then not also serve as a liberal basis on which immigration might be constrained?

For Carens, the answer, perhaps unsurprisingly, is: it depends. It depends upon the nature of the interests at stake and the underlying basis for the exclusion. It depends, that is, upon the extent to which entry is sought to escape severe social ills, such as extreme poverty or intense political oppression. And it depends upon the extent to which exclusion simply reflects a collective desire for cultural homogeneity, or "an attachment to what is one's own," rather than a discriminatory presumption that a particular racial or ethnic group is inferior or otherwise undeserving of membership.[138] This, Carens maintains, may only be ascertained in the light of a careful, contextual assessment. Carens, for instance, points to the White Australia policy—really a series of policies, operative beginning in the late nineteenth and lasting into the mid-twentieth century, that sought the exclusion of non-white persons from the continent—as a decidedly racist and so indefensible form of exclusion, tied to the domination of long oppressed groups. And yet he also suggests that restrictions on immigration to Japan, insofar as such constraints are applicable on a universal basis to members of all non-Japanese racial and ethnic groups, may be legitimate from a liberal perspective, at least when we put to one side real-world questions of economic need and political oppression.[139]

Even given all of Carens's qualifications, however, I must admit to skepticism over the notion that cultural preservation might serve as a liberal ground for restrictive national immigration policies. We can, as I think I have in these pages,

---

[138] Ibid., pp. 38–9.

[139] Ibid.

acknowledge the critical importance of culture as a context of choice that serves liberal purposes, without condoning official state policies that exclude individuals on the basis of their race or ethnicity (or lack thereof). Even if it is true that Japanese exclusion is based not on a sense that non-Japanese are inferior, but merely on cultural self-attachment, the fact that it is a state that is acting makes a critical difference.

Religious and other cultural groups, as well as private associations, may require the power of exclusion as part of an effort in collective self-preservation or expressive freedom.[140] But nations are different. Membership within the broader polity often will be a precondition even for the exercise of most rights, and thus for access to the sorts of opportunities and personal liberties that enable liberal self-invention. As a general matter, then, inclusion itself often will be (at least) instrumentally conducive to liberal norms. Indeed, a disposition toward inclusion is reflected deeply within liberal thought as well, as for instance in the classical contractarian idea that legitimate government is founded only upon the consent of the governed,[141] or in the Rousseauian notion that law's claim to social obedience rests upon one's having participated in some genuine sense in the making of law.[142] Of course, neither Locke nor Rousseau nor even Mill really meant to advocate universal inclusion in the political state.[143] Nonetheless, the inclination toward extensive inclusion is manifest at the core of their and other liberal thought.

---

[140] Amy Gutmann provides an illuminating treatment of the relationship between exclusion from private associations and liberal egalitarian principles, noting the essential tension that comes with a vigorous freedom of association: "Freedom of association entails some substantial freedom to exclude people; yet to enjoy equal freedom of association, individuals must also be free from discrimination ... Some individuals express their identities by becoming members of voluntary groups that discriminate, whereas other individuals are blocked from expressing their identities by being excluded from these very same groups." Amy Gutmann, *Identity in Democracy* (Princeton, NJ: Princeton University Press, 2003), p. 87. Gutmann's proposed resolution is official toleration of discriminatory exclusion from private associations, combined with a prohibition on state subsidization of such associations and public pressure against the messages expressed. Ibid., p. 112.

[141] See John Locke, *The Second Treatise of Government* (1690), in *Two Treatises of Government*, Peter Laslett, ed. (Cambridge: Cambridge University Press, 1960), ch.VIII: "no one can be . . . subjected to the political power of another without his own consent"; Thomas Hobbes, *Leviathan* (1651), Richard Tuck, ed. (Cambridge: Cambridge University Press, 1996), ch.XXX: "no law can be unjust. The Law is made by the Soveraign Power, and all that is done by such Power, is warranted, and owned by every one of the people; and this which every man will have so, no man can say is unjust."

[142] See Rousseau, *On the Social Contract*, Bk.I, ch.7: "whoever refuses to obey the general will will be forced to do so by the entire body"; and Bk.II, ch.6: "The populace that is subjected to the laws ought to be their author."

[143] For a generally helpful discussion of the "problem of inclusion" in democratic theory, see Robert A. Dahl, *Democracy and its Critics* (New Haven, Conn.: Yale University Press, 1989), pp. 119–31.

"Evidently the moral value of democracy," Robert Dahl wrote, "and thus much of its justification, will vary according to its inclusiveness."[144]

Democratic political membership brings with it an array of rights and opportunities far broader than membership in any cultural group. Treating national borders as we do cultural borders makes the state complicit in unwarranted discrimination and places too many critical resources out of the reach of too many people. Narrowly construed restrictions on immigration that are genuinely necessary to preserve liberal institutions, current members' security, or public order—constraints, that is, that serve liberty and equality—may be consistent with liberal principles. But exclusion on the basis of preservation of cultural difference would exact too great a sacrifice in constitutive autonomy and equality of opportunity.

As we close this chapter on the relationship between liberalism and membership, however, recall that political membership, even when held open in accordance with liberal principles, remains a group-differentiated right. And citizenship, as with all group-differentiated rights, necessarily constitutes an aspect of its bearers' social identities. In this, we see once again an essential conundrum in the relationship between group-differentiated rights and individual constitutive autonomy. Political membership both defines persons and yet also enables self-definition. Group-differentiated rights will sometimes sacrifice constitutive autonomy, but may be essential to human well-being, nonetheless. Liberal membership privileges constitutive autonomy, but must, even just to avoid undermining its own commitments, countenance a certain degree of involuntary construction of the self. For with inclusion comes definition; persons will at times be included, and to that extent partially constituted, specifically in order to secure to such persons the capacity for further self-invention.

In this chapter, we have witnessed the sense in which liberalism places paramount value in constitutive autonomy and yet seen too the reality of liberal values in conflict. Indeed, it is in significant part the plural and conflicting nature of liberal values that engenders such great controversy over group-differentiated rights. Group-differentiated rights, through the processes of inclusion and exclusion, sort and construct individuals as members of particular social groups. Liberal membership demands individual constitutive autonomy but also commends inclusion and the need for certain differentiated rights even where constitutive autonomy will, to some extent, be sacrificed. Where individuals are well-positioned to react against legal constructions, the cost of such constructions will be comparatively less severe. Moreover, under certain circumstances the advantages engendered by differentiated treatment will, even where individual

---

[144] Ibid., p. 99; see also ibid., p. 129: "Experience has shown that any group of adults excluded from the demos—for example, women, artisans and laborers, the unpropertied, racial minorities—will be lethally weakened in defending its own interests." See also Iris Marion Young, *Inclusion and Democracy* (Oxford: Oxford University Press, 2000), p. 53.

constitutive autonomy is constrained, exceed the associated costs. Meaningful assessment of group-differentiated policy therefore requires careful attention to the contexts within which the need for differentiated treatment is said to arise. In this book's final chapter, I will suggest three forms that group-differentiated claims might take, and from which we might begin to discern, contextually, the legitimacy of the rights-claims involved. First, though, there exists an important objection to this liberal conception of membership—indeed, an objection challenging even the characterization of this conception *as* liberal—that remains to be considered.

Chapter 6

The Universalist Critique

Liberal theory today, for the most part, has come round to the view that some degree of state accommodation of minority cultural practice is required as a matter of justice. Debate then shifts to determining the best justifications for, and the appropriate extent of, differentiated policy. A significant holdout, in this respect, is Brian Barry. Barry has sought to challenge the predominant view by re-invoking a purportedly "liberal egalitarian" objection to multicultural policy.[1] He argues that liberal principles of justice entail not a differentiated but a universalistic conception of citizenship: "The core of this conception of citizenship, already worked out in the eighteenth century, is that there should be only one status of citizen (no estates or castes), so that everybody enjoys the same legal and political rights."[2] Thus invoking formal equality, Barry condemns in particular those group-differentiated rights that ground their differentiation on the basis of cultural attachments, including religious practices. Rights accorded on the basis of cultural membership, Barry argues, contradict egalitarian liberal norms, ignore enlightenment virtues and the lessons painfully there learned, and, as such, risk a reprise of the sort of sectarian conflict that characterized pre-liberal eras.[3]

Where some theorists of difference indeed may have misguidedly abandoned liberalism on their march to justify multicultural political programs,[4] Barry has rather too adamantly remained tethered to an exceedingly proceduralist, and so unduly thin, conception of liberalism. Barry is correct to criticize difference theorists for some of the more extreme and illiberal elements of their political agendas, but, as we have already seen, many more moderate proposals for cultural recognition and accommodation have sought and found a congenial home in a less impoverished conception of liberalism. Just below, in the first part of this chapter, I outline the major strands of Barry's universalistic conception of justice, as well as the sense in which he relates that conception to group-differentiated claims for religious freedom. Then, in the second part, I assess the cogency of Barry's

---

1 See Brian Barry, *Culture and Equality: An Egalitarian Critique of Multiculturalism* (Cambridge, Mass.: Harvard University Press, 2001).

2 Ibid., p. 7.

3 Ibid., pp. 20–21.

4 Although there is a great deal that is of value in her work, I think this is ultimately true of Iris Marion Young. See Iris Marion Young, *Justice and the Politics of Difference* (Princeton, NJ: Princeton University Press, 1990).

justification of social and economic rights in light of his denunciation of multicultural and difference theory. In the final part, I suggest why, in contrast to Barry's proceduralist approach, we do better by asking whether differentiated citizenship policies threaten to impede individual constitutive autonomy.

Universalistic Liberalism

Barry's egalitarian critique of multiculturalism is grounded in his universalistic conception of justice, developed particularly in his earlier work, *Justice as Impartiality*.[5] Barry's representation of justice as defined by that set of principles capable of earning the universal assent of reasonable persons is derived in significant form from Rawls, though he has parted company both with the later Rawls and with Rawls's most famous invention, the "original position."[6] In brief, in an effort to arrive at principles the fairness of which reasonably can be endorsed by all, Rawls posits the original position as a hypothetical situation in which a collection of persons, ignorant of their own particular characteristics, attachments and conceptions of in what a valuable life would consist, collectively arrive at general prescriptions for a just society.[7] The genius of Rawls's device is, of course, that, ignorant of their own identities, the persons in the original position cannot pursue their particular ends but will instead have a strong incentive to consider the plight of every person, since they might in fact be any person. Barry finds fault with this ideal, suggesting that while the principles derived through Rawls's apparatus might command universal assent behind a "veil of ignorance," once that veil is lifted, and the participants again become aware of their particular statuses, it becomes perfectly rational for individuals to disavow their prior assent.[8]

Like Rawls, though, Barry is most fundamentally interested in deriving principles of justice that will allow persons with highly divergent interests, attitudes and conceptions of the good to live together amicably—and amicably not simply because a peaceable existence is forced upon them, but because everyone will be capable of recognizing that whatever disputes do arise will be adjudicated according to principles that all can appreciate as fair.[9] But unlike Rawls's strategy of hypothetical self-ignorance, Barry attempts to deal with the inevitable persistence of conflicting conceptions of the good by inquiring what it is that even persons highly aware of their own strong differences might agree upon as a fair

---

[5] See Brian Barry, *Justice as Impartiality* (Oxford: Clarendon Press, 1995).

[6] Barry, *Justice as Impartiality*, ibid., pp. 57–61. For further discussion of Rawls's influence on Barry, see Barry, *Culture and Equality*, pp. 16, 331 n.27.

[7] See John Rawls, *A Theory of Justice* (Cambridge, Mass.: Harvard University Press, 1971), pp. 136–42.

[8] Barry, *Justice as Impartiality*, p. 59.

[9] Ibid., p. 77.

way of conducting public life.[10] To take one example that becomes particularly prominent in Barry's subsequent critique of multiculturalism, it naturally will be the case that among different religious groups there will be many different modes of expressing one's faith. An Orthodox Jew or Muslim might seek to observe religious dietary laws, a Sikh might seek freedom to wear a turban and possibly a *kirpan*, a Native American might seek freedom to ingest peyote, and so on.[11] Any claim by any particular group that their mode of religious practice is uniquely good, and, as such, should be protected to the exclusion of any of the others, is obviously unlikely to command universal assent.[12] What is required, then, says Barry, is a move among all groups to a higher level of abstraction.[13] We must seek a principle that no member of any particular religious group, including that group composed of persons who wish for themselves to remain free of religious doctrine, could reasonably reject.[14]

The first step in locating such a principle is recognizing the central role that religious belief may play in persons' lives. As Barry suggests, "From the point of view of virtually any conception of the good, the possibility of practising the form of religious worship in which one believes (or practising none if one=s beliefs lead in that direction) will be regarded as an important component of the good life."[15] Given this critical commonality among persons, the second step then involves deriving a principle with respect to freedom of religious worship that is able to elicit general consent. Neither eating only foods prepared in a certain fashion, nor the wearing of certain clothing, nor the universal absence of any of these religious requirements, can elicit such consent. Rather, it is only the more general prescription, the *equal freedom of all* to practice, or, as the case may be, not practice, their religion, that cannot reasonably be rejected. "If freedom to worship in the way you think right is of great importance to your own ability to live what you regard as a good life, then you are asked to accept that it is important to others too."[16]

Given the extent to which he acknowledges the critical importance of religious freedom to human well-being, Barry's sweeping rejection of religious conduct exemptions from generally applicable laws might strike some as incongruous. On the one hand, Barry argued quite strenuously in *Justice as Impartiality* that

---

10 Ibid., p. 67.

11 These and other religious claims are treated throughout *Culture and Equality*. See, e.g., Barry, *Culture and Equality*, pp. 40–50.

12 Barry, *Justice as Impartiality*, p. 82.

13 Ibid., p. 84.

14 Ibid., p. 67. In this sense, Barry's theory of justice is derivative of Thomas Scanlon's reconstruction of Rawls's contractualist ideas. See Thomas Scanlon, "Contractualism and Utilitarianism," in Amartya Sen and Bernard Williams, eds., *Utilitarianism and Beyond* (Cambridge: Cambridge University Press, 1982), pp. 103–28.

15 Barry, *Justice as Impartiality*, p. 82.

16 Ibid., p. 84.

"religious belief . . . is at the core of self-identity, and [that] if its expression is denied it leaves a gap in life that cannot be filled in any alternative way."[17] And yet, on the other hand, a substantial portion of his more recent work is dedicated specifically to rejecting claims of religious groups for public accommodation of their religious practices.[18] Indeed, the argument here is not simply that claims for religious conduct exemptions often constitute bad policy decisions (though that argument is nearly ever-present as well). Rather, Barry argues that the accommodation of religious practice is simply not a concern from the perspective of liberal justice, at all.[19] Thus, where a particular religious practice has been prohibited generally, Barry would deny even that an exemption from the more general law *might* be required as a matter of justice. And he would do so now despite his previous recognition of the "gap in life" this denial would cause at the very "core of self-identity."

How is it that Barry can both affirm the critical importance for human life of religious exercise, and yet deny that public accommodation of religious practice is a concern of liberal justice? The answer lies, it would seem, in the extreme stress that Barry's theory of justice places on the universalistic treatment of difference. Recall that, as derived by Barry, the basic prescription regarding religious freedom capable of commanding universal assent, and so of constituting a principle of liberal justice, is the equal freedom of all to practice or not to practice their religion. A policy that would afford a special exemption to any particular religious group would not be affording equal freedom to all, but, rather, would be treating one group more favorably than the rest.[20] Thus, the move asserted by Barry from a lower to a higher level of generality—in this case, from a group specific claim of free religious practice to the more general claim of equal religious freedom for all—results also in a requirement that, as a matter of justice, different groups must face uniform laws.

Yet, what sort of liberalism is it that excludes from consideration a matter that cuts to the very "core" of individual well-being? It is, as Barry has readily admitted, a theory of "strictly limited ambitions."[21] And so what then becomes of those many questions that are not susceptible to analysis strictly on the basis of substantive principles that can command universal (reasonable) assent? In that broad range of substantive issues, where individuals reasonably will disagree regarding morally charged outcomes, Barry asserts that resort must be had to fair decision procedures. And in what will these procedures consist? Fair decision

---

17 Ibid.

18 See especially Barry, *Culture and Equality*, Chapters 2 and 5. Barry also claimed that justice requires uniform laws across religious organizations in *Justice as Impartiality*, p. 164.

19 Barry, *Culture and Equality*, p. 33.

20 See Barry, *Justice as Impartiality*, p. 164; Barry, *Culture and Equality*, p. 34.

21 Barry, *Justice as Impartiality*, p. 113.

procedures are those that accord to each citizen an equal right to participate in democratic politics.[22]

Barry thus finds in Justice Scalia's reasoning in *Smith*—the well-known case in which the Supreme Court disapproved of a balancing test for free exercise claims, and with it the prospect of judicially mandated religious conduct exemptions from generally applicable laws—an approach quite congenial to his own.[23] After *Smith*, a statute would be deemed violative of the Free Exercise Clause only if the statute expressly discriminated against, as opposed merely to burdening, religious practice.[24] In this sense, both Scalia's and Barry's interpretations of the Free Exercise Clause emphasize the universalistic legal treatment of individuals over particularized claims to religious freedom. Further, both encourage resort on the part of burdened religious practitioners to legislatively, as opposed to judicially, crafted remedies.[25] An initial problem with this approach is that it arguably reduces the Free Exercise Clause to a gloss on the Equal Protection and Due Process Clauses, since those clauses already protect against overt discrimination.[26] A more practical problem, however, is that since the vast majority of religious practitioners likely to run afoul of generally applicable laws will be members of minority religious groups, the true prospect for effective political remedies will be more limited. Although Barry partially refutes this contention, claiming that at least well-organized minority religious groups will be successful in the political arena, Scalia has explicitly acknowledged the, at times, insurmountable obstacles such groups would face.[27]

---

22 Barry, *Culture and Equality*, p. 79.

23 See *Employment Division v. Smith*, 494 U.S. 872 (1990).

24 For an example of such a case, see *Church of the Lukumi Babalu Aye, Inc. v. Hialeah*, 508 U.S. 520 (1993), in which a city ordinance designed solely to suppress a particular religious sect's practice of animal sacrifice was deemed violative of the Free Exercise Clause.

25 See *Smith*, 494 U.S. at 890: "a society that believes in the negative protection accorded to religious belief can be expected to be solicitous of that value in its legislation"; Barry, *Culture and Equality*, pp. 169–73.

26 For arguments along these lines, see Larry Alexander, "Good God, Garvey! The Inevitability and Impossibility of a Religious Justification of Free Exercise Exemptions," *Drake Law Review* 47 (1998), p. 35, maintaining that "the heart of the Free Exercise Clause is the right to judicially mandated exemptions from general laws for those whose religion mandates conduct contrary to such laws. And *Employment Division v. Smith* cut the heart out of the Free Exercise Clause;" "The Supreme Court, 1989 Term: Leading Cases: I. Constitutional Law; C. Free Exercise of Religion," *Harvard Law Review* 104 (1990), p. 206: "Interpreted strongly, this conclusion reduces the free exercise clause to a virtual nullity."

27 Barry's position is stated in *Culture and Equality*, p. 39: "Any open political system . . . is inevitably subject to lobbying by minority groups with a special interest in some aspect of public policy. It very often happens that there is no similarly well-organized group on the other side." For Scalia's position, see *Smith*, 494 U.S. at 890: "It may fairly be said that leaving accommodation to the political process will place at a relative disadvantage

Notice, then, just how far we have come from Barry's initial affirmation of religious freedom. Freedom to worship (or not to worship) according to the tenets of one's faith is of great, and even self-defining, importance to all persons. Yet, because the value of any particular religious practice is incapable of garnering universal assent, liberal justice must remain remote from the claim of any given group to the free practice of their religion. Instead, the practitioners' claim, which in all likelihood will be brought by a minority religious group, must be decided according to majority will. Barry's conception of liberal justice is thus open not only to the charge that it is radically underdeterminative on a great number of critical social questions, but that on many of those questions it sacrifices individual freedom to majority will.

At the same time, however, that Barry maintains that claims for religious conduct exemptions cannot be justified on the basis of principles of liberal justice, he is also compelled to acknowledge that a given statute might "bear[] particularly harshly on some people, [and] that is at the very least a reason for examining it to see if it might be modified so as to accommodate those who are affected by it in some special way."[28] In such an event, though an exemption will not be required as a matter of justice, Barry suggests that an exemption might be justifiable on the basis of prudence or generosity.[29] For example, Barry actually endorses a current exemption from legal regulations governing the construction industry in Great Britain that permits members of the Sikh religious sect to continue to wear turbans rather than hard hats on work sites.[30] Absent the exemption, many Sikhs would be forced to choose between continuing to observe their religious obligations and continuing to maintain their livelihood. Yet, Barry's purpose in describing the hard hat exemption is not to propose it as a generalizable model for the alleviation of special hardship, but rather to suggest the remarkable rarity of justifiable conduct exemptions even on prudential grounds. Indeed, this apparently is the *only* individualized exemption that gains Barry's favor, and it does so only because nearly half of all male Sikhs living in Great Britain are employed in the construction trade.[31]

---

those religious practices that are not widely engaged in . . ."

[28] Barry, *Culture and Equality*, p. 38.

[29] Ibid., p. 39.

[30] Ibid., p. 49.

[31] Ibid. Barry also acknowledges the justifiability of an exemption from laws governing employment discrimination to enable religious groups, in a collective capacity, to employ only members of their own religion as leaders. See ibid., pp. 167–8.

Universalism and Difference

Interestingly, Barry's hostility does not extend to all group-differentiated rights. In fact, Barry is quick to defend rights that attach on the basis of social classifications such as race, gender, disability or economic status.[32] It is only rights that attach on the basis of cultural membership that give Barry such pause. What justifies this distinct treatment? According to Barry, it is only because socially-differentiated rights are universalistic and temporary that special treatment for these categories of persons is justified. In contrast, since culturally-differentiated rights are particularistic and permanent these cannot be countenanced by liberal justice.[33]

But are these characterizations fair? In what sense may rights that attach on the basis of disability or economic status be considered mere stop-gaps? At least as presently conceptualized, such rights would seem highly unlikely to, as Barry maintains, "make the need for that special treatment disappear as rapidly as possible."[34] Disability and economic rights surely are designed to remedy disadvantage, but, at least without radical reconceptualization, they are as surely incapable of eradicating the need for economic assistance or social accommodation of disability. And while particular preferential programs indeed may be designed to lead to their own termination, the conditions that give rise to the need for affirmative governmental remedies in general hardly seem transitory. Moreover, we might question whether it is really fair to characterize, as Barry does, cultural rights as permanent. Members of a particular religious or cultural group are likely to assert claims for exemptions or self-determination only so long as there are in place generally applicable laws that frustrate their aspirations. A view that conceptualizes religious and cultural group claims to special treatment as permanent does so only by assuming contrary status quo positions as an appropriate baseline.[35]

Likewise, Barry's characterization of socially-differentiated rights as universalistic, while deeming culturally-differentiated rights as particularistic, seems flawed. In what sense are rights that attach on the basis of race, gender,

---

[32] For discussion of the distinction between social and cultural categories, see *supra*, Chapter 4.

[33] See Barry, *Culture and Equality*, pp. 12–13, arguing that "special treatment for members of disadvantaged groups is justifiable only for as long as the inequality persists. We may say, therefore, that the objective of special treatment for members of disadvantaged groups is to make the need for that special treatment disappear as rapidly as possible . . . It is instructive to contrast this with the case made by multiculturalists for granting special rights to groups defined by their distinctive cultural attributes. This special rights will, according to their advocates, be needed permanently."

[34] Ibid., p. 13.

[35] C.f., Cass Sunstein, *The Partial Constitution* (Cambridge, Mass.: Harvard University Press, 1993), characterizing as error the assumption of the status quo as a neutral position in constitutional interpretation.

disability or economic status universalistic? Notice that Barry does not claim that such rights are "universal," because, of course, each of these rights remains dependent on a particular classification. In characterizing these non-cultural rights as "universalistic," then, Barry's point seems to be that, though these rights are afforded only to particular classes of persons, they nonetheless provide universally desirable benefits: "the beneficiaries are assumed to be people who want the same things as the rest of the population and simply lack the resources that would enable them to enjoy more of these things."[36] But notice how the universalistic nature of these desires depends in part upon the level of abstraction at which they are conceptualized. For instance, if we conceive of the desire of wheelchair-bound persons for unimpeded entry to a municipal building as a general claim for free accessibility, then the claim does seem universalistic. It is fair to assume that most people value accessibility. However, if we conceptualize the claim at a more narrow degree of abstraction—as a specific claim, say, for a ramp—then the claim loses its universalistic flavor. For we do not all strongly value the construction of ramps; indeed, one can imagine an (admittedly callous but not wholly unreasonable) objection on aesthetic grounds. To be clear, my point is not that we should conceptualize the claims of the disabled this narrowly, only that the universalistic character of the claim is more contingent than Barry lets on.

Now consider once again, at the other extreme, Barry's characterization of religious conduct exemptions. In conceptualizing claims for religious exemptions as particularistic—for example, as a highly particularized claim to wear a yarmulke or a turban—Barry has assumed a relatively lower level of abstraction. If, instead, as with the non-cultural group claims above, religious conduct exemptions were conceptualized as general claims to act freely, then such claims could lay claim to being "universalistic" as well. So what is it that justifies this more specific conceptualization for cultural practices, but the more general conceptualization for non-cultural aims? At least as between culturally and socially-differentiated rights, the forced move to a higher level of abstraction seems to be justified by nothing more than Barry's own perception of the rationality of particular positions.

In addition to distinguishing between cultural and social group-differentiated rights on the basis of the universal desirability of the benefits received, Barry also claims a critical distinction exists between the rights-claimants themselves in terms of their capacities to enjoy the benefits secured by such rights. In the absence of socially-differentiated rights, members of groups differentiated according to race, gender, disability, or economic status would "simply lack the resources" to take advantage of a free social life.[37] On the other hand, Barry maintains that cultural rights-claimants do not lack the capacity to enjoy the benefits afforded by the

[36] Barry, *Culture and Equality*, p. 116; see also ibid., p. 13: "'disadvantage' is defined in universal terms—as the lack of things (resources and opportunities) whose possession would generally be agreed to be advantageous."

[37] Ibid., p. 116.

rights they seek. Rather, the benefits are denied them on the basis of their own religiously or culturally based *preferences*.[38] Again, though, we need to be careful to discern precisely what it is that Barry is claiming here. Barry is not claiming that religious belief and cultural allegiance are merely matters of choice.[39] He does not, therefore, suggest that persons are wholly free to choose their own attachments and commitments. Barry does, however, equate *beliefs* with preferences for purposes of discerning the justifiability of cultural rights, and he does so specifically in light of the common distinction beliefs and preferences share as against choices.

Barry's argument is that since both beliefs and preferences (his example is a preference for vanilla ice cream) are "almost impossible to change," then "beliefs and preferences are in the same boat" vis-à-vis rights-claims.[40] Insofar as we would not afford a group-differentiated right merely on the basis that the members of a particular group "have a preference for vanilla over strawberry ice cream," we should also not afford a group-differentiated right on the basis of religious belief or cultural practice. Instead, when laws of general applicability place persons at a disadvantage in virtue of their religiously or culturally-based attachments, we are to view the disadvantage merely as a morally unregrettable "side-effect" of the law, no different, as a matter of justice, from, for example, the "much more severe impact [that laws against sexual violence have] on those who are strongly attracted to rape and paedophilia."[41] Indeed, according to Barry, the costs imposed on members of religious and cultural groups result not from the generally applicable laws that impinge upon their practices but from the practitioners' own "expensive tastes."[42] As such, general laws that have a differential impact on persons in virtue of their religious beliefs or cultural practices are, as a matter of justice, no more a cause of concern than are, say, general traffic laws that have a differential impact on persons in light of their preference for fast cars.[43]

Now, this is all, of course, just a bit too facile. The commonality that beliefs and preferences share in contradistinction with choices demonstrates no more (and no less) than that neither beliefs nor preferences are easily changed. But this relatively slim concurrence provides little traction on the serious issues presented by the claims of religious and cultural practitioners. The positive legal argument for the differential treatment of beliefs and preferences is that we do not, as a general matter, privilege personal preference in the form of constitutional rights, whereas the Constitution does privilege religious and associational freedom. Indeed, the Supreme Court in *Wisconsin v. Yoder* noted this distinction explicitly

---

38 Ibid., pp. 32–6.
39 See ibid., p. 35.
40 Ibid., p. 36.
41 Ibid., pp. 25, 34.
42 Ibid., p. 40.
43 See ibid., p. 34.

when it suggested that "the traditional way of life of the Amish is not a matter of personal preference, but one of deep religious conviction, shared by an organized group and intimately related to daily living."[44]

Moreover, at least part of the reason why we do, as a matter of positive constitutional law, privilege religious and associational freedom but not mere personal preference, is that beliefs and cultural attachments are critically distinguishable from preferences on a normative level as well. Religious beliefs and cultural commitments tend to constitute aspects of practitioners' identities and self-concepts in a far deeper sense than do (most) personal preferences. Of course, there is a personal dimension to individual identity; as discussed in a previous chapter, our preferences and desires partially determine the person we are.[45] At the same time, however, our beliefs and other cultural attachments serve as critical centers for a whole range of meaningfully constitutive aspects and life influences. To take up Barry's example again, an individual's preference for a particular flavor of ice cream is unlikely to constitute a meaningful aspect of that individual's identity, but that same individual's attachment to her native tribe is likely to play an enormous role in the constitution of her social identity and self-concept. The argument for or against culturally-differentiated rights cannot be made to turn, as Barry would have us believe, on a simple correlation between preferences and beliefs. By summarily dismissing religious and other cultural freedoms from the realm of liberal justice, Barry's position would radically curtail the self-inventive capacity of individuals in ways that matter greatly.

There is a final leg to Barry's universalist attack on cultural rights. He argues that one mark in favor of socially-differentiated rights is their assimilationist effect on otherwise socially marginalized individuals. "If such policies succeed," Barry writes, "they will tend to decrease social isolation and enable their beneficiaries to make the transition all the way into the mainstream society."[46] This is a valid claim; the inclusionary influence of socially-differentiated rights is indeed conducive to liberal purposes. But Barry's further contention, that this "assimilationist virtuous circle is in sharp contrast with the rationale of the kind of

---

44 *Wisconsin v. Yoder*, 406 U.S. 205, 216 (1972).

45 See the discussion on personal identity contained in the present volume at Chapter 4. For further discussion of the influence of personal beliefs and desires on human identity, see Joseph Raz, "Liberating Duties," *Ethics in the Public Domain: Essays in the Morality of Law and Politics*, rev. ed. (Oxford: Clarendon Press, 1994), p. 38: "That is why, on the whole, we identify with our desires and beliefs: what we are is partly determined by what they are." For a more general treatment of the collective and personal dimensions of human identity, see K. Anthony Appiah, "Identity, Authenticity and Survival: Multicultural Societies and Social Reproduction," in Amy Gutmann, ed., *Multiculturalism* (Princeton, NJ: Princeton University Press, 1994), p. 151. On the impact of social perceptions on self-understanding; see Charles Taylor's essay, "The Politics of Recognition," in the same volume.

46 Barry, *Culture and Equality*, p. 116.

group-based policies advocated by the theorists of multiculturalism,"[47] in practice often proves false. Exemptions such that Jews might wear yarmulkes in the armed forces, or so that Muslim school girls might wear a traditional chador in class, in effect rather clearly enable the integration of members of particular cultural groups into the broader fabric of social life.[48] If the integration made possible by socially-differentiated rights is considered valuable, then cultural rights with similar effects must, at least in this respect, be deemed conducive to liberal purposes as well.

In Barry's defense, the motivation behind his universalistic brand of liberalism is manifestly not to injure minority religious and cultural groups, but to moderate the sort of social conflict that did in fact injure minority religious and cultural groups in the pre-liberal past. "In fact," Barry claims his favored "model of citizenship was developed in response to the wars of religion that made much of Europe a living hell in the sixteenth and seventeenth centuries. If it could bring those conflicts to an end—and on the whole it did—it is not at all apparent why it should not be up to the task of coping with religious and cultural differences now."[49] Hence, complete relegation of religious and cultural group difference to private life, and with it, the acute depoliticization of cultural difference, is seen by Barry as the best way to ensure the continued existence of a public climate in which minority groups can endure.[50]

"In contrast," Barry claims, "the 'politics of difference' is a formula for manufacturing conflict, because it rewards the groups that can most effectively mobilize to make claims on the polity . . ."[51] And here Barry would seem to have a point, at least with respect to some of the more illiberal claims made by difference theorists. Take for example the rather extreme charge, asserted by certain of those who press for a politics of difference, that a lack of group proportionality in positions of high social status *automatically* entails injustice.[52] Now we need to be careful about what specifically this claim entails. This claim does not assert that group disproportionality in positions of high status might be an *indication* of discrimination and injustice. That claim Barry's liberalism clearly can accommodate.[53] This claim also does not assert merely that a program of affirmative action is required as a matter of justice. Again, Barry concedes the

---

[47] Ibid.

[48] See *Goldman v. Weinberger*, 475 U.S. 503 (1986), denying an exemption from military regulation prohibiting the wearing of religious symbols while on duty. In the now notorious *l'affaire du foulard*, Muslim school girls who sought to wear a traditional *chador*, or headscarf, in a public school outside of Paris were unsuccessful in obtaining an exemption. See Anna Galeotti, "Citizenship and Equality: The Place for Toleration," *Political Theory* 21 (1993).

[49] Barry, *Culture and Equality*, p. 21.

[50] See ibid., p. 325.

[51] Ibid., p. 21.

[52] See Young, *Justice and the Politics of Difference*, p. 29.

[53] See Barry, *Culture and Equality*, p. 93.

likelihood, and the legitimacy, of this prospect as well (while citing, on the other hand, Iris Marion Young's assertion that even "strong affirmative action" would provide an insufficient remedy).[54] Rather, difference theorists, following Young, press a conception of social justice commensurate only with a strict equality of outcomes, regardless of the cause for the inequality.[55] The question arises, though, whether different outcomes across cultural groups might be the result of cultural norms themselves, and, if so, whether this, without more, can reasonably be stated as an occasion of injustice.

In his critique of Young's demand for the imposition of strictly equal success rates across groups, Barry observes that there likely will be cultural group-based affinities that do not coincide with conventional conceptions of what constitutes a successful career or life-plan.[56] To appreciate Barry's point, imagine that a given individual's culture places great value in the intimate relationship that is said to exist between human beings and the land. It is not unimaginable, then, that a greater than representative proportion of persons from this particular cultural group might become involved in careers tied to the land, say as park rangers, landscape architects, environmental consultants, etc. What then is the appropriate response to the significantly smaller relative proportion of persons from this cultural group in, say, the medical profession? A disproportionately low number of persons from a particular group might be an indication of discrimination, and to the extent that it is discrimination on the basis of cultural group membership that is causing the imbalance, then, Barry claims, in accordance with liberal justice, the law should provide a remedy. Further, we may for a number of reasons decide that a program of affirmative action is required, perhaps on the basis of past discrimination or because it would be beneficial for members of this cultural group to see doctors within their cultural communities. To the extent that the imbalance in the medical profession is due to a lack of educational opportunities or other resources in the given community necessary to qualify for entrance, public policies should be addressed to remove these impediments. Finally, we might press for even more fundamental economic reforms, such that the lack of proportionality between professions will not result in highly disproportionate rates of income. All of this is potentially consistent with Barry's conception of justice.[57] "The egalitarian liberal position," says Barry, "is that justice requires equal rights and opportunities but not necessarily equal outcomes defined over groups."[58] What is beyond the scope of liberal justice, however, is that which the aspirations of difference theorists like

---

[54] Ibid., pp. 13, 94, citing Young, *Justice and the Politics of Difference*, p. 199.

[55] See Young, *Justice and the Politics of Difference*, p. 29.

[56] Barry, for instance, points again to the disproportionate number of Sikhs in Britain that cluster in the construction industry. See Barry, *Culture and Equality*, p. 98.

[57] See ibid., pp. 90–98, 108.

[58] Ibid., p. 92.

Young would apparently require: the imposition of "an identical distribution of achievement-motivations within each group."[59]

A second strikingly illiberal plank in the recent multiculturalist literature with which Barry takes special issue involves testing the limits of freedom of speech against cultural group-based sensitivities. This issue arose in the last decade particularly in light of the uproar caused by the publication of Salman Rushdie's novel, *The Satanic Verses*.[60] Bhikhu Parekh has argued that the right to freedom of speech has been justified only in light of the personal interests of intellectual elites (i.e., the writers themselves), and that free speech must instead be "balanced against . . . [the] self-respect and dignity of individuals and groups."[61] A related argument, pressed by Susan Mendus, maintains that because beliefs are essential to religious practitioners, "to undermine and despise their beliefs is simultaneously to undermine and despise their selves. Freedom of speech should be devoted to, and also limited by, the promotion of mutual understanding between different communities of believers."[62] With respect to both of these claims, however, we can readily concede that one's membership in a particular religious or cultural group may constitute a critical aspect of that individual's identity, while at the same time remaining extremely anxious over the extraordinary constraints on speech contemplated by these arguments. If countenanced, the group dignity argument could, in effect, provide a rationale for the curtailment of any speech critical of any religious or cultural practice. In response, Barry defends a broad right to freedom of speech specifically on the basis that criticism of group-oriented beliefs and practices is itself valuable. "The case against all this," he writes, "is that a society owes its members the opportunity—whether they choose to avail themselves of it or not—of changing their minds in matters of religious belief, and that this entails more than the absence of legal sanctions against apostasy."[63]

Thus, even while many of the distinctions he draws between culturally and socially-differentiated rights seem specious, Barry's response to liberalism's more

---

[59] Ibid., p. 95.

[60] See Salman Rushdie, *The Satanic Verses* (New York: Viking, 1989). For discussions of the political theoretical issues raised by the Rushdie affair, see especially the three volumes of papers delivered at seminars before the British Commission for Racial Equality, each of which was edited by Bhikhu Parekh, *Law, Blasphemy and the Multi-Faith Society* (1990), *Free Speech* (1990), and *Britain: a Plural Society* (1990). For a useful critical review of these works, see Peter Jones, "Rushdie, Race and Religion," *Political Studies* 38 (1990).

[61] Bhikhu Parekh, *Rethinking Multiculturalism: Cultural Diversity and Political Theory* (Cambridge, Mass.: Harvard University Press, 2000), p. 320. This argument is addressed in Barry, *Culture and Equality*, p. 30.

[62] Jones, "Rushdie, Race and Religion," p. 689. Note, however, that Jones was merely describing, rather than pressing, the argument advanced by Susan Mendus in "The Tigers of Wrath and the Horses of Instruction," in Bhikhu Parekh, ed., *Free Speech* (1990), pp. 3–17.

[63] Barry, *Culture and Equality*, p. 30.

extreme multicultural critics can be, at times, quite edifying. The essential question we are left with, however, is how to defend liberal justice against Barry's own formal egalitarianism.

Formal Equality and Constitutive Autonomy

The precept of formal justice that similar cases be treated similarly excludes certain forms of procedural injustice. But the precept, in itself, provides no assurance of substantive justice, for its application will of course turn on what we take to be relevant similarities and differences among persons. Formal justice is, in this sense, a formula in need of substantive principles. Formal equality, the notion that all persons, merely as such, should receive the same legal rights, is one such principle. This substantive perspective, as we have seen, constitutes the core of Barry's denunciation of multiculturalism, which in turn is grounded in his universalistic conception of justice. While noting below the continuing significance of formal equality to any assessment of group-differentiated rights, I shall suggest that we do better, from the perspective of liberal justice, by asking whether differentiated rights threaten to impede individual constitutive autonomy.

Whereas formal equality, as a substantive conception of justice, proves ultimately too thin, recourse to egalitarian formalism surely has served to promote justice in a number of important contexts. In the United States, for example, the invalidation of formal legal distinctions founded upon the basis of race, gender, national origin and similar categories, has been accomplished, in large part, through appeals to the criticality of universal human qualities. In this sense, the universalist teaching of the fundamentally equal worth of human beings *qua* human beings is indeed capable of preventing significant harm. As counterpoint, recall Taney's framing of the issue for decision in *Dred Scott*. In that case, Taney asked whether the descendants of persons brought to this country as slaves might ever be entitled to political membership and, hence, constitutional rights.[64] The universalistic conception of justice, mandating formally equal rights, would, of course, require that the issue be answered affirmatively. Taney, however, concluded that the rights granted under the U.S. Constitution need not be afforded to "that unfortunate race . . . so far inferior, that they had no rights which the white man was bound to respect."[65]

In one of the first casebooks to focus exclusively on the role of race in American law, Derrick Bell pronounced *Dred Scott* "the most frequently overturned decision" in American constitutional history.[66] To the extent that the

---

64 See *Dred Scott v. Sandford*, 60 U.S. (19 How.) 393, 403 (1856).

65 Ibid. at 407.

66 Derrick A. Bell, *Race, Racism and American Law* (Boston: Little Brown, 1973), p. 21.

decision established the constitutionality of the institution of slavery, it was explicitly overruled by the Thirteenth Amendment to the U.S. Constitution.[67] To the extent that the decision legitimized the exclusion of persons of African descent from holding citizenship, it was overturned three years later by the first clause of the Fourteenth Amendment.[68] And to the extent that the decision excluded African-Americans more generally from bearing rights, it was formally reversed by a series of Reconstruction legislation. As Donald Fehrenbacher described it:

> Blacks were expressly guaranteed equal rights before the law and placed on a level of equality with white persons in regard to contracts, litigation, property-holding, inheritance, and access to facilities used by the public (such as railroads, inns, and theaters). In more indirect language, blacks were also made eligible to vote and participate in jury service on the same terms as white persons; their privileges and immunities as citizens of the United States were protected against impairment by state governments . . . the Reconstruction program constituted a blueprint for a social revolution of truly remarkable proportions.[69]

Less fortunately, much of this blueprint for formal equality was wiped clean in the latter part of the nineteenth century as the Supreme Court consistently upheld legislation that continued to exclude and segregate African-Americans.[70] Indeed, the broader range of invidious racial distinctions was not finally curtailed until the school desegregation cases and the civil rights acts of the latter half of the twentieth century.[71] Yet, though they were late in coming, these and other similar measures proscribing most racial distinctions in the law demonstrate that the universalist's aspiration toward formal equality can indeed result in the elimination of significant instances of injustice and substantial practical hardships.

At the same time, however, the inegalitarian nature of the distribution of rights and benefits that results from such formal distinctions is not the only, and, I would argue, not the most significant, moral cost imposed by such differentiated social policy. Individuals of African descent were not simply denied equal civil and political rights. Rather, because these rights legally vest in "citizens" and "persons" merely as such, their denial refuted the citizenship and even the

---

[67] See U.S. Const. amend XIII: "Neither slavery nor involuntary servitude, except as a punishment for crime whereof the party shall have been duly convicted, shall exist within the United States, or any place subject to their jurisdiction."

[68] See U.S. Const. amend XIV, sec. 1, cl.1: "All persons born or naturalized in the United States, and subject to the jurisdiction thereof, are citizens of the United States and of the State wherein they reside."

[69] Don E. Fehrenbacher, *The Dred Scott Case: Its Significance in American Law and Politics* (New York: Oxford University Press, 1978), p. 581.

[70] See, most famously, *Plessy v. Ferguson*, 163 U.S. 537 (1896).

[71] See *Brown v. Board of Education*, 349 U.S. 483 (1954); Civil Rights Act of 1964; Voting Rights Act of 1965.

humanity of such individuals. And while the legal construction of a class of individuals as "non-persons" is surely at one extreme, exclusion from legal rights on the basis of race, gender, religion and similar categories approached, until recently, a veritable norm in American public law.[72]

In an insightful analysis of the nature of inequality, Thomas Scanlon delves beneath such instances of discrimination, arguing that among the most telling objections to this sort of unequal treatment is the perpetuation of stigmatizing differences in social and political status. "One possible reason for objecting to these differences," Scanlon writes, "would be the belief that it is an evil for people to be treated as inferior, or made to feel inferior. Social practices conferring privileges of rank or requiring expressions of deference are objectionable on this ground, for example."[73] Scanlon thus conceptualizes objections to discriminatory treatment, in contrast to Barry's overly facile emphasis on formal equality, in virtue of the striking stigmatic effect and experiential harm caused by such discrimination. Yet, though an unquestionable improvement on Barry's analysis, Scanlon continues to interpret objections to stigmatization as grounded purely in egalitarianism.[74] This seems a mistake, however, for stigmatization, in addition to raising egalitarian concerns, also imposes on its victims a critical moral cost in constitutive autonomy.

Categorical denials of citizenship, and, even more so, the basic humanity of classes of persons, certainly represent deplorable instances of formal and substantive inequality, but the exclusions themselves have been grounded ultimately in much deeper constitutive assumptions regarding the inherent worth or capacities of those denied rights. Individuals historically disqualified from the right to vote, for instance, were not excluded simply on account of their membership in a particular racial, gender or religious group; the exclusions were justified on the basis of presumptions that members of such groups would not possess the moral, civic and intellectual characteristics required of the electorate. Consider, as well, laws of relatively (indeed, shockingly) recent vintage that excluded women from service in the American jury system.[75] Clearly, such a distinction in the law imposes a moral cost by treating similarly situated persons unequally. Again, however, inequality is not the sole moral harm associated with this differential treatment. The law in distinguishing among persons for jury

---

[72] See Rogers M. Smith, *Civic Ideals: Conflicting Visions of Citizenship in U.S. History* (New Haven, Conn.: Yale University Press, 1997).

[73] T.M. Scanlon, "The Diversity of Objections to Inequality," The Lindley Lecture, University of Kansas (1996), p. 3. A reprint of this lecture is available from the Department of Philosophy at the University of Kansas.

[74] At different points, Scanlon describes objections to stigmatization as one of "the clearest expressions of egalitarianism," as "clearly egalitarian," "more truly egalitarian," and even the "most purely egalitarian" objection to inequality. Ibid., pp. 2–6.

[75] In fact, state laws to this effect were not finally deemed unconstitutional until 1975. See *Taylor v. Louisiana*, 419 U.S. 22 (1975).

service on the basis of gender also expresses constitutive misconceptions regarding women *vis-à-vis* men; namely, that jury service demands virtuous traits which men possess but women do not. Once again, social perceptions, and with them aspects of the individual identities of men and women, may be constituted according to legal distinctions rather than constructed autonomously. The categorical exclusion of women from this civic function, like the categorical exclusions from constitutional rights discussed above, is surely violative of egalitarian norms, but the exclusion also imposes a critical moral cost in self-invention.

The universalist notion that all persons, merely as such, should receive the same rights has indeed performed significant work in promoting substantive justice in a number of contexts. In each of the above contexts, however, the alternative to formal equality would have been the perpetuation of a legally constructed second-class form of citizenship. Within the contexts so far considered, the worst that can be said of the universalist perspective is that its excessive focus on the loss differentiation inflicts in formal equality caused it to miss an even greater loss in constitutive autonomy. Yet, since that constitutive loss was *accompanied* by an instance of formal inequality, closing the inegalitarian breach functioned also as a check on the involuntary legal construction of persons. This easy correlation between formal equality and constitutive autonomy does not survive other contexts, however.

To appreciate why this is so, recall the treatment offered by Barry of religious liberty in light of the substantive principle of formal equality. According to the universalist perspective, the legal accommodation of a particular religious practice is not required as a matter of justice where that practice is incapable of garnering universal assent. Hence, where a generally applicable law mandates that helmets be worn while riding a motorcycle, the universalist would deny that an exemption for Sikh men, such that they might continue to wear turbans, would be required as a matter of justice. Yet note here the moral cost that, in the context of religious free exercise, *formal equality imposes*: in each such case the constitutive autonomy of religious practitioners is curtailed. Conduct exemptions permit members of cultural groups to differentiate themselves, and in the process autonomously to construct cultural identities. In the context of the exclusion of women from jury service considered above, the violation of formal equality was attended by a loss in self-invention. Yet in the context of a minority cultural group seeking accommodation of a particular religious practice, it is the decision to uphold formal equality that begets the constitutive loss. By focusing so intently on formal equality as the predominant criterion of just social policy, the universalist position simultaneously precludes an important source of self-invention.

Differentiated rights thus often arise in circumstances of cultural pluralism where the congenial association we witnessed between formal equality and constitutive autonomy quickly collapses. Yet, neither is the correlation of these principles a simple switch that may be turned either on or off; indeed, the relationship between formal equality and constitutive autonomy can be irreducibly contingent. Consider differentiated rights designed to remedy the effects of previous legal or other social exclusionary practices on a particular social group. Where, for example, a right of affirmative action is afforded exclusively to the members of a subordinated social group, the departure from formal equality is blatant and purposive, and the legal differentiation is usually justified with reference to notions of substantive equality. Such rights acknowledge that members of groups subject to oppression are differently situated, and so must at times be treated differently in order to be treated equally. But here too the loss in formal equality is not the only moral cost at issue. For this legal categorization too, though clearly an effort to improve the situation of subordinated persons, results in the further legal construction of a social group.

Scanlon similarly, though he continues to conceptualize the values at stake purely in terms of equality, to the exclusion of self-inventive autonomy, notes the prospect of a moral trade-off attending to such efforts: "Overcoming [discrimination] may represent a gain in fairness, but there may be no decrease, and perhaps even an increase, in objectionable consequences of [stigmatization]."[76] Just as in the exclusionary jury classification described above, individual bearers of affirmative rights are defined in part by law as members of a particular social category. And yet just as in the context of a cultural or religious group seeking accommodation of a particular group practice, the imposition of formal equality over affirmative rights would deny oppressed persons the capacity for a more equal and autonomous life. Indeed, as described in the next chapter, what may ultimately distinguish this circumstance of social differentiation from the exclusionary and cultural contexts considered above is the extent to which the apparent loss of constitutive autonomy exacted by socially-differentiated rights may in fact place rights-bearers in a position further to invent themselves in other social spheres.

Formal inequality is a moral cost of differentiated citizenship policy, but it is rarely the only or the most crucial consideration. Where a category of persons is subordinated by the law, the requirement of formal equality may be instrumental in securing to such persons the capacity for self-invention. Where a religious or other cultural group seeks accommodation of an unpopular practice, however, the imposition of formal equality might sacrifice that same capacity. And where social policy offers special assistance to oppressed persons, the cost in formal equality may be accompanied by a loss of self-invention in a particular sphere but a gain in that value overall. The universalist's adoration of formal equality above all else fails to capture the complex moral calculus inherent in group-differentiated policy. Moreover, it ignores the sense in which that calculus remains fundamentally dependent upon social context. A meaningful assessment of group-differentiated rights from a liberal perspective requires a careful balance of moral values, with particular attention to the potential for individual constitutive autonomy. Further,

---

[76] Scanlon, "The Diversity of Objections to Inequality," p. 14.

such an assessment must be attuned to the particular circumstances within which claims for differentiated treatment may be said to arise. It is to these matters that we now turn.

Chapter 7

Three Models of Group-Differentiated Rights

Rights, we have seen, distribute membership. In accordance with the precept of formal justice, rights-claimants are included or excluded on the basis of investitive conditions reflective of the substantive commitments of the legal system at issue. But not all inclusions, and not all exclusions, are alike. Consider, for example, the following three types of rights: (a) a right granted to persons generally, except married women, to own real property; (b) a right, granted to persons who share a particular trait that has served previously as the basis for discriminatory exclusion, to a preference in the competition for college admissions; and (c) a right granted to persons of a particular religious faith not to send their children to public school despite a generally applicable law mandating that they do so. As we have seen, all three rights will result in the further construction of social groups that inform aspects of their individual members' social identities. But the first group is constructed in virtue of a decision within a legal system to exclude a particular class of persons on the basis of an ascribed characteristic; the second group is constructed affirmatively to include a particular class of persons on the basis of an ascriptive characteristic previously deemed relevant; and the third group is composed of a class of individuals granted the freedom to exclude themselves from an otherwise quite ordinary aspect of social life.

In this final chapter, then, I want to propose three models, broadly consistent with the examples just mentioned, of the process by which social and cultural groups and identities are constructed by law. The models should prove useful both in further describing the nature of group-differentiated rights and in assessing the extent to which such rights are consistent with a liberal conception of membership. My contention will be that the group-differentiated form of right imperils the capacity of persons for self-invention, but that the extent of any such loss is contingent upon the particular model invoked.

The Constitution of Social Groups: Ascriptive Exclusion

We have noticed that any right granted will of necessity be granted to a class of persons. Rights-claimants able to demonstrate sufficient congruity between their own particular circumstances and the criteria indicated by a right's investitive conditions will be *included* in a class of rights-bearers. Rights-claimants who fail to meet such investitive criteria, and so are deemed in some important respect dissimilar from those entitled to exercise the right, are thereby *excluded* from the class. Where the interest protected by a right is of critical importance, inclusion in or exclusion from the class of rights-bearers may dramatically affect a rights-claimant's social identity. Moreover, where the dissimilarity between the classes of persons included and excluded from the right is founded upon an ascribed characteristic (e.g., a moral or intellectual trait associated with the right-claimant's race or gender), both the inclusion and the exclusion will result in the construction of social groups characterized according to the particular capacity or incapacity involved. Membership in such an ascriptive social group will contribute both to social and self-perceptions of any individual member's identity.

Consider, for example, the evolution of the class of persons granted the right to vote in the United States. The U.S. Constitution, perhaps surprisingly, nowhere affirmatively defines investitive conditions for the right to vote in national elections. Instead, reflective of a broader federalist tendency in this sphere, general qualifications for voting rights are determined in accordance with state law. Thus, American suffrage at the founding remained conditioned on state imposed landed property qualifications, usually combined with specific legal exclusions for persons who were not free, white, male and often also adherents of a particular religion; that is, for persons who were not "freeholders." The Commonwealth of Virginia, for example, "specifically denied the suffrage to free blacks, mulattos, Native Americans, women, minors, and all non-Protestants, with Catholics expressly banned."[1] Each such categorical exclusion from the right to vote was justified on the basis of inegalitarian assumptions regarding the excluded persons' race, culture, gender, religion or economic status. Persons who fell within these categories, it was thought, could not possibly possess the moral, civic and intellectual traits required to fulfill the critical function of the electorate. As a result, each such person was, by law, ascriptively excluded from the class of political membership in the United States. At the same time, persons thus ascriptively excluded were simultaneously included in a social group (or groups) constructed according to the characteristic (race, gender, etc.) which served as the basis for the assumed incapacity. And membership in each such social group, together with its inegalitarian ascriptive subtext, would thus come to define an aspect of each individual member's particular identity.

On the opposite side of this rights equation, the categorical inclusion of freeholders was justified on the basis of similarly inegalitarian, though now more sanguine, ascriptive assumptions regarding the intellectual and moral capacities and civic propensities of persons who were free, white, male, landed, and of the right religion to serve as the population's political class. Membership in this social

---

[1] Rogers M. Smith, *Civic Ideals: Conflicting Visions of Citizenship in U.S. History* (New Haven, Conn.: Yale University Press, 1997), p. 58.

group, composed of full "citizens," together with its inegalitarian but now positive ascriptive subtext, would come then to constitute an aspect of each individual *citizen's* identity.[2]

Indeed, not only the legal system's political membership but also in a broader sense its constitutional (some might say moral) membership has been constituted according to comparable ascriptive inclusionary and exclusionary decisions. With the exception of a very few rights for which one indeed must be a "citizen," the U.S. Constitution invokes only a single investitive criterion: to exercise most constitutional rights one merely must be a "person."[3] Hence, the exclusion of classes of individuals from this most general sphere of membership carries with it even more radical constitutive consequences. And yet categories of human beings throughout the nation's history have been deemed "non-persons" for constitutional purposes. The most notorious such instance, of course, occurred in the *Dred Scott* case—the decision, you will recall from our discussion above, in which Chief Justice Taney distorted a seemingly technical question of diversity jurisdiction in order to justify the institution of slavery itself.[4] In consequence of the Court's decision in *Dred Scott*, all individuals of African descent were ascriptively excluded from the class of "persons" deemed competent to bear rights.[5]

So too have members of numerous other social categories been excluded from constitutional rights on the basis of ascriptive presumptions. Individuals with disabilities, for example, were long subject to ascriptive classification as non-persons for constitutional purposes.[6] In the *Insular Cases*, the Supreme Court

---

[2] For a detailed analysis of the inegalitarian ascriptive tradition in American citizenship laws, see ibid.

[3] Compare, e.g., U.S. Const., art.II, sec.1, cl.5, limiting eligibility for the office of President to citizens, and amend. XV, affording the right to vote to citizens, with amend. XIV, affording equal protection and due process to persons, and amend. I, affording general rights to freedom of speech and religion. While First Amendment freedoms are not afforded explicitly to persons, that is the most natural inference from the text.

[4] See *Dred Scott v. Sandford*, 60 U.S. (19 How.) 393 (1856); Alexander M. Bickel, *The Morality of Consent* (New Haven, Conn.: Yale University Press, 1975), pp. 36–7: "A majority of the Supreme Court seized on the concept of citizenship in the *Dred Scott* case, in a futile and misguided effort, by way of a legalism and an unfounded legalism at that, to resolve the controversy over the spread of slavery."

[5] See *Dred Scott*, 60 U.S. at 409, asking "whether the general terms used in the Constitution of the United States, as to the rights of man and the rights of the people, was intended to include [slaves], or to give them or their posterity the benefit of any of its provisions."

[6] See Martha Minow, *Making All the Difference: Inclusion, Exclusion, and American Law* (Ithaca, NY: Cornell University Press, 1990), pp. 101–20; see also *Buck v. Bell*, 274 U.S. 200 (1927); *City of Cleburne v. Cleburne Living Center*, 473 U.S. 432 (1985), granting equal protection rights to the mentally disabled, though confirming that other constitutional rights may be withheld.

notoriously affirmed the power of Congress to govern the inhabitants of "unincorporated territories," such as Puerto Rico, Guam and the Philippines, without according to such persons constitutional protections.[7] Congressional discretion was required, said the Court, for fear that otherwise citizenship would vest in territorial residents "absolutely unfit" to exercise such rights.[8] More generally, while resident aliens, as a class, technically have been deemed the bearers of rights afforded constitutional persons since the late nineteenth century,[9] the continued refusal of the Supreme Court in light of the plenary power doctrine to exercise meaningful judicial review over immigration decisions has engendered a morally ambiguous distinction between the status of non-citizens at the border and those who happen already to be located inside the country.[10] Each of these exclusions, based upon inegalitarian ascriptive assumptions, has had grievous effects on the social and self-conceptions of the members of the groups involved.[11]

---

[7] The designation *Insular Cases* refers to a series of cases decided in 1901 in which the U.S. Supreme Court determined the constitutional status of the territories acquired by the U.S. as a result of the Spanish-American War and the 1898 Treaty of Paris. See *De Lima v. Bidwell*, 182 U.S. 1 (1901); *Goetze v. United States*, 182 U.S. 221 (1901); *Grossman v. United States*, 182 U.S. 221 (1901); *Dooley v. United States* 182 U.S. 222 (1901); *Armstrong v. United States*, 182 U.S. 243 (1901); *Downes v. Bidwell*, 182 U.S. 244 (1901); *Huus v. New York and Porto Rico Steamship Company*, 182 U.S. 392 (1901); *Dooley v. United States*, 183 U.S. 151 (1901); *Fourteen Diamond Rings v. United States*, 183 U.S. 176 (1901).

[8] See *Downes*, 182 U.S. at 306. While a form of U.S. citizenship was conferred upon the residents of Puerto Rico by the Jones Act of 1917, they nonetheless continued to be excluded from voting and other constitutional rights held by full U.S. citizens. See, e.g., *Balzac v. Porto Rico*, 258 U.S. 298 (1922), denying the constitutional right to a jury trial. For helpful general treatments of the constitutive influence of the *Insular Cases* and their progeny, see Efren Rivera Ramos, *The Legal Construction of Identity: The Judicial and Social Legacy of American Colonialism in Puerto Rico* (Washington, D.C: American Psychological Association, 2001); Smith, *Civic Ideals*, pp. 429–39.

[9] See *Yick Wo v. Hopkins*, 118 U.S. 356 (1886), deeming resident aliens constitutional persons entitled to rights of equal protection; *Wong Wing v. United States*, 163 U.S. 228 (1896), deeming Fifth Amendment Due Process Clause applicable to aliens.

[10] See T. Alexander Aleinikoff, "Detaining Plenary Power: The Meaning and Impact of Zadvydas v. Davis," *Georgetown Immigration Law Journal* 16 (2002), p. 366. Moreover, even while both aliens present in the U.S. and U.S. citizens may be deemed "persons" for purposes of receiving due process protection, the substance of due process protections afforded aliens and citizens may differ. See, e.g., *United States v. Ju Toy*, 198 U.S. 253 (1905), holding that for aliens who have not acquired residence, the decision of an administrative officer constitutes due process.

[11] See, e.g., Ian Haney Lopez, *White By Law: The Legal Construction of Race* (New York: New York University Press, 1996); Smith, *Civic Ideals*; David M. Engel and Frank W. Munger, *Rights of Inclusion: Law and Identity in the Life Stories of Americans with Disabilities* (Chicago: University of Chicago Press, 2003); Ramos, *The Legal Construction*

It should be noted, however, that the paradigm of ascription in the law is not itself necessarily illiberal. At least when viewed in an instrumental sense, ascriptive norms might also foster liberal membership. That is, where emphasis is placed not on involuntary human characteristics which sustain exclusionary practices but on the ascription of universalistic and egalitarian human traits that support inclusionary aspirations, liberal goals may be served rather than frustrated. For illustration we might return to the evolution of the class of persons granted political membership in the United States, where more recent developments seem to have been shaped by just such egalitarian ascriptive inclinations. Although state law ostensibly retains the dominant role in defining the investitive conditions for the electorate, through a progressive series of amendments the U.S. Constitution has made the right to vote more inclusive by gradually proscribing barriers to the franchise. With each such amendment—the Fifteenth (1870), eliminating race as an investitive criterion; the Nineteenth (1920), eliminating sex as a barrier; the Twenty-Fourth (1964), eliminating economic obstacles; and the Twenty-Sixth (1971), extending the franchise to eighteen-year olds—inegalitarian ascriptive categories have been unraveled, and the sphere of political membership expanded.[12] Along similar lines, the Supreme Court's decision that racially segregated educational institutions violate the Equal Protection Clause was grounded in the conviction that segregation is unjust because it inherently signals inferiority.[13] These illustrations are emblematic of a broader expansion in our civic and constitutional membership that has occurred specifically in light of the notion, ascribed to all citizens, that all human beings are of fundamentally equal worth.

We have so far been discussing exclusively American public law, but the same ascriptive process has been reflected in private law, in the form either of specific statutorily prescribed legal disabilities or common law incapacity or incompetency doctrine. As described by Martha Minow, "The law grants rights of autonomy and self-determination to most but devises special rules for those whom the legal system deems incapable of exercising these qualities."[14] For example, alongside rules restricting the legal capacity of "infants" and the "insane" to enter into enforceable agreements, we have seen that "married women" were in most states similarly deemed incompetent to contract or to be in legal possession of property. In this sense, the law reflected the strikingly inegalitarian, ascriptive notion that a

of Identity. These recent analyses of the constitutive effects of ascriptive exclusions bring to mind DuBois's century old insight into the "strange meaning of being black" in America: "It is a peculiar sensation, this double-consciousness, this sense of always looking at one's self through the eyes of others, of measuring one's soul by the tape of a world that looks on in amused contempt and pity." W.E.B. Dubois, *The Souls of Black Folk* (1903) (New York: Penguin, 1989), p. 5.

12 See U.S. Const. amend. XV, XIX, XXIV and XXVI.

13 See *Brown v. Board of Education*, 349 U.S. 483 (1954).

14 Minow, *Making All the Difference*, pp. 126–7.

woman would cease to possess a separable identity upon marriage.[15] Indeed, the constitutive effects of the incapacity doctrine in Anglo-American private law have been quite wide-ranging. At various times legal rules have classified sailors, Jews, Quakers, the disabled, lepers, aliens, prisoners, excommunicates, and many other categories of persons, as legally incompetent for a wide variety of purposes.[16] Most of these illiberal distinctions, of course, have since been invalidated. But even arguably progressive reforms, such as the Married Women's Property Acts which granted women the right to own and transfer property, continued in various respects to reflect inegalitarian ascriptive notions. Indeed the first such act, enacted in Mississippi in 1839, was intended primarily to guarantee the authority of women over slaves.[17] And state laws excluding women from service on juries were not finally deemed unconstitutional until as recently as 1975.[18]

Just as in the sphere of political membership discussed above, however, more progressively egalitarian ascriptive stories increasingly have served inclusionary ends in the private arena as well. This is particularly apparent in the sort of logically general right commonly enacted to protect particular categories of persons from discrimination. Typically, such rights list a series of human characteristics proscribed as the basis for the denial of certain opportunities or services, for example in access to employment or housing.[19] The rights are logically general, in that the characteristics listed apply in some respect to all persons; everyone, that is, is considered to have a, or to be a member of some,

---

[15] See ibid., p. 128.

[16] See W.S. Holdsworth, *History of English Law*, Vol. 9 (London: Methuen, 1966), pp. 3–4, 91–9, cited in Minow, *Making All the Difference*, p. 127.

[17] Smith, *Civic Ideals,* p. 233.

[18] See *Taylor v. Louisiana*, 419 U.S. 22 (1975). See also Akhil Reed Amar, *The Bill of Rights: Creation and Reconstruction* (New Haven, Conn.: Yale University Press, 1998), p. 274, suggesting that the Nineteenth Amendment be interpreted as having conferred on women a right to jury service.

[19] This is true both of federal and state civil rights and antidiscrimination law. See, e.g., 42 U.S.C. §2000e, outlawing discrimination in employment. Consider, for illustration, Maryland's Antidiscrimination Act: "It is unlawful for an owner or operator of a place of public accommodation or an agent or employee of the owner or operator, because of the race, creed, sex, age, color, national origin, marital status, sexual orientation or disability of any person, to refuse, withhold from, or deny to such person any of the accommodations, advantages, facilities and privileges of such place of public accommodation." 2001 Md. Chap. 340. This is also true of current Supreme Court practice with respect to constitutional equal protection. The Fourteenth Amendment's Equal Protection Clause is even more logically general than most civil rights legislation, since the Clause does not provide even a list of characteristics which should trigger scrutiny. Nonetheless, the Court's current interpretive practice incorporates heightened degrees of scrutiny for certain "suspect classifications," such as race, nationality and gender. For the classic defense of this practice, see John Hart Ely, *Democracy and Distrust: A Theory of Judicial Review* (Cambridge, Mass.: Harvard University Press, 1980).

gender, race, nationality, sexual orientation, ethnicity, etc. Of course, such rights against discrimination on the basis of group membership clearly are enacted primarily to ensure the fair and equal treatment of the individual members of subordinated social groups, the individuals most likely to suffer discrimination. But in so doing, logically general legal rights against discrimination express inclusionary ascriptive norms. Women, African-Americans, homosexuals, etc., may not be excluded on the basis of those differentiating characteristics, but instead are ascribed egalitarian, universalistic human traits mandating equal treatment in the provision of services and opportunities.[20]

The denial of personal liberties and opportunities to categories of individuals on the basis of ascriptive characteristics resembles, and indeed to some extent perpetuates, ancient and feudal forms of differentiated citizenship.[21] And yet we have seen this same tendency toward ascriptive exclusion articulated historically through American public and private law. Liberal membership requires genuine equality of treatment and broad deference to individual agency in the construction of one's self. Individuals must, to the greatest extent possible, remain free to define and rationally to revise their own identities consistent with their own sense of virtue and their own freely chosen attachments. Where universalistic, egalitarian ascriptive accounts are invoked as part of an effort more broadly to include persons as rights-bearers, liberal membership, at least instrumentally, is served. In each of the rights-exclusion cases described above, however, individuals were sorted and aspects of human identity defined by law on the basis of inegalitarian, socially ascribed criteria. Whether distinctions are drawn on the basis of gender or race, ethnicity or alienage, economic or marital status, or indeed by virtue of any characteristic that serves to distinguish classes of persons, the construction of social groups and human identities by ascriptive exclusion is inconsistent with a liberal conception of membership.

Moreover, while the inegalitarian norms that served to legitimize the ascriptive exclusionary form of group-differentiated right have largely been rejected within contemporary liberal democratic legal systems, there remain a number of areas in which ascriptive exclusion persists. I shall mention two prominent such instances here. In the first, the Supreme Court recently affirmed the exclusion of children from citizenship on the basis of an arguably unwarranted assumption regarding parenting and gender; the second, involving the rights of gay and lesbian couples to marry, promises to be among the most contentious legal and political issues of the early twenty-first century.

---

[20] It remains true, of course, that even such broadly inclusive rights nevertheless exclude categories of persons. At the very least, persons outside the particular legal system remain unprotected.

[21] See Robert W. Gordon, "Critical Legal Histories," *Stanford Law Review* 36 (1984); see also the essays collected in Virginia Hunter and Jonathan Edmondson, eds., *Law and Social Status in Classical Athens* (Oxford: Oxford University Press, 2000).

Title III of the Immigration and Naturalization Act is one of the few remaining sections of the federal code in which rights are vested on the basis of an explicit gender classification.[22] Section 1409 of the Act sets forth the conditions under which out-of-wedlock foreign-born children with one American parent will be granted citizenship. If a child is born outside the U.S., and her unwed *mother* is an American citizen, the child is automatically entitled to citizenship so long as the mother, at any point in her life, resided in the U.S. for a minimum of one year. An unwed *father* who is an American citizen, however, may not pass on citizenship to his child in the same way. Rather, several additional conditions must be met, including documentation of the father's express agreement to support the child financially until the child reaches the age of eighteen.[23] Section 1409 was recently challenged on equal protection grounds, and affirmed by the Supreme Court, in *Nguyen v. INS*.[24] The Court deemed the gender-based distinction substantially related to the important governmental goal of ensuring a meaningful parent-child relationship.[25] In consequence, children born to American fathers may continue to be excluded from citizenship on the basis of an ascriptive presumption that mothers are more likely than fathers to develop meaningful bonds with, and so be willing financially to support, their children.

The Supreme Court's recent, broadly drawn, decision in *Lawrence v. Texas* striking down state anti-sodomy laws as a violation of substantive due process, arguably has placed the Court on a collision course with the issue of same-sex marriage.[26] Several western democratic countries, including France, Denmark, Iceland, Germany, Portugal, Finland, Sweden and Norway, have recently established parallel institutions to marriage for same-sex couples.[27] In the United States, with somewhat varying effects, California now recognizes same-sex domestic partnerships, Hawaii recognizes reciprocal beneficiaries, and Vermont recognizes civil unions.[28] Same-sex *marriage* itself, however, as of this writing, is recognized only in the Netherlands, Belgium, Canada, and, most recently,

---

[22] Immigration and Nationality Act §309, 8 U.S.C. §1409 (2000 & Supp. 2003); see also *Miller v. Albright*, 523 U.S. 420, 461 (1998) (Ginsburg, J., dissenting).

[23] 8 U.S.C. §1409(a).

[24] *Nguyen v. INS*, 121 S.Ct. 2053 (2001).

[25] Ibid. at 2061.

[26] See *Lawrence v. Texas*, 539 U.S. 2472, 2498 (2003) (Scalia J., dissenting): "Today's opinion dismantles the structure of constitutional law that has permitted a distinction to be made between heterosexual and homosexual unions, insofar as formal recognition in marriage is concerned."

[27] See William N. Eskridge, Jr., *Equality Practice: Civil Unions and the Future of Gay Rights* (New York: Routledge, 2002), p. 116; Yuval Merin, *Equality for Same-sex Couples: The Legal Recognition of Gay Partnerships in Europe and the United States* (Chicago: University of Chicago Press, 2002), pp. 238–9.

[28] Eskridge, *Equality Practice*, p. 234.

Massachusetts.[29] In the section below, I treat state efforts to afford governmental recognition and benefits to same-sex couples, short of marriage, as group-differentiated forms of affirmative rights. Notice here, though, that such differential treatment is only necessary in light of the inegalitarian ascriptive exclusion of same-sex couples from the right to marry. "Same-sex couples," William Eskridge has argued, "who are acknowledged to form similar commitments and families, get another institution that is presented as marriage without the name."[30] But names, or social labels, can matter; they can signify status and define social identity. This exclusion, and the exclusion of children from citizenship on a parent gender-differentiated basis, demonstrates the formal persistence in modern American law of a second-class form of citizenship violative of liberal membership.[31]

The structural and constitutive aspects of ascriptive group-differentiated rights described above are also instructive in assessing the two other forms of group-differentiated rights that compose this chapter. Rights that seek specially to affirm the status of individual group members, and rights that would enable members of particular cultural groups to self-exclude, share with ascriptive rights a formal resemblance and an influence upon their claimants' social identities. And yet, in each case, the cost imposed in terms of the principles which define a liberal conception of membership is importantly different.

---

[29] See *Goodridge v. Department of Public Health*, 2003 Mass. Lexis 814 (Supreme Judicial Court of Mass., November 18, 2003), holding that Massachusetts law precludes denial of "the protections, benefits, and obligations conferred by civil marriage to two individuals of the same sex who wish to marry." Most recently, in response to a legislative inquiry regarding the constitutionality of civil unions, the Massachusetts Supreme Judicial Court further clarified its holding in *Goodridge*, explaining its conclusion that the Commonwealth's marriage licensing law, to the extent it failed to extend the status of civil marriage to same-sex couples, violated the Constitution of the Commonwealth of Massachusetts. See Opinions of the Justices to the Senate, SJC-09163, Massachusetts Supreme Judicial Court (February 3, 2004). On same-sex marriage in Canada, see *Halpern v. Toronto*, 2003 WL 34950 (Ontario Ct. App., 2003), holding that the existing common-law definition of marriage as a union between a man and a woman violates equality rights on basis of sexual orientation under Canadian Charter of Rights and Freedoms. On same-sex marriage in the Netherlands and Belgium, see Eskridge, *Equality Practice*, pp. ix, 116.

[30] Ibid., p. 133.

[31] For an argument against same-sex marriage, grounded in a traditional conception of the marital relationship as inherently heterosexual, see Robert P. George, *The Clash of Orthodoxies: Law, Religion, and Morality in Crisis* (Wilmington, Del.: ISI Books, 2001), pp. 75–89.

The Constitution of Social Groups: Affirmation

We have seen that every positive rights-inclusion begets a rights-exclusion. That is, a certain class of rights-claimants will be described by a right's investitive criteria, and so be included as rights-bearers, whereas all other rights-claimants not so described will be excluded from the right. We have further noticed that, where the decision to exclude is sustained on the basis of an ascribed characteristic, this process will constitute at least two social groups, membership in which will constitute an aspect of each individual member's social identity. At times, however, a right will be granted only to a particular subset of persons specifically in an attempt to reverse the inegalitarian consequence of a previous ascriptive exclusion, or to remedy the exclusionary effect of social practices other than law itself. And yet even this effort, an effort ultimately to include otherwise subordinated persons, will of necessity result in the legal system excluding a category of persons.

Although formally similar, this type of legal exclusion is of a substantively different nature than the ascriptive exclusionary process discussed above. The exclusion of a dominant class from a right granted to oppressed persons may be justified not on the basis of negative inegalitarian characteristics ascribed to the excluded class, but rather on the ground that the particular remedy afforded the included class will be conducive to genuine equality of treatment for all. In such a case, the exclusion may function affirmatively to include a category of persons in need of special protection.[32]

The modifier "affirmative" used to describe the effect of this form of right will bring immediately to mind disputes over the legitimacy of "affirmative action." These include the well-known disputes concerning preferential treatment for underrepresented categories of persons in, for example, college admissions, employment, or government contracting. And, indeed, a right to affirmative action, on the basis of, say, past or continuing racial discrimination, clearly would fall within this category.[33] As with the logically general rights against discriminatory treatment discussed above, rights to affirmative action might be justified on the basis of ascriptive inclusionary narratives regarding the fundamentally equal worth of all human beings. Yet unlike those general rights, rights to preferential treatment lack universalizable investitive criteria. That is, rights to affirmative action are granted only to a particular subset of persons,

---

[32] See, e.g., Justice Ginsburg's comments in dissent in *Gratz v. Bollinger*, 123 S. Ct. 2411, 2444 (2003) (Ginsburg, J., dissenting): "In implementing this [constitutional] equality instruction, as I see it, government decisionmakers may properly distinguish between policies of exclusion and inclusion . . . Actions designed to burden groups long denied full citizenship stature are not sensibly ranked with measures taken to hasten the day when entrenched discrimination and its after effects have been extirpated."

[33] See, e.g., *Grutter v. Bollinger*, 123 S. Ct. 2325 (2003).

namely those persons subject to prior inequitable treatment. That legal classification thus results in the construction of a social group the defining characteristic of which will be the particular trait which serves as the basis for the differentiation, whether it be race (as, e.g., in the case of African-Americans), nationality (e.g., Native Americans) or indeed any other characteristic that might serve to distinguish classes of persons. Further, each rights-bearer's membership in such a group will constitute an aspect of that individual member's social identity, both in terms of the (racial, national, etc.) categorization itself and the associated social and personal cognizance of subordination and, more hopefully, the progressive movement the remedy represents toward a more egalitarian norm.

Notice, then, that just as in the ascriptive exclusionary cases discussed above, rights to affirmative action sacrifice not only formal equality of treatment but also, potentially, individual constitutive autonomy. Individual affirmative rights-claimants are sorted, and defined, by law as members of particular social groups. Considered in isolation, this constitutive perspective, perhaps more than any other, has the potential to undermine the project of affirmative action. For it reveals a deep sense in which such differentiated policy may harm the very people it is designed to support.[34] The idea is that individuals who fall within the class described by such rights, including those who pre-right would have qualified even absent a preference, will be perceived post-right as substandard. Indeed, the notion that affirmative action programs may exacerbate already dangerous social stigmas is increasingly acknowledged as a potential moral harm by proponents and detractors of preferential policies alike. This concern led Supreme Court Justice Clarence Thomas in one case to claim that such "programs stamp minorities with a badge of inferiority," and in another that "because of this policy all [blacks] are tarred as undeserving."[35] Glenn Loury has similarly noted: "One such reason for questioning the wisdom of affirmative action is that the widespread use of preferences can logically be expected to erode the perception of black competence."[36] Ronald Dworkin has raised the same issue,[37] as have the authors

---

[34] See Amy Gutmann's analysis in "How Affirmative Action Can (and Cannot) Work Well," Robert Post and Michael Rogin, eds., in *Race and Representation: Affirmative Action* (New York: Zone Books, 1998).

[35] *Adarand Construction, Inc. v. Pena*, 515 U.S. 200, 241 (1995) (Thomas, J., concurring); *Grutter*, 123 S. Ct. at 2362 (Thomas J., dissenting); see also *Richmond v. J.A. Croson Co.*, 488 U.S. 469, 493 (1989): "Classifications based on race carry a danger of stigmatic harm. Unless they are strictly reserved for remedial settings, they may in fact promote notions of racial inferiority . . ."; *Regents of the University of California v. Bakke*, 438 U.S. 265, 298 (1978): "preferential programs may only reinforce common stereotypes holding that certain groups are unable to achieve success without special protection."

[36] Glenn C. Loury, "How to Mend Affirmative Action," *The Public Interest* (Spring, 1997), p. 38; see also Charles Murray, "Affirmative Racism," in Nicolaus Mills, ed., *Debating Affirmative Action: Race, Gender, Ethnicity, and the Politics of Inclusion* 207 (New York: Delta, 1994), p. 207, suggesting that "the evil of preferential treatment [is that

of *The Shape of the River*, the most comprehensive empirical study of affirmative action policies in higher education to date: "The very existence of a process that gives explicit consideration to race can raise questions about the true abilities of even the most talented minority students ('stigmatize' them, some would say)."[38]

Yet, while even empirical studies friendly to preferences have demonstrated the "all too real" nature of the stigmatic costs associated with such rights,[39] there is also evidence that affirmative inclusion of underrepresented minorities engenders conditions in which associated stigmas may be broken down.[40] That is, increasing interaction across social groups, and exposing members of dominant groups to the diversity of viewpoints within subordinated groups, may help to diminish stereotypes.[41] Moreover, even conceding the probability that programs that privilege minorities may, in the process, perpetuate negative stereotypes does not necessarily condemn such programs. The bare existence of a policy cost does not entail abandonment of the policy. It merely, at least where the cost is a serious one, mandates a shift in the weighing of the critical interests at stake.

Differentiated rights to affirmative action, to the extent that they signify their bearers as inferior, present the prospect of a substantial loss in constitutive autonomy. Such rights partially construct the individuals they benefit, and any calculus of affirmative action that fails to take account of this moral cost would be seriously remiss. But these rights also only arise in virtue of a more pervasive, long-standing series of legal and social constructions of their beneficiaries. To assess affirmative rights without considering the historically contingent nature of such rights is to mistake cause for effect, and racial consciousness for racism.[42] The real point of such rights is to afford the members of long subordinated groups the same opportunities and liberties enjoyed by members of more dominant social

---

it] perpetuates the impression of inferiority."

[37] See Ronald Dworkin, *Sovereign Virtue: The Theory and Practice of Equality* (Cambridge, Mass.: Harvard University Press, 2000), p. 389: "Does affirmative action do more harm than good, because it enrolls some blacks in studies beyond their capacities, or stigmatizes all blacks as inferior, or makes the community more rather than less conscious of race?"

[38] William G. Bowen and Derek Bok, *The Shape of the River: Long-Term Consequences of Considering Race in College and University Admissions* (Princeton, NJ: Princeton University Press, 1998), pp. 264–5.

[39] Ibid., p. 265.

[40] See the evidence discussed in *Grutter*, 123 S. Ct. at 2334.

[41] See ibid., pp. 2339–40, suggesting that "the Law School's [preferential] admissions policy promotes 'cross-racial understanding,' helps to break down racial stereotypes, and 'enables [students] to better understand persons of different races.'"

[42] Along these lines, Stephen Carter has commented: "To pretend . . . that the issue presented in *Bakke* was the same as the issue presented in *Brown* is to pretend that history never happened and that the present doesn't exist." Stephen Carter, "When Victims Happen to be Black," *Yale Law Journal* 97 (1988), pp. 433–4.

groups.[43] Hence, the sacrifice that preferential treatment entails in formal equality *may* be warranted by a gain in substantive equality. And the loss in constitutive autonomy *may* be at least partially offset, as beneficiaries gain the capacity further to invent themselves in other spheres. Ultimately, any reasoned assessment of affirmative action must proceed on a case-by-case basis. We cannot say, as a general matter, that every affirmative action program warrants the cost; the resolution will depend always upon the particular circumstances at issue.[44]

While the notion of affirmative inclusion is perhaps most obviously evident in the context of rights to affirmative action, this model of constitutive right is apparent in a number of other contexts as well. Above we considered the exclusion of gay and lesbian couples from the right to marry.[45] With legally constituted marriage comes a broad series of legal rights and entitlements not afforded unmarried couples, from visitation, evidentiary and decisional privileges to the receipt of governmental benefits to standing to bring suit in the event of injury to one's spouse.[46] Recognizing that, in terms of commitment and significance to the individuals involved, gay and lesbian relationships stand on an equal-footing with heterosexual relationships, individual states have initiated efforts to remedy the practical effects of the exclusion of homosexual couples from the right to marry.[47]

Among the most far-reaching of these state laws is the Vermont Civil Unions and Reciprocal Beneficiaries Law, which, in an effort to protect the interests of gay and lesbian couples, constitutes a new form of legal relationship, the "civil union."[48] The law grants to individuals who choose to form such a union rights to all the legal benefits to which married couples are entitled. Yet the right to form a civil union is itself limited exclusively to couples "of the same sex."[49] Marriage

---

43 See K. Anthony Appiah and Amy Gutmann, *Color Conscious: The Political Morality of Race* (Princeton, NJ: Princeton University Press, 1996), p. 131, arguing that the "strongest argument for preferential treatment from the perspective of anyone committed to justice as fairness is that it paves the way for a society in which fair equality of opportunity is a reality rather than merely an abstract promise." See also Will Kymlicka, *Multicultural Citizenship: A Liberal Theory of Minority Rights* (Oxford: Clarendon Press, 1995), pp. 67–8, suggesting that: "Demands for affirmative action within the mainstream economy are evidence of a desire to integrate into the institutions of the larger society . . ."

44 Indeed, the Court referenced the importance of context in *Grutter*, see 123 S. Ct. at 2338: "Context matters when reviewing race-based governmental action under the Equal Protection Clause."

45 See *supra*, this chapter.

46 For an illustrative list of legal rights and benefits afforded legally married couples in the District of Columbia, see William N. Eskridge, Jr., *The Case for Same-sex Marriage: From Sexual Liberty to Civilized Commitment* (New York: Free Press, 1996), pp. 66–7.

47 See Eskridge, *Equality Practice*, p. 234.

48 15 Verm. Stat. Ann. §1201.

49 15 Verm. Stat. Ann. §1201(4).

retains its traditional definition under the Act as "the legally recognized union of one man and one woman."[50] Hence, while the purpose of the legislative right is affirmatively to include gays and lesbians as members in the broader category of civil rights-bearers, the distinction drawn between civil unions and traditional marriages nevertheless perpetuates the legal, as opposed to autonomous, construction of dual social groups and identities. Arguably analogous to the separate but formally equal treatment afforded African-Americans in the nineteenth century, state laws that create differentiated institutions for gay and lesbian couples signify the inferiority of the individuals involved in those relationships.[51] While these differentiated rights concededly provide critical practical benefits, unlike with rights to affirmative action, the same benefits could be made available even absent the differentiation.[52]

Certain rights that proscribe discriminatory treatment also take differentiated form in an effort affirmatively to include subordinated persons. The Americans with Disabilities Act, as we have seen, mandates that employers and providers of services to the public alter business practices reasonably to accommodate disabled persons.[53] The accommodation might be as simple as providing signs in Braille, or ramp access to a building. Alternatively, the law might require an employer to re-assign a disabled worker to a position compatible with that worker's disability, or force a reluctant provider of health services to treat an HIV-infected patient.[54] Clearly, such rights are intended affirmatively to integrate individuals with disabilities more comprehensively into social life. The aim, as Martha Minow has articulated it, is to "invent other practices that treat difference as just the variety of human experience, rather than the basis for dividing people into the class of the normal and the abnormal."[55]

Yet, affirmative inclusionary solutions founded in law tend to perpetuate rather than to eliminate such distinctions. Rights under the Disabilities Act are granted exclusively to "disabled" persons, or persons who exhibit a "physical or mental impairment that substantially limits one or more of the major life activities of such individual."[56] Hence, the individual with a visual impairment, the individual who

---

[50] 15 Verm. Stat. Ann. §1202(2). Compare the Netherlands' Act on the Opening Up of Marriage, Staatsblad van het Koninkrijk der Nederlanden, 2001, nr. 9 (11 January), Article 30(1): "A marriage can be contracted by two persons of different sex or of the same sex."

[51] Eskridge, *Equality Practice*, pp. 134–5; see *Plessy v. Ferguson*, 163 U.S. 537 (1896).

[52] For an argument that official recognition of same-sex marriage, in virtue of law's educative function, will undermine the institution of marriage, see George, *The Clash of Orthodoxies*, pp. 86–7.

[53] 42 U.S.C. §12182; see also the Age Discrimination in Employment Act, 29 U.S.C. §623.

[54] See *Bragdon v. Abbott*, 118 S.Ct. 2196 (1998).

[55] Minow, *Making All the Difference*, p. 94.

[56] 42 U.S.C. §12102(2)(A).

seeks reasonable accommodation of a psychiatric condition, the pre-symptomatic HIV-infected dental patient, and any number of other persons who make claims under the Act, will only be successful to the extent that they fall, together, within the investitive criteria indicated above. That is, they will only be considered rights-bearers to the extent that they can be legally classified, and thus collectively be defined, as "disabled."[57]

As above, however, the bare fact that an individual will be defined in part by law does not in itself suggest that a group-differentiated right is necessarily inconsistent with a liberal conception of membership. That determination will depend on whether the moral cost in constitutive autonomy is sufficiently offset by the advantage inclusion brings. As an initial matter, as with rights to affirmative action considered above, the right itself may be conducive to genuine equality of opportunity. Additionally, in granting persons defined as disabled such opportunities, the right might afford individuals the freedom more fully to construct their own identities in other spheres. Consider, in this regard, a fictional person. Call him Herbert. Imagine that Herbert has contracted an illness and on that basis has been discriminated against in the provision of services and employment. Post-right, Herbert, partially in virtue of a legal construction, may be perceived as a "disabled" person, but he may now also be perceived as a disabled person employed as an airline mechanic who is able to take clarinet lessons and visit a lodge in the Adirondack mountains. In other words, it is only one aspect of Herbert's identity that has been involuntarily constructed, and that involuntary construction may prove instrumental in Herbert's further self-invention.

There are other prominent examples of rights that categorize in an effort affirmatively to incorporate a category of persons more extensively into the broader community's social life.[58] But rights such as these are and generally should be rare. In part, this is because of the need pursuant to formal justice to justify any such differential treatment. In part also, however, this is because any such right constricts autonomous self-construction. Any right granted exclusively to a particular class of persons will constitute a social group, the central

---

[57] For a valuable empirical study of the constitutive effects of the Americans with Disabilities Act on the social identities of disabled persons, see Engel and Munger, *Rights of Inclusion*.

[58] Special minority cultural and social group representation rights are an important example. On the representation of cultural groups, see Chandran Kukathas, "Are There Any Cultural Rights?," *Political Theory* 20 (1992); Kymlicka, *Multicultural Citizenship*, pp. 131–51. For a discussion of representation rights in the context of subordinated social groups, see Iris Marion Young, *Justice and the Politics of Difference* (Princeton, NJ: Princeton University Press, 1990), pp. 183–91, and *Inclusion and Democracy* (Oxford: Oxford University Press, 2000), pp. 121–53; Anne Phillips, *The Politics of Presence: Issues in Democracy and Group Representation* (Oxford: Clarendon Press, 1995); Melissa S. Williams, *Voice, Trust, and Memory: Marginalized Groups and the Failings of Liberal Representation* (Princeton, NJ: Princeton University Press, 1998).

characteristic of which will define an aspect of each individual member's identity. Yet while rare, while in need of critical justification, and while inherently constitutive, such rights are often among the most crucial to liberal justice. Through the exclusion of most others, this type of group-differentiated right aspires to protect subordinated persons. Hence, although any such right will in a formal sense treat persons unequally, this formal inequality may be necessary in light of social conditions to ensure genuine equality of opportunity. Moreover, although any such group-differentiated right will inherently come to define an aspect of its rights-bearer's identity, that particular loss in self-invention may be more than offset by a gain in constitutive autonomy more generally. In that sense, rights which seek affirmatively to include members of subordinated groups often will be conducive to liberal membership.

The Constitution of Cultural Groups: Self-Exclusion

In contrast both to rights that ascriptively constitute individuals as members of social groups, and rights that seek affirmatively to include persons on the basis of their group-membership, are rights that permit individual members of groups, or the groups themselves in a collective capacity, the freedom to exclude themselves from some aspect of social life. Typically, rights such as these are claimed by members of ethnic, national or other types of cultural groups seeking recognition or accommodation of group practices or identities.[59] Unlike ascriptive and affirmative rights, such culturally-differentiated rights often directly foster constitutive autonomy by enabling cultural group members to construct their own particular social identities in contrast to broader social groups. Yet cultural rights may also facilitate the intra-group repression of more vulnerable individuals and sub-groupings within cultural groups, and where this is the case the moral costs apparent in the ascriptive differentiated citizenship model are merely revived at a different level.[60]

---

[59] For a helpful typology of cultural rights, see Jacob T. Levy, "Classifying Cultural Rights," in Ian Shapiro and Will Kymlicka, eds., *NOMOS XXXIX Ethnicity and Group Rights* (New York: New York University Press, 1997), pp. 22–66.

[60] One might also conceptualize the family as the most basic cultural group, in the sense that families develop particular practices and strongly enculturate beliefs and values. For an argument to this effect, see Nomi Maya Stolzenberg, "A Tale of Two Villages," in *Ethnicity and Group Rights*, p. 314. Rights to family privacy, which in essence signify rights of parents to control the upbringing of their children, might then also be construed as group-differentiated rights that enable cultural self-exclusion. See, e.g., *Meyer v. Nebraska*, 262 U.S. 390 (1923); *Pierce v. Society of Sisters*, 268 U.S. 510 (1925). And, as with other cultural rights, rights to family privacy might also enable intra-group oppression of more vulnerable members. See, e.g., Susan Moller Okin, *Justice, Gender, and the Family* (New York: Basic Books, 1989), describing the risk that family privacy creates for women and

In the United States, religious conduct exemptions constitute perhaps the most prominent example of this form of group-differentiated right. The need for such exemptions is said to arise because generally applicable laws at times conflict with the obligations of a particular religious group. Where this is the case, religious practitioners face an intractable choice between obeying the dictates of the law or the dictates of their conscience. For this reason, beginning in the early 1960s, and continuing for approximately three decades, religious practitioners in the U.S. could seek judicially fashioned exemption rights as a potential remedy, at least where the governmental interest represented by the general law did not outweigh the practitioners' interest in freely practicing their religion.[61] In *Wisconsin v. Yoder*, for example, the Supreme Court overturned the convictions of Amish parents who had been prosecuted for refusing to send their children to school beyond the eighth grade, as required by a purportedly neutral state compulsory attendance law.[62] The Court in *Yoder* accepted the argument made by the Amish parents that their children's continued attendance in school was contrary to their way of life and that this way of life was itself integrally related to Amish religious beliefs. The Amish parents were thus granted an exclusive right to an exemption from a generally applicable law on the basis of their religious group membership. They were granted, in effect, the freedom further to exclude themselves from the broader stratum of American society.

In its 1990 decision in *Employment Division v. Smith*, the Supreme Court reversed course, essentially precluding judicially fashioned religious conduct exemptions of the type granted in *Yoder*.[63] At the same time, however, the *Smith*

children, and Anne C. Dailey, "Constitutional Privacy and the Just Family," *Tulane Law Review* 67 (1993), depicting law's role in the formation of family life and the ensuing conflict between personal and familial autonomy. This work describes the family as an agent of socialization in Chapter 3, and explores the legal construction of the family above in the treatment of same-sex marriage, and below in the analysis of exemptions from generally applicable laws mandating public school attendance.

61 See, e.g., *Sherbert v. Verner*, 374 U.S. 398 (1963), granting an exemption from an unemployment compensation law requirement that applicants must be available to work on Saturdays, in contravention of religious practices; *Goldman v. Weinberger*, 475 U.S. 503 (1986), denying an exemption from military regulation prohibiting the wearing of religious symbols while on duty.

62 *Wisconsin v. Yoder*, 406 U.S. 205 (1972).

63 See *Employment Division v. Smith*, 494 U.S. 872 (1990). In *Smith*, two members of a Native American tribe sought an exemption from a generally applicable criminal statute proscribing the use of peyote. The two individuals had been discharged from their jobs, and were denied unemployment compensation, based on their having violated the statute. The Court not only rejected this particular claim for an exemption, but also the prospect of any judicially created free exercise exemption right. Rather than explicitly overrule their opinion in *Yoder*, however, the Supreme Court in *Smith* somewhat speciously attempted to distinguish the *Yoder* exemption as a "hybrid" right protecting not only a religious free

decision explicitly countenanced legislatively produced exemptions, and indeed the number of legislative exemptions granted to particular religious groups has greatly exceeded the pace at which the judiciary ever approved religiously based exemption rights.[64] This trend reflects recent accommodationist policies in virtually all western liberal democratic states. Sikh men, for example, have successfully sought exemptions on religious grounds in Great Britain and Canada so that they may continue to wear turbans despite generally applicable laws mandating hard hats in the construction industry and motorcycle helmets on the public highways.[65] Similarly, religious Jews and Muslims have been granted exemptions in nearly all western countries from generally applicable legislation regulating the slaughtering of animals.[66]

Religious conduct exemptions vest in individuals specifically in virtue of their membership in a particular group. The social differentiation drawn between the minority cultural group and the dominant culture enables cultural group members further to construct their particular identities. Indeed, constitutive self-exclusion operates on a collective level as well. For example, communally asserted land or water use rights, and rights to collective self-determination, similarly enable cultural (usually internal national) groups to self-exclude and self-define.[67] To be sure, many culturally-differentiated rights in effect permit members of minority cultural groups to participate more fully in the social life of the dominant culture. One of the religious conduct exemptions indicated above, for instance, was sought by a Sikh male specifically so that he could *join* the Royal Canadian Mounted

---

exercise interest but also a parental substantive due process interest in directing the education of their children. 494 U.S. at 881.

[64] Even at the height of its purportedly accommodationist period the Supreme Court actually ruled in favor of persons seeking religious exemptions in only a small number of cases. See John E. Nowak and Ronald D. Rotunda, *Constitutional Law*, 6th ed. (St. Paul, Minn.: West, 2000), p. 1377. For discussions of Amish efforts to achieve exemptions through the political process, see Brian Barry, *Culture and Equality: An Egalitarian Critique of Multiculturalism* (Cambridge, Mass.: Harvard University Press, 2001), pp. 179–81, and the essays collected in Donald B. Kraybill, *The Amish and the State* (Baltimore, Md.: John Hopkins University Press, 1993).

[65] See Bhikhu Parekh, *Rethinking Multiculturalism: Cultural Diversity and Political Theory* (Cambridge, Mass.: Harvard University Press, 2000), pp. 243–8. Similar exemptions have been granted to accommodate the traditional Sikh practice of wearing a *kirpan*, or short sword, in public. See Barry, *Culture and Equality*, p. 51.

[66] Ibid., p. 41. Muslim school girls who sought to wear a traditional *chador*, or headscarf, in a public school outside of Paris were less successful in obtaining an exemption. See Anna Galeotti, "Citizenship and Equality: The Place for Toleration," *Political Theory* 21 (1993).

[67] On collective rights to land, see Allen Buchanan, "The Role of Collective Rights in the Theory of Indigenous Peoples' Rights," *Transnational Law and Contemporary Problems* 3 (1993). On collective rights to self-government, see Avishai Margalit and Joseph Raz, "National Self-Determination," *Journal of Philosophy* 87 (1990).

Police.[68] Yet alongside this vital integrationist aspect, exemption rights permit individuals to detach themselves from most others, and in the process to constitute further their particular cultural identities. The same may be said of other rights that take culture as the basis for their differential treatment. For example, language rights (to multilingual ballots, schools, court interpreters) permit speakers of minority languages to participate more fully in, and hence to become more fully integrated into, the dominant societal culture.[69] Yet language rights serve also to accommodate the preservation and further construction of particular cultures and cultural identities, particularly those of internal national minorities.[70]

A dilemma, though, arises when the collective constitutive autonomy secured by culturally-differentiated rights is used by elites or majorities within minority cultural groups to subordinate more vulnerable members. For example, the accommodation claim at issue in *Yoder* may be viewed as subordinating the interests of Amish children in receiving a general education to the cultural claims of their parents and their religious group.[71] More directly, at times the *nomos* or traditional precepts of certain cultures—the precepts for which members may seek accommodation rights—explicitly prescribe repression of individual members and internal sub-groupings, most particularly women. State accommodation thus serves at times to perpetuate already existing power hierarchies and, with them, intra-group repression. "[H]ow" then, as Ayelet Shachar has asked, "do we protect group members from routine violations of their citizenship rights, when those violations arise from the traditional practices of the group which we have already sanctioned through accommodation?"[72]

In her treatment of the problem of multicultural vulnerability, Shachar suggests that two primary theoretical responses, both of which serve also as a source for a dominant legal approach, have been proposed to solve this dilemma. The first, labeled by Shachar the "re-universalized citizenship" response, maintains that where the good of a particular individual and that of her cultural group conflict, the state must privilege the interests of the individual even if the result is a radical

---

68 Parekh, *Rethinking Multiculturalism*, p. 244.

69 See, e.g., the essays collected in Will Kymlicka and Alan Patten, *Language Rights and Political Theory* (Oxford: Oxford University Press, 2003).

70 In the American context, I have in mind here particularly Native Americans, including Alaskans. See Kymlicka, *Multicultural Citizenship*, pp. 79–80.

71 See, e.g., Kent Greenawalt, "Freedom of Association and Religious Association," in Amy Gutmann, ed., *Freedom of Association* (Princeton, NJ: Princeton University Press, 1998), p. 124; Richard Arneson and Ian Shapiro, "Democratic Autonomy and Religious Freedom: A Critique of *Wisconsin v. Yoder*," in Ian Shapiro and Russel Hardin, eds., *NOMOS XXXVIII: Political Order* (New York: New York University Press, 1996). Refusals on religious or other cultural grounds of medical treatment by parents on behalf of their children raise similar issues. See, e.g., Barry, *Culture and Equality*, p. 303.

72 Ayelet Shachar, *Multicultural Jurisdictions: Cultural Differences and Women's Rights* (Cambridge: Cambridge University Press, 2001), p. 3.

severance of the individual from her culture.[73] Derivative of this first theoretical response, the "secular absolutist" legal model declines to accommodate the traditional practices of cultural groups, electing instead to preserve full state authority over, and so protection of, group members.[74] In strong contrast, the theoretical response termed "unavoidable costs" by Shachar contends that the multicultural state must be severely constrained from intervening between a cultural group and its members, even given pervasive individual rights violations.[75] This second response, then, provides the underlying theoretical basis for the "religious particularist" legal model, which (predictably) grants far more extensive authority to cultural groups to pursue traditional beliefs and practices.[76]

Now, of course, these positions are essentially re-labeled reiterations of, on the one hand, pre-multicultural, universalistic liberalism, and, on the other, the toleration perspective on liberal multiculturalism.[77] Nevertheless, Shachar's insightful criticism of certain aspects of the leading proponents' theories is worthy of attention. For example, Shachar seems clearly right in suggesting that Susan Moller Okin's sweeping view that multiculturalism is necessarily degrading to women fails to account for potential female agency, and so too radically discounts the prospect of cultural change in virtue of that agency.[78] Similarly, Shachar demonstrates that Kukathas's position rests on some arguably dubious assumptions: first, because while he relies heavily on individual freedom of association to justify multicultural accommodation, most cultural group members join at birth rather than as a result of any explicit consensual act; and second, because while cultural membership may as a matter of justice entail recognition and accommodation, so too might membership in other social identity (e.g., gender) groups.[79]

---

[73] See ibid., pp. 65–8. For an illustration of this response, see Barry, *Culture & Equality*.

[74] See Shachar, *Multicultural Jurisdictions*, pp. 72–8.

[75] Ibid., pp. 68–70. For an illustration of this response, see Kukathas, "Are There Any Cultural Rights?"; and Chandran Kukathas, "Cultural Toleration," in Ian Shapiro and Will Kymlicka, eds., *NOMOS XXXIX: Ethnicity and Group Rights* (New York: New York University Press, 1997).

[76] See Shachar, *Multicultural Jurisdictions*, pp. 78–85.

[77] See the discussion of universalistic liberalism above in Chapter 6, and the depiction of liberal multicultural theorists who privilege toleration or diversity above in Chapter 5. Shachar's own theory, I contend below, is essentially a working out of the autonomy perspective on liberal multiculturalism, also discussed in this work at Chapter 5, and proposed, most prominently, by Will Kymlicka. See Kymlicka, *Multicultural Citizenship*.

[78] For Shachar's critique of Okin, see *Multicultural Jurisdictions*, p. 66. For Okin's views, see Susan Moller Okin, "Is Multiculturalism Bad for Women?," *Boston Review* 22 (1997).

[79] Shachar's critique of Kukathas appears in *Multicultural Jurisdictions*, p. 70.

Though she does not mention it in connection with her analysis of these two radically divergent theoretical responses, Shachar is also critical of a third, more moderate, response to the problem of multicultural vulnerability. This third theoretical response—labeled at one point by Shachar as "weak multiculturalism"[80]—is in fact none other than the autonomy perspective on liberal multiculturalism, described above, and conveyed most prominently by Will Kymlicka.[81] Yet, Shachar's critique of Kymlicka's theoretical approach is strange indeed, for Shachar's own prescriptive legal model appears to be grounded in Kymlicka's liberal multicultural theory.

Recall that Kymlicka's theory of multicultural accommodation calls for equality between cultural groups, in the form of "external protections," but rejects claims pressed by cultural groups that would violate individual members' general rights, on the ground that such "internal restrictions" are inconsistent with liberal autonomy.[82] Most claims for exemption rights (excluding those that harm children), and for rights to the use of particular languages or natural resources, fall within the former category. The sorts of claims that fall within the latter category range from constraints on internal criticism of group customs to practices involving physical mutilation.[83] Shachar contests Kymlicka's "too simple distinction between 'external' and 'internal' aspects of accommodation" on two grounds.[84] First, Shachar challenges the "viability" of the distinction itself, arguing that the powers afforded to cultural groups in the name of external protections might also be used by the group to impose internal restrictions.[85] Second, Shachar claims that Kymlicka's approach, grounded as it is in liberal autonomy, is self-defeating, insofar as it advocates the extension of external protections notwithstanding potential restrictions on individual freedom.[86] But Shachar's critique of Kymlicka is misleading on both counts. Kymlicka's theory clearly does account for the possibility that "external protections can open the door to internal restrictions."[87]

---

80 Ibid., p. 29.

81 See *supra*, Chapter 5; Kymlicka, *Multicultural Citizenship*.

82 Ibid., pp. 35–44.

83 See Amy Gutmann, "The Challenge of Multiculturalism in Political Ethics," *Philosophy and Public Affairs* 22 (1993).

84 Shachar, *Multicultural Jurisdictions*, p. 42.

85 See ibid., p. 30.

86 Kymlicka's model, Shachar says, "contradicts its own central tenet when it advocates accommodation even in cases where putting legal authority in the hands of the identity group means exposing certain group members to routine in-group violations of their individual citizenship rights." Ibid., p. 29.

87 Kymlicka, *Multicultural Citizenship*, p. 43; see also ibid., p. 40, acknowledging the possibility that "polyethnic rights [might] be used to impose internal restrictions"; and ibid., p. 42: "This distinction between internal restrictions and external protections . . . is not always easy to draw. Measures designed to provide external protections often have implications for the liberty of members within the community."

More importantly, Kymlicka is manifestly hostile to the prospect of accommodative policy serving as cover for intra-group rights violations.[88]

Yet, while Shachar has not demonstrated that Kymlicka's theory is misguided, she may indeed have revealed a sense in which his approach is incomplete. For while Kymlicka is clearly sensitive to the relationship between external protections and internal restrictions, he has not, to date, offered a *means* to detach cultural accommodation from intra-group repression. Indeed, the most sensible reading of the approach adopted by Shachar may be as an institutional working out of Kymlicka's autonomy perspective on multicultural accommodation. Both Shachar's concern for the vulnerability of particular categories of individuals, and her insight that state protection of cultural groups might exacerbate unjust restrictions on the liberty of individual members, are already manifest in Kymlicka's work. Hence, despite Shachar's, at times peculiar, efforts to distance and distinguish herself from Kymlicka, it does seem as if Kymlicka supplies the theoretical response to the problem of multicultural vulnerability that serves to underlie Shachar's own innovative legal model.

Shachar critiques the two dominant responses to the problem of multicultural vulnerability for imposing upon cultural group members an unfortunate and unnecessary ultimatum. Under either approach, it's "either your culture or your rights":

> Both approaches offer a misguided 'either/or' resolution to the paradox of multicultural vulnerability. Both require that women and other potentially at-risk group members make a choice between their rights as citizens or their group identities. But this amounts to a choice of penalties . . . Neither the 're-universalized citizenship' option nor the 'unavoidable costs' approach has satisfactory answers to offer women and other members who legitimately wish to preserve *both* their cultural identities *and* to challenge the power relations encoded within their minority groups' traditions.[89]

In order, then, to transcend an ultimately insufferable choice between one's culture and one's freedom from cultural oppression—and so to permit vulnerable individuals to continue to find meaning in their group memberships while

---

[88] See ibid., p. 153, arguing that internal restrictions "are inconsistent with any system of minority rights that appeals to individual freedom or personal autonomy." Indeed, in an interesting exchange with Shachar, Kymlicka makes this point clear: "It's clear that the capacity to impose internal restrictions is inextricably bound up with the acquisition of external protections, and so we need to analyse them together. However, my claim is that the goal, from a liberal point of view, is (a) to ensure that groups have the external protections they need, while (b) creating the institutional safeguards which prevent groups from imposing internal restrictions." Will Kymlicka, "Comments on Shachar and Spinner-Halev: An Update from the Multiculturalism Wars," in Christian Joppke and Steven Lukes, eds., *Multicultural Questions* (Oxford: Oxford University Press, 1999), p. 127 n.7.

[89] Shachar, *Multicultural Jurisdictions*, p. 71.

simultaneously maintaining access to their general rights—Shachar suggests we must take an institutionalist turn. We must reexamine our assumptions with respect to jurisdiction itself, or the legal-institutional doctrine delineating public decisional authority. Contrary to the preconceptions underlying the currently dominant legal and theoretical paradigms, it is not the case, says Shachar, that cultural group members must be subject solely to one source of legitimate authority, either the state or the group. Indeed, "in today's day and age, no single authority can expect to be the sole source of legal norms and institutions affecting its members."[90] Instead, Shachar contends, the only practicable solution to the paradox of multicultural vulnerability lies in a scheme of *joint* governance.

A joint governance approach is grounded in what Shachar terms a "'cultural' understanding of institutions."[91] The approach recognizes that individuals may concurrently belong to, and so derive rights and obligations from, multiple communities. It thus seeks a solution to the complicated problem of multicultural accommodation and individual vulnerability by engendering interaction, and at times even open competition, between different sources of jurisdiction. Before rendering her own preferred joint governance structure, Shachar describes four already existing legal-institutional models that exhibit features of joint governance. The critical commonality among the four designs considered consists in the idea that each may provide a means to escape the intolerable either/or dichotomy imposed by the more extreme universalistic and particularistic approaches described above. Under a joint governance institutional model, the expectation is that one may have one's rights and one's culture too.

The first, and to those familiar with American governmental structures, most recognizable, form of joint governance is a "federal-style accommodation" approach, under which legal authority is allocated across different levels of government. This devolution of jurisdictional authority to more local agencies may provide an enhanced degree of collective autonomy to *nomoi* groups with substantial populations in a given region, while simultaneously constraining repressive group practices by virtue of generally applicable individual rights. Yet the very aspect of federalism that potentially yields more expansive cultural freedom serves also to limit the structure's efficacy more generally: the accommodationist resources of federalism are limited to territorially-based groups.[92]

The second joint governance scheme, which Shachar describes as "temporal accommodation," divides authority over individual group members between the state and the cultural group according to certain time intervals linked to those traditions conceived of as most critical to the preservation of the group's *nomos*. Shachar in fact suggests that *Wisconsin v. Yoder* might be viewed as an illustration

---

90 Ibid., p. 15.

91 Ibid., p. 89.

92 See ibid., pp. 94–5.

of temporal accommodation, insofar as the Amish children involved in the case fell within the jurisdiction of state educational authorities until eighth grade, but the cultural group beyond that point.[93] Yet, as above, the same aspect of temporal accommodation that serves to maintain the group *nomos* also condemns the scheme; for during the period of time that members remain subject to the jurisdictional authority of the group, individuals necessarily also remain vulnerable to culturally-enacted repression.[94]

The third form of joint governance, termed "consensual accommodation," allocates a one-time choice among jurisdictional frameworks to each individual. So, for example, a member of a particular religious group might decide to be married in accordance with her group's traditions, or she may instead opt for a state-sanctioned ceremony. The authority selected would then also have jurisdiction over the dissolution of that relationship. A virtue of the consensual accommodation model, then, is its aspiration to promote individual agency in the affirmation of cultural attachments. Yet, as with other consent-derivative structures, the consensual approach presupposes that choice is truly free—at best an arguable supposition in the realm of cultural membership, and doubly so with respect to vulnerable group members. Moreover, the conclusive nature of the choice fails to protect individual members from the unforeseeable consequences of their jurisdictional decisions. While, Shachar observes, "[i]t might seem like a merely symbolic and natural decision at the time, to preserve the traditions of one's forebears by celebrating marriage in accordance with the group's practices,"[95] the constraints imposed by one's culture on divorce or childrearing might be far less bearable. Indeed, the one-time character of the jurisdictional decision merely resurrects, rather than remedies, the either/or culture/rights conundrum.

The final model considered and abandoned by Shachar is the "contingent accommodation" model. Here jurisdictional autonomy is devolved from the state to *nomoi* groups in particular legal contexts deemed essential to the group's cultural identity, but only so long as the group's implementation of its authority rises above state-defined minimum standards.[96] The most immediate problem with this approach is the almost certain perpetuation of cultural partiality, in light of the state's singular role in delineating standards. Ian Shapiro, among other theorists, has sought to redress such bias, while still checking cultural repression, through the creation of multidimensional regulatory structures.[97] Under such an approach, matters would be divided as subject either to state or cultural primary jurisdiction, but with the alternate authority serving in a "back-up" role as a source of

---

[93] Ibid., p. 98; *Wisconsin v. Yoder*, 406 U.S. 205 (1972).

[94] Shachar, *Multicultural Jurisdictions*, p. 103.

[95] Ibid., p. 108.

[96] Ibid., p. 109.

[97] See Ian Shapiro, *Democratic Justice* (New Haven, Conn.: Yale University Press, 1999).

secondary jurisdiction. Thus, the cultural entity might exercise primary authority within a context critical to its *nomos*, and the state would retain primary jurisdiction within contexts more generally critical to human well-being, but in each case a secondary authority would strive to ensure the legitimacy of the decision reached.

Despite the promise she sees in this sort of dynamic interactive approach to joint governance, Shachar questions the contingent model's practicability: for example, would state or cultural norms determine error? While the state might surely intervene in cultural affairs, by what mechanism could the cultural group intervene in state affairs? Moreover, by leaving the division of primary authority to state and cultural auspices, the virtue of individual agency raised by the consensual model is sacrificed. Individual members are thus "forced to play the role of whistleblowers (informing the other jurisdictional authority of violations of their rights by the other entity), instead of being allowed to work as authors" of the institutional structure designed to protect their own interests.[98]

Hence, all four extant models of joint governance present institutional structures designed, in recognition of persons' multiple attachments, to compel interaction between state and cultural sources of authority. While each approach presents certain virtues, each also, in its own way, fails ultimately to accommodate cultural differences while simultaneously protecting vulnerable group members from cultural repression. In what then lies the solution to the paradox of multicultural vulnerability? The fatal flaw, Shachar believes, common to each institutional design so far considered, lies in the failure of each approach to hinge the accommodation of traditional group practices on the reduction of intra-group repression.[99] To do so, says Shachar, we need an institutional structure of joint governance specifically designed to induce cultural elites, and to empower vulnerable individuals, to transform their cultures from within.

As with the four institutional schemes described above, indeed incorporating certain of their more salutary aspects, Shachar's "transformative accommodation" model embraces the notion of multiple sources of authority linked to persons' "multiple identity-creating affiliations."[100] What distinguishes transformative accommodation from previously considered joint governance models, according to Shachar, are three core principles. First, the transformative model would divide jurisdiction between the state and cultural groups not merely *along* traditional subject matter lines (e.g., education, family law, criminal justice), but also *within* each social context. Thus, neither the state nor the group would maintain exclusive jurisdiction with respect to, say, marriage; instead, the cultural group might retain power over issues of status and membership, while the state might exercise authority over the distribution of property. The point of this first condition, which

---

98 Shachar, *Multicultural Jurisdictions*, p. 113.
99 Ibid., pp. 89, 113.
100 Ibid., p. 118.

Shachar terms "the 'sub-matter' allocation of authority," is both to permit concurrent state and cultural influence over group members and to compel interaction among those sources of authority.[101]

Shachar's second principle she calls the "no monopoly" rule. "According to this rule, neither the group nor the state can ever acquire exclusive control over a contested social arena that affects individuals both as group members and as citizens."[102] But this requirement, in effect, seems merely a corollary of the first; allocating jurisdiction within contested social contexts according to "sub-matters," and mandating that no single authority maintain monopoly power over any contested social context, seem but two sides of the same coin.[103] Shachar's third principle, "the establishment of clearly delineated choice options," does a bit more work. With this condition, Shachar's model offers members of cultural groups a wholly new option, and a new instrument for change: it offers at-risk individuals a *partial* exit. Individual members, Shachar proposes, "must have clear options which allow them to choose between the jurisdiction of the state and the *nomoi* group. Choice here means that they can remain within the sub-matter jurisdiction of the original power-holder (approval) or that they can resist that jurisdictional authority at predefined 'reversal' points (disapproval)."[104] According to Shachar's theory, the opportunity to invoke a partial exit would enable vulnerable individuals to exercise their rights as citizens of the state without sacrificing their cultural identity. Even more, by affording individuals the option to choose between cultural and state sources of authority, this model would engender competition between jurisdictions, and, with it, the capacity for cultural transformation.

One example, indeed one that recurs in Shachar's treatment, is the traditional Jewish notion of an "anchored woman," or an *agunah*.[105] Under Jewish law, a married woman cannot initiate a religious divorce (a *get*), and so become free to re-marry within her faith, without first obtaining her husband's consent.[106] The consequences of the doctrine are frequently quite severe; a recalcitrant or abusive husband might engage in blackmail, leaving an *agunah* with no choice beyond ceding undeserved (typically, property or custodial) rights or abandoning her

---

[101] Ibid.; see also ibid., p. 120: "Meaningful consideration of marriage and divorce rules thus requires a consideration of both jurisdictions: the authority which governs each distinct legal sub-matter, as well as the complementary authority which jointly governs (or 'co-prevails') in a contested social arena."

[102] Ibid., p. 121.

[103] Shachar notes well the inevitable inefficiencies that would be associated with a joint governance model, like hers, that requires interaction across jurisdictions to resolve fully any dispute. She contends that on balance any loss in judicial economy is more than compensated for by the gain registered from a critical review of cultural traditions and (somewhat vaguely) of federalist institutional structures more generally. Ibid., pp. 130–31.

[104] Ibid., p. 122.

[105] See ibid., pp. 57–60, 133–5.

[106] For the biblical source of this doctrine, see Deuteronomy 24:1.

cultural membership. Consider, though, how the situation might change under an accommodation model that empowers vulnerable individuals by offering them clearly delineated choice options. The *agunah* seeking a divorce would be afforded an opportunity partially to exit; that is, to sever her current relationship pursuant to state jurisdiction. She would then be free (by force, if necessary) to re-marry in accordance with her cultural traditions.[107] Hence, the partial exit might enable a vulnerable member of a cultural group to exercise her general rights as a citizen of a liberal state, yet also retain her particular cultural identity.

Shachar's most critical point here, though, is not merely that partial exits be made available, but that where partial exits are made available, they will rarely be needed. Faced with the prospect of selective exit, indeed faced with exit by the biological and social "bearers" of the group's *nomos*, cultural leaders will have a strong incentive to reinterpret their texts and traditions in ways that enable them to reverse oppressive and discriminatory practices.[108] "Avoiding the reversal of jurisdiction becomes a matter of self-interest to the group, since it allows the group to protect whatever degree of self-regulating power it has already secured over its members, rather than risk losing it piecemeal."[109] The partial exit is thus not an end in itself, but an instrument of cultural change. It is a risk imposed upon cultural elites, the avoidance of which entails the avoidance of cultural repression. Moreover, by devolving jurisdictional decisions to individuals themselves, the transformative model creates "a dynamic new space for meaningful participatory group membership."[110] The transformation of culture is thus accomplished not merely from on high, but broadly in virtue of the actions and expectations of all group members, including those individuals historically more vulnerable. In that sense, Shachar's design might be said to aspire to democratize culture.

One obvious criticism, then, sure to be leveled against Shachar by the proponents of a more accommodating approach to cultural practice (e.g., the toleration perspective), would consist in the notion that any state-imposed cultural change, regardless of the particular agents of that change, necessarily fails to treat cultural groups justly.[111] A culture transformed from within, but only in virtue of a structural remedy imposed from without, is no different, according to this "non-interventionist" view, than a culture transformed directly by the state. Shachar has

---

[107] See Shachar, *Multicultural Jurisdictions*, p. 135: "At this point, the state will acquire (group-backed) authority to enforce the removal of all barriers to remarriage (even if the marriage was originally created by religious solemnization)."

[108] As Shachar describes them, "*Nomoi* communities are living entities. They are not suicidal in nature. Most have ample resources for re-interpretations which permit them to preserve their *nomos* while adaptively responding to change." Ibid., p. 140.

[109] Ibid., p. 125.

[110] Ibid., p. 123.

[111] Shachar notes that, in this sense, her transformative model might be perceived "as indirect intervention into the group's 'private' affairs, a multicultural state acting *ultra vires*." Ibid., p. 126, n. 20.

a response to this view, however. She asserts that cultural practice, at least in modern multicultural states, is critically enmeshed within a broader social context: "the group and the state are both viable and mutable social entities which are constantly affecting each other through their ongoing interactions."[112] Indeed, Shachar suggests that it may in fact be interaction with an overly accommodationist state that unnaturally arrests the otherwise "organic processes of [cultural] change."[113] In response to a state which affords expansive jurisdiction to groups on the basis of cultural difference, cultural elites have incentives to maintain such differences in order to maintain their authority, even where the maintenance of difference entails the maintenance of oppressive practices.[114] Hence, Shachar notes an important, if rather ironic, sense in which transformative accommodation might actually enable, rather than subvert, the normal processes of collective cultural self-determination. Of course, in light of the uniformly anti-repressive ends she expects her model to provoke, to accept Shachar's premise (that state-imposed cultural transformation merely frees the culture to evolve as it naturally would) one would also have to believe that cultures naturally evolve in a unilinear, and uniquely progressive, fashion.

Yet even placing alternative perspectives to one side, Shachar's model is problematic on its own terms. Recall that, as articulated by Shachar, transformative accommodation is premised on three (really just two) principles: (1) the "sub-matter allocation of authority"; (2) the "no monopoly rule"; and (3) "the establishment of clearly delineated choice options."[115] The first two principles, as we have seen, combine to encourage interaction between the state and cultural groups from a structural perspective. The third is intended to provide individuals with an instrument of cultural and political change.

Shachar has thus proposed a highly interactive design pursuant to which *both* cultural groups *and the state* will be induced better to serve individual members.[116] Yet virtually all of Shachar's analysis is inclined toward cultural group adaptation. Even assuming the accuracy of her view that cultural group leaders, facing selective exit, will reinterpret their traditions, in what sense would we expect the state to react? Given that the paradox of multicultural vulnerability only arises once the state has demonstrated its willingness to accommodate repressive cultural practices, why would we suddenly expect the state to seek to protect vulnerable members? In Shachar's terms, how will minority cultural group members be able

---

[112] Ibid., p. 118.

[113] Ibid., p. 85.

[114] Shachar terms this phenomenon "reactive culturalism." See ibid., pp. 35–7.

[115] Ibid., p. 118.

[116] See ibid., p. 117: "transformative accommodation seeks to adapt the power structures of both *nomoi* group and state."

to "discipline" the state with the threat of "opting-out,"[117] when the state has already shown itself uninterested in their plight?

Moreover, the principles that compose Shachar's model, and that serve to construct her transformative accommodation design, presuppose state-cultural group *negotiation*; both the initial allocation of sub-matter jurisdiction, and the delineation of reversal points, will be subject to bargaining among state and cultural authorities.[118] Shachar assumes that each authority would seek jurisdiction in sub-matters most central to its core mission; hence, the group would likely seek influence over questions pertinent to its survival, while the state would aim toward acquiring jurisdiction over issues of civic participation. Yet, other than noting that at-risk group members must not be "den[ied] voice," that "generosity at the negotiation stage is required from the state as the stronger party," and that vaguely-stated "incentives" exist for authorities to self-regulate and so "engage in constructive dialogue," there is little in Shachar's model to institutionalize this critical process.[119] Surely there will be matters deemed crucial within *both* state and cultural spheres (e.g., both state and cultural sources of authority might view jurisdiction over education as indispensable).[120] On such contested matters, what process will be invoked to resolve disputes? Would the state simply prevail, in virtue of its greater power (perhaps a reasonable, but unexplained result)? Or might something in the way of a neutral arbiter be appointed? Beyond the few indistinct stipulations noted above, Shachar merely declares that the process of allocating authority and identifying choice options be approached "carefully" and with "precision."[121]

Finally, and perhaps most significantly, Shachar's treatment of individual will is overly facile. Clearly, competition between state and cultural sources of authority will only be engendered, and so cultural transformation realized, where group members have options. But the *presence* of options is merely a necessary, not a sufficient, condition for competition.[122] For a model premised on competition to be effective, individuals must not only have clearly delineated choice options but also *the capacity to exercise* such options. There are, though, reasons to expect that capacity to be limited in the multicultural context. First,

---

[117] Ibid., p. 122.

[118] Ibid., pp. 128–30.

[119] See ibid.

[120] In her appendix, Shachar helpfully describes various potential products of a joint governance scheme in the context of education, see ibid., pp. 154–60, but she fails, here and elsewhere, to describe adequately the means by which a dispute among sources of authority over the initial allocation of sub-matter jurisdiction in the educational context would be resolved.

[121] Ibid., pp. 128–9.

[122] Shachar appears to recognize this point, see ibid., p. 138, and yet she nonetheless fails to incorporate directly into her model any provision that would guarantee the agency required for competition to take place.

constitutive attachments, while revisable, are nonetheless are often quite difficult to abandon. Even (perhaps particularly) the more vulnerable members of *nomoi* groups may feel deeply obligated to conform to religious and other cultural dictates. Second, individuals socialized within a particular *nomos* to be compliant—individuals socialized into vulnerability, that is—may have a particularly difficult time suddenly exercising agency.[123] Hence, for the most vulnerable members of cultural groups to exercise even a partial exit, much more in the way of state sponsored resources and intervention will often be required. While the married woman in the *agunah* illustration depicted above might have been in a position to make a genuine choice, individuals involved in more extreme cultural contexts almost surely would not.

Imagine, for example, the following paradigm: In a local jurisdiction, governed according to a strict interpretation of cultural law, one woman, call her Amina, has given birth to a child outside of wedlock; another woman, Mukhtaran, happens to be related to a young boy seen in the company of a girl from a higher caste. Tribal authorities sentence Amina, after allowing her an interval of one year to wean her child, to death by stoning. They order Mukhtaran to submit to a gang-rape.[124] How might these women, at the time their brutal and repressive penalties were imposed, have exercised an option to switch to a public source of authority? How might these women, existing in highly isolated and potentially remote communities, even have learned that such an option existed? In addition to sub-matter allocations and clearly delineated choice options, a model premised on individual agency in a multicultural context must, at a minimum, provide for the sort of social, educational and financial resources at-risk group members will require to recognize, and be capable of taking advantage of, jurisdictional options.[125]

Insofar, then, as a given culturally-differentiated right distinguishes among persons specifically to permit the members of a cultural group the freedom to self-exclude, the right may critically enable individuals further to construct their own cultural groups and identities. Cultural self-exclusion, thus, often facilitates the

---

[123] The reference here is to the well-developed literature on unseen dimensions of power. See Steven Lukes, *Power: A Radical View* (London: Macmillan, 1974); John Gaventa, *Power and Powerlessness: Quiescence and Rebellion in an Appalachian Valley* (Urbana, Ill.: University of Illinois Press, 1980). Shachar notes this literature in a tangential context, see *Multicultural Jurisdictions*, p. 136, n.36, but fails to apply its teachings to her core assumptions.

[124] The scenarios depicted are drawn from actual stories. See Norimitsu Onishi, "Mother's Sentence Unsettles a Nigerian Village," *The New York Times*, September 7, 2002, p. A3; Beena Sarwar, "Brutality Cloaked as Tradition," *The New York Times*, August 6, 2002, p. A15.

[125] Shachar's treatment of these critical issues is fleeting, at best. See *Multicultural Jurisdictions*, pp. 124, 138–9. Her project would be better served had she built these as preconditions directly into her model.

capacity to self-define that is so central to a liberal conception of membership. But that constitutive capacity loses its liberal coherence when aspects of individual identities are constructed involuntarily, as they are when cultural groups use accommodationist policy to subjugate vulnerable members. Joint governance approaches, and the transformative accommodation model in particular, offer some hope of fostering individual constitutive autonomy in a cultural context. Yet, at least in the absence of significantly enhanced educational and economic provisions for the most vulnerable members of cultural groups, culturally-differentiated rights would still require careful monitoring to ensure that they do not facilitate intra-group repression.

Group-Differentiated Rights and Self-Invention

All legal rights categorize claimants. Group-differentiated rights, we have seen, do this and more. Such rights serve also further to constitute aspects of human identities. From a liberal perspective, this loss of constitutive autonomy would seem presumptively unjust. Yet we have also seen that the group-differentiated form of right in fact subsumes three distinct models of rights, and that each model bears a different relationship to a liberal conception of membership.

Where classes of individuals are excluded from, and so defined by, rights on the basis of inegalitarian ascriptive characteristics, the principles that compose a liberal conception of membership are radically contravened. In a similar sense, when rights are granted affirmatively to members of subordinated social groups, an aspect of their bearers' social identity is constituted in part by law. Yet that particular moral cost may be more than offset by a gain in substantive equality, which itself might engender constitutive autonomy in other social spheres. Finally, legal rights that take culture as the basis of their differentiation often foster constitutive autonomy by enabling members further to construct their own cultural groups and identities. At times, however, culturally-differentiated rights facilitate internal repression of vulnerable group members, and where this is the case such rights merely resurrect a form of illiberal differentiated membership at another level.

Group-differentiated rights, then, may both constrain and at times foster self-invention. The process of discerning the moral implications of particular instantiations of this form of right will likely continue to occupy theorists and state actors for so long as social and cultural group differences remain socially salient. That is, perhaps indefinitely. Even as social conditions evolve, however, the more valuable inquiries into the legitimacy of differentiated policy will be marked by two indispensable characteristics. First, they will persistently renew, while critically reflecting upon, the liberal commitment to individual autonomy in the construction of the self. And, second, they will attend closely to the particular social contexts in which group-differentiated interests ordinarily arise. For neither human dignity as a value in itself, nor the essentially local character of human relations, is fast approaching transformation.

Index